Rebel Politics

David Brenner

Rebel Politics

A Political Sociology of Armed Struggle in Myanmar's Borderlands

SOUTHEAST ASIA PROGRAM PUBLICATIONS
an imprint of
Cornell University Press
Ithaca and London

First published 2019 by Cornell University Press

Library of Congress Cataloging-in-Publication Data
Names: Brenner, David, 1986– author.
Title: Rebel politics : a political sociology of armed struggle in Myanmar's
    borderlands / David Brenner.
Description: Ithaca : Southeast Asia Program Publications, an imprint of Cornell
    University Press, 2019. | Includes bibliographical references and index.
Identifiers: LCCN 2018059407 (print) | LCCN 2018060258 (ebook) |
    ISBN 9781501740107 (pdf) | ISBN 9781501740114 (epub/mobi) |
    ISBN 9781501740084 | ISBN 9781501740084 (cloth) |
    ISBN 9781501740091 (pbk.)
Subjects: LCSH: Karen National Union. | Kachin Independence Organisation. |
    Political violence—Burma—Karen State. | Political violence—Burma—Kachin
    State. | Insurgency—Burma—Karen State. | Insurgency—Burma—Kachin State. |
    Karen (Southeast Asian people) —Burma—Politics and government. | Kachin
    (Asian people) —Burma—Politics and government. | Karen State (Burma) —
    History—Autonomy and independence movements. | Kachin State (Burma) —
    History—Autonomy and independence movements. | Karen State
    (Burma) —Ethnic relations. | Kachin State (Burma) —Ethnic relations.
Classification: LCC DS528.2.K35 (ebook) | LCC DS528.2.K35 K74 2019 (print) |
    DDC 959.105/3—dc23
LC record available at https://lccn.loc.gov/2018059407

To my friends in Myanmar and its borderlands

CONTENTS

ACKNOWLEDGMENTS

Over the six years I have worked on this book I have received infinite trust, encouragement, and support from family, friends, colleagues, my supervisor, and my friends in Myanmar. My debt of gratitude to those who helped me is considerable. But if I can convey even a small portion of it to those who have been most important to this journey, then it is certainly worth doing so.

A thousand thanks go to my doctoral supervisor, Jürgen Haacke, to whom I am most indebted for his trust, patience, and numerous efforts on my behalf. I learned a lot from his expertise on Myanmar as well as his knowledge of critical social theory, which inspired the conceptual framing of my analysis. He let me run on a long leash when I wanted to, while giving me direction when I needed it. Moreover, it is no exaggeration to say that this book would be lacking in some respects without his close reading of my often confused drafts and his extensive critical and constructive feedback.

The London School of Economics (LSE) was a special place in which to pursue the bulk of research underpinning this book. It not only funded my doctoral studies and field research with a generous grant but also was an exceptional space to meet like-minded people. Among them were many friends who entertained my rambling ideas in workshops or at the pub. Many thanks go to Aaron McKeil, Maggy Ainley, Anissa Haddadi, Gustav Meibauer, Kelly-Jo Bluen, Mark Kersten, Sophie Haspeslagh, Florian Weigand, Harsh Agarwal, Tanguy Sene, Mohammed Azhar Hussain, and Irina Muñoz. My special thanks go to Sam Vincent. From the early days of our studies Sam was willing to let me bounce my ideas off him, ideas that were necessary to shaping this book. My research also benefited greatly from the critical input of many other academics and friends. I want to offer my sincere gratitude to everyone who offered their wise advice and kind friendship. I very much enjoyed exchanging thoughts about development and conflict with James Putzel, from whom I learned a lot in his seminars, at the pub, and over barbequed "redneck birds" in his garden. Hans Steinmüller was another source of inspiration. As a political anthropologist he helped me digest my fieldwork and welcomed me into a lively crowd of anthropologists despite my disguise as a "newspaper scientist." Bill Callahan provided helpful feedback for shaping the ethnographic character of my work, while making sure that it still speaks to the concerns of international relations scholars. I am greatly indebted to David Rampton, a brilliant scholar on nationalism and conflict. He sacrificed much time in patiently reading through my ideas, half-baked though they were then. Without his comments on my work and mentoring on many other academic queries, I would have gotten lost more than once. Moreover, I want to take this opportunity to thank Kate Meagher, with whom I initially started to work on a very different project. She taught me a great deal about the sociology of power, and my thought remains influenced by her excellent research on informal politics.

Regular discussions with other academics and researchers have also been instrumental in my shaping of this book. Jonathan Goodhand and Klaus Schlichte both engaged critically and constructively with earlier versions of the book as the examiners of my doctoral thesis. Their excellent scholarship on armed conflict has inspired my own work in many ways, and I feel very lucky that they took interest in my research. During my first job at the University of Surrey my colleagues and friends in the Department of Politics have supported me in my fieldwork and encouraged me as I was writing this book. My special thanks go to Ciaran Gillespie, Roberta Guerrina, Alia Middleton, and Laura Chappell for their kind support. This book has benefited from the critical reading of several editors and reviewers. Portions of chapters 1, 3, and 4 were previously published in *Contemporary Politics, Conflict, Security and Development,* and *Asian Security.* The peer review processes were very helpful in clarifying my ideas. I am very grateful for the generous feedback and support of Sarah Grossman, the managing editor of the Southeast Asia Program Publications at Cornell University Press, and for the help of Kate Epstein and Lawrence Kenney with copyediting. Most helpful were the insightful discussions I had with Myanmar researchers, sessions that were crucial for reflecting on the findings of my fieldwork and for putting my thoughts on Kachin and Karen politics into perspective with wider developments in Myanmar. I particularly want to thank Lee Jones and Karin Dean for their critical reflections and suggestions for improving the book as well as all the other friends from whose expertise I learned, including Danseng Lawn, Martin Smith, Laur Kiik, Tony Neil, Kevin McLeod, Alicia de la Cour, Mandy Sadan, Matthew Walton, Enze Han, Giuseppe Gabusi, and Stefano Ruzza.

I owe the greatest thanks to my family. Without their love and support I would not have been able to start this research in the first place. My deepest gratitude goes to my parents, who managed to raise me and get me through school despite the occasional hiccups. My mother, Gabi, nurtured my early interest in politics with her outstanding ability to communicate the complex and often tragic history of our world to children of all ages. My father, Hardy, has always supported me and encouraged me to pursue my interests—however odd some of them must have seemed to him—knowing from his own experience that this is the only way to achieve success and joy in one's life. Both of my parents have always been in my corner. I also thank my uncle, Micha, who, as an academic, understood my journey and always offered helpful advice and encouragement along the way. Moreover, my thanks go to my sisters, Miriam and Jael, my cousin Simone, my grandma Henny, and my aunt Michelle for their love despite my quirks. Throughout this project my thoughts have been with my late grandfather Hermann, one of the kindest and wisest persons I have ever known. A Polish Jew who lived during the Holocaust, he unfortunately experienced the worst of humankind. I feel incredibly privileged that he told me about his personal life. He left a deep impression on me.

Most important, this book would not exist but for the incredible trust and selfless support I received from the many friends I met during my research in Myanmar and its borderlands as well as in the diaspora in London. The political situation in Myanmar is unfortunately still too unstable, insecure, authoritarian, and unpredictable to mention the names of the people at the very center of this book. Nevertheless, I want to express my utmost gratitude to everyone who helped make my fieldwork happen, even more so as many of them continue to be affected by the ongoing armed conflict, discrimination, and oppression. Their support not only facilitated my travels, access, and interviews. The fact that I was in their caring hands also made me feel safe during my work in unstable and violent environments. Their willingness to share their analyses and permit me to enter their everyday lives was vital in helping me gain insights into the complex local politics, societies, and cultures. Moreover, getting to know them was a most humbling, formative, and enjoyable experience for me as a person. With great fondness I will always remember my journeys with the crew of the Karen Education Department. I admire their passion for delivering, at great personal sacrifice, education to some of the most marginalized communities in war-torn eastern Myanmar. I cherish my memories of the many celebrations held with my friends in Kachin and Karen States; my seminar participants in Kachin State, who challenged Western orthodoxies in the study of politics in the most inspiring ways; the beautiful excursions with the "Picnician Gang" of Laiza; and the long nights of critical discussions about local and world politics with my dear friends in Myitkyina as well as the Kachin community in Hounslow. I will remain eternally grateful for their friendship. They are among the most generous people I have ever met. I hope they will soon be able to live their lives in peace. I dedicate this book to them.

ABBREVIATIONS

AFPFL   Anti-Fascist People's Freedom League

BGF   Border Guard Force

BIA   Burma Independence Army

CPB   Communist Party of Burma

CSO   civil society organization

DKBA   Democratic Karen Buddhist Army

EEDY   Education and Economic Development for Youth

FDI   foreign direct investment

IDP   internally displaced person

KAF   Kawthoolei Armed Forces

KIA   Kachin Independence Army

KIO   Kachin Independence Organization

KNDO   Karen National Defence Organisation

KNLA   Karen National Liberation Army

KNU   Karen National Union

KSDP   Kachin State Democracy Party

MEC   Myanmar Economic Corporation

NCA   Nationwide Cease-Fire Agreement

NDA-K   New Democratic Army-Kachin

NLD   National League for Democracy

SLORC   State Law and Order Restoration Council

UMEHL   Union of Myanmar Economic Holdings Limited

UNFC   United Nationalities Federal Council

UWSA   United Wa State Army

Rebel Politics

INTRODUCTION

In June 2011 a seventeen-year-long cease-fire collapsed in Myanmar.[1] A new, violent chapter began in one of the world's longest-running civil wars. Following years of relative stability in the country's northern borderlands with China, heavy fighting broke out between rebels of the Kachin Independence Organization (KIO) and Myanmar's military. This resumption of armed conflict represented a break with KIO leaders' long participation in negotiations with Myanmar's military rulers. That it coincided with the end of decades-long military dictatorship and remarkable democratic transition makes it seem even more peculiar. Only months earlier Sr. Gen. Than Shwe, the dictator of Myanmar from 1992 to 2011, had paved the way for far-reaching political reforms. He appointed a new, semicivilian government led by President U Thein Sein, a retired army general. The new administration initiated a peace process and, during its term from 2011 to 2016, signed a range of new cease-fires with several other ethnic rebel groups.

The new cease-fires included a January 2012 agreement with Myanmar's oldest rebellion, the Karen National Union (KNU), which had fought in the country's war-torn eastern borderlands since the country gained independence in 1948. This was especially notable because the KNU had remained the last sizable rebellion locked in combat throughout the 1990s and 2000s, a time when the military and most other ethnic armed groups in Myanmar, including the KIO, signed cease-fires and engaged in dialogue. Since 2011–12 this landscape of conflict has turned upside down. The KNU has come to champion the nationwide peace process, and eastern Myanmar has enjoyed fragile yet unprecedented stability. The KIO has returned to the trenches, leading a new coalition of ethnic armed groups consisting of Kokang, Palaung, Arakan, and Shan movements into battles more severe than any northern Myanmar has seen since the late 1980s.

This book investigates the reasons for the waves of war and peace in Myanmar's borderlands since 2011. It is based on six years of research, including nine months of fieldwork inside the KNU in the Thai–Myanmar borderlands and the KIO in the Chinese–Myanmar borderlands in 2013 and 2014 as well as frequent shorter research trips since. The book aims to recalibrate the conventional but limited prism through which most Western observers have looked at Myanmar: civil–military relations in the country's center, particularly the contestation between the former democracy idol Aung San Suu Kyi and Myanmar's powerful generals. Viewed from this vantage point, the reescalating conflict in the northern borderlands seemed like a glitch in the country's wider move toward democracy, reconciliation, and peace. After all, national reforms should have opened a window of opportunity for armed resistance groups to engage at the negotiating table. The KNU cease-fire of 2012 and the subsequent Nationwide Cease-Fire Agreement (NCA) signed by eight armed groups and the government in 2015 initially appeared to confirm it had succeeded. As per the conventional narrative, the landslide electoral victory of Suu Kyi and her National League for Democracy (NLD) in 2016 seemingly marked another milestone in the transformation of an impoverished, conflict-ridden country into a peaceful and prosperous democracy.

Contrary to expectations, ethnic conflict has not ended since Suu Kyi came to power. In fact, it has escalated. Most prominently, Myanmar's military has continued indiscriminately targeting civilians in ethnic minority communities during atrocious counterinsurgency campaigns. While media attention has focused mostly on the dire plight of the Rohingya Muslims in Rakhine State, other ethnic minorities have experienced similar abuse. Army offensives against rebel positions in the north of the country have in fact displaced hundreds of thousands since 2011. At the same time, ethnic rebels have remobilized on a large scale. Movements like the KIO demonstrate a revived revolutionary spirit, military strength, and organizational discipline. Moreover, they enjoy vast popular support among large parts of ethnic minority communities, form complex alliances, and engage the Myanmar army in fierce combat. A closer look at nationwide peacemaking efforts is also sobering. The KNU is the only sizable rebel group that signed the NCA in 2015. Most other signatories are counterinsurgency militias for the military or have no substantial armed wings. At the time of writing, the most powerful ethnic rebel armies remain on the battlefield. Unfortunately, the reescalation of conflict and violence was not an anomaly. The country is not transitioning toward peace and reconciliation. Rather, the norm in Myanmar's borderlands is conflict and violence.

VIEW FROM THE BORDERLANDS

In order to understand the dynamics of protracted armed conflict in Myanmar, this book shifts the center of analysis away from the conventional perspective of national level politics. It focuses on the politics of armed struggle in the country's war-torn borderlands, many parts of which remain inaccessible to most international observers, including scholars, journalists, diplomats, and humanitarians. These far-flung mountains and forests have been the epicenter of decades-long civil war and have given birth to an enormous array of nonstate armed groups. The most powerful of these armed groups are ethnonational rebel movements that emerged as a result of militarized and violent identity formation processes that positioned Burma's ethnic groups against each other during British colonial rule and the Second World War. These conflicts led to countrywide violence on the eve of independence in 1948, despite an initial settlement between the Burmese independence hero Gen. Aung San and representatives of several ethnic minorities. This so-called Panglong Agreement of 1947 stipulated equal treatment of all ethnic groups and power-sharing arrangements, including regional autonomy provisions under a federal constitution. The agreement remains the reference point for most ethnic minorities today. Captured by an ethnocratic military elite comprised of the ethnic Bamar majority, the postindependence state has not followed through on its promises.

Since the failure of Panglong, guerrilla armies have sprung up across almost all of Burma's borderlands, where most ethnic minorities are located. Many of these insurrections developed political wings and administrative capacities, maintaining extensive parallel governance systems and generating revenue and public goods in territories they liberated from the central government. Over the course of decades-long civil war, smaller militias also began to operate in Burma's border areas after larger movements fragmented. Some splinter groups fight for the counterinsurgency, others act as vigilantes, and still others follow mainly criminal agendas. Often these lines are blurred. Precise figures on Myanmar's nonstate armed groups and their combatants are impossible to find. In 2015 the local information platform Myanmar Peace Monitor of the local Burma News International network counted 18 ethnic rebel movements, 13 of which had bilateral cease-fire agreements with the government. Their military strength, territorial control, and political weight vary from groups commanding fewer than 100 soldiers and possessing no territorial foothold to groups with armies several thousand combatants strong that govern sizable pockets of territory, including towns, forests, and mountain ranges. In addition, the platform recorded 58 progovernment militias, including 23 so-called Border Guard Force (BGF) militias, each with more than 326 soldiers, and 35 so-called People's Militia groups and other counterinsurgency militias, each with up to 100 soldiers and less formalized command structures (Burma News International 2015).

My research concentrated on two of the oldest and most important rebel movements: the Kachin and Karen rebellions. Despite their contrasting strategies on the battlefield and at the negotiating table in 2011–12, the KIO and the KNU exhibit many similarities. These include their ideological and organizational character as well as comparable challenges in their structural environment. Ideologically, both are ethnonational movements fighting for greater autonomy for their respectively claimed ethnic constituency from the ethnocratic political order in Myanmar. In terms of organizational structure, both rely on popular support from local communities. Although both groups rejected Maoist ideology and expressed an affinity for Western capitalism during the Cold War, Maoist ideas of guerrilla warfare and mass mobilization heavily influenced their organizational structures and relationships to local rural communities. They developed pronounced political wings and administrative capacities with which they administer pockets of territory. Both groups have been operating within the same rapidly changing context of Myanmar in transition. Similar political and economic pressures and incentives operate on both, including the introduction, since the end of the Cold War, of ever-increasing investments in infrastructure and resource industries in the Myanmar borderlands with China and Thailand.

To develop a grounded understanding of the Kachin and Karen struggles, I embedded myself in both movements for nine months in 2013 and 2014 and one month in 2017. During this time I conducted several dozen formal interviews with KIO and KNU leaders and other social elites. My close-range research in the two movements allowed me to live and travel with a variety of people involved in or intimately related to the Kachin and Karen armed struggles. This experience enabled me to accumulate a wealth of informal conversations and observations on a daily basis. It also gave me the privilege of developing friendly relationships with many participants and supporters of the rebellions, including with local youth and ordinary rebel soldiers, over the course of my research. This was crucial to gaining an understanding of their lifeworlds, including their perspectives and analyses of their situation, and thus of the social context within which political violence takes place. In fact, had these daily encounters not taken place it would have been impossible for me to write this book. To gain initial access to the movements, I first sought contact with the Kachin and Karen diasporas in the UK and Thailand, presenting myself as an academic researcher interested in and sympathetic to the struggle of their communities in Myanmar. As it turned out, my background in higher education and the social sciences enabled me to foster a reciprocal relationship with both movements during my field research. I spent four months supporting the efforts of the KNU's educational arm by surveying

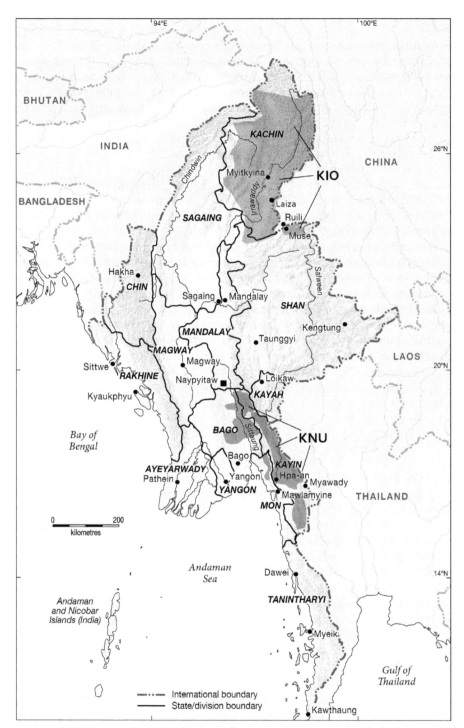

Map 1 The Kachin and Karen rebellions. The gray areas in Myanmar's northern borderlands with China denote the region where the Kachin Independence Organization (KIO) operates. The gray areas in Myanmar's eastern borderlands with Thailand denote the region where the Karen National Union (KNU) operates. Both movements control pockets of territory in these borderlands, but most of their territories overlap with the territorial control and areas of operation of other armed actors, including the Myanmar army, other ethnonational rebel movements, counterinsurgency militias, and criminal syndicates. *Source:* Adapted from CartoGIS Services, College of Asia and the Pacific, Australian National University.

its extensive parallel schooling system in the "liberated areas" of Karen State for a needs assessment. For several weeks I also conducted a course for KIO officers and affiliated humanitarian and development workers in government- and rebel-held areas of Kachin State at the behest of the KIO leadership. Both of these activities bore fruit in terms of my research.

Assisting the KNU's education efforts afforded me access to the head of the organization's education arm, an elderly Karen headmaster and senior rebel leader, and to his closest companions, many of whom were young, passionate teachers with whom I developed amicable relations. Some of these teachers held military positions in the rebellion's armed wing. I spent many days at their workplaces learning about the challenges of education provision in rebel-held schools. Assessing part of their rebel governance system enabled me to develop a deep understanding of the politics of rebellion and cease-fire in various parts of Karen State, including the relations between the KNU and local communities in different rebel brigade areas. I spent many nights in the living quarters of my Karen friends, where discussions of high-level politics unfolded over food, beer, and betel nut. Our conversations often turned to the hardships of war as well as everyday concerns and aspirations, including love, marriage, and family. My work surveying the school system called on me to travel extensively to small towns and refugee camps on the Thai side of the border as well as to villages and camps in eastern Myanmar's Karen State, where I met many other supporters, affiliates, members, and leaders of the Karen rebellion.

My teaching of informal college-level courses, which consisted of about twenty classes given to groups of young men and women in Kachin State, came about when I spent three months in both government-held and rebel-held areas of northern Myanmar. During this time a Kachin officer who was interested in learning more about academic inquiry into war and peace asked me to conduct seminars on the subject. The KIO valued these seminars for several reasons. First, they offered insight into the Western peace-building, development, and aid industry that had been operating in Myanmar since 2011. Second, they shed light on some of the pressing problems Kachin communities face via comparisons with those of other countries, such as Afghanistan's opium industry and the threats it poses to peace. Third, given that Myanmar has banned the teaching of political science in its universities since the military dictatorship, many seminar participants were genuinely interested in learning about Western political concepts. Beyond requiring me to travel to various KIO-held places, including the Kachin capital of Laiza and its surroundings, the KIO operational headquarters, an officer school, and frontline positions, the seminars gave me invaluable insights into the perspectives of KIO members and affiliates. Over barbeque and beer I made friends with the seminar participants, who invited me into their homes and circles of friends. They took me on fishing and picnicking excursions and taught me how to play an air guitar while singing revolutionary songs in karaoke bars.

My seminar teaching for the KIO and surveying of KNU schools shaped the ways in which the members of the two rebel movements perceived me and my research and ultimately the knowledge production in this book. The access I enjoyed to the two rebellions poses questions about bias and misrepresentation. In this context, triangulation of data was pivotal to my efforts to construct a plausible, balanced account. Of great value in this respect were discussions with other academic and nonacademic researchers, both verbal and via their writings. In addition, I sought information from local experts who were a little further from the heat of the conflict and indeed of the many conflicts within both movements. These included local church leaders, community elders, members of local civil society, and the diaspora community in the UK and Thailand. Many of these people had close links to and deep insights into the movements. Most of my interlocutors, both formally inside and outside of the Kachin and Karen rebel movements, engaged in sophisticated analyses of such issues as Myanmar's difficult political transition, the dynamics of conflict, local economies and incoming foreign investments, changing geopolitics, the ongoing peace process, and the internal politics of armed struggle. Their analyses had a profound influence on my understanding, and to a great extent my book presents the outcome of these extensive discussions. With the exception of high-profile leaders and elites who agreed to be named in the text I have made sure to protect all my sources. I have attached fictional names to everyone else.

The Karen and Kachin movements make for a good comparison. That said, similar armed movements engage in civil wars worldwide. Some of the most protracted ethnonational conflicts in recorded history have affected South and Southeast Asia, including the many rebellion in northeastern India, the Tamil conflict in Sri Lanka, Malay Muslim separatism in southern Thailand, and the Moro secessionist movements in the southern Philippines. Many of them emerged on the fringes of the state but have become increasingly squeezed by geopolitical change and economic transitions, as movements in Myanmar have (Parker, Colleta, and Oppenheim 2013). In addition to shedding light on Myanmar's little-understood civil war, this book adds to scholars' limited understanding of armed struggle in contemporary Asia. More generally, the intimate insights I gained during my time with the KIO and KNU contribute to our conceptual understanding of political violence by highlighting the hidden social fabric and everyday practices of rebellion.

THE POLITICS OF REBEL MOVEMENTS

Beyond scholars' limited knowledge of rebellion in Myanmar, the puzzle at the center of this book points to a more general shortcoming within security, conflict, and peace studies. The traditional theories in this area struggle to explain the strategies of rebel movements and are thus inadequate to decoding why the KNU would engage in negotiations with the state at the same time that the KIO leaves the negotiating table and returns to the battlefield. Rebel movements are often conceptualized as monolithic actors that act according to a unified strategic rationale in order to maximize their power vis-à-vis the incumbent state. This simplification is common in large statistical studies because unitary actor assumptions enable scholars to model the collective behavior of armed groups in theoretically parsimonious ways on the basis of quantitative data. The same understanding, however, underpins some of the most prominent arguments by conflict-resolution scholars. For instance, Zartman's "mutually hurting stalemate" defines a situation as ripe for mediation at the point that warring factions perceive the continuation of violence as detrimental to their interests (for example, Zartman 1989; see also Stedman 1997; for a good critique, see Pearlman 2009).

While models based on unitary actor assumptions make sense on paper, they often struggle to account for the empirically observable conduct of rebel groups. As Charles Tilly writes, this is so because "coherent, durable, self-propelling social units—monads—occupy a great deal of political theory but none of political reality" (2008b, 69). Many nonstate armed groups behave in ways that seem suboptimal when measured against their assumed strategic objectives with regard to their external environments (see Pearlman 2009; Bakke, Cunningham, and Seymour 2012). As early as the 1970s James Scott criticized this reduction of multidimensional movements into presumably coherent entities. In a study of peasant revolutions in eastern Asia he questioned the then-prevalent binary categorization of revolutionary movements into communists or nationalists. To him, such broad-brush labeling was a form of "instant analysis" that centers on the decisions of a few elites but ignores "a large stratum of revolutionary actors" (Scott 1979, 98). He suggested that the internal politics of rebellion, especially a movement's grassroots and their often uneasy relations with their leaders, hold the key information about violent insurrections.

Since Scott's vital insight, the study of civil wars has expanded widely. Scholars in various disciplines have pondered the causes, dynamics, and potential solutions of armed conflict. Instead of disaggregating rebel movements and investigating elite–grassroots relations, however, most analyses have continued to operate on a macrolevel, conceptualizing rebel groups as unitary actors. This has recreated highly simplistic intellectual binaries, most prominently Mary Kaldor's distinction between political old wars, fought by noble soldiers, and apolitical new wars, fought by predatory criminals (Kaldor 1999). This dichotomy dovetails with Paul Collier's (2000) claim that economic greed rather than political grievances drives contemporary rebel groups (for critical discussions, see Kalyvas 2001; Cramer 2002; Keen 2012). While such reductionist, Eurocentric narratives add little analytical value to our knowledge of civil war, they had a profound impact on public discourse, adding to the criminalization of rebel movements that government officials often characterize as terrorist in the context of the global war on terror (Keen 2006). Framing rebels as terrorists or criminals is, however, conceptually incorrect and analytically unhelpful. Although no authoritative definition of rebellion exists in scholarship or international law, rebel movements typically have such political goals as secession or the overthrow of the incumbent government and strategies that include guerrilla warfare against state forces and, often, the control of rural territory. Rebellion, then, contrasts with nonstate armed groups that pursue purely criminal agendas, including criminal gangs and mercenaries, or that target mainly civilians rather than the state, such as terrorists (for a good discussion, see Krause and Milliken 2009).

Conceptual clarity is also pivotal for understanding political violence in Myanmar, where the military, as noted, brands resistance against its abuses of ethnic minority communities as terrorism (Brenner 2017). Researchers, myself among them, have often used the term *insurgency* when writing about ethnic rebel groups like the KNU or KIO (see Smith 1999; Selth 2002). While the English concept of insurgency is closely related to rebellion, I refrain from using that term in this book. Concepts don't travel conveniently across language barriers, and *insurgency* translates most closely into Burmese as *thaung kyan thu*. This term, which the Myanmar army uses pejoratively, highlights the violent methods of ethnic rebels, not their political goals. Members and supporters of ethnonational rebel movements themselves prefer *taw hlan-ye tha ma*, which points to the idea of progressive politics and might best be translated into English as *revolutionaries*. In fact, the Myanmar army also uses this term when referring to its own roots in the anticolonial struggle against British imperialism. I do not use *revolution* because in English it does not sufficiently capture the armed aspects, guerrilla methods, and organizational modes of political struggle of the Kachin and Karen movements. I prefer *rebellion,* which stresses both the political and military aspects. The closest literal equivalent to the English word *rebel* in Burmese might then be *thu-pone.* Although the term is not necessarily pejorative, the Myanmar military uses it when denouncing ethnic resistance. Nonetheless, I feel *rebellion* offers the greatest clarity, and therefore I use it interchangeably with nonstate armed groups, rebel movements, armed struggle, and armed resistance to refer to the KNU and KIO.

My choice of terminology emphasizes my intention to challenge the bird's-eye views and reductionist assumptions of most aggregate studies of civil war. In doing so, my research contributes to recent microlevel studies on political violence that have rejected the notion that civil wars are simply binary contests between monolithic state and nonstate actors (Kalyvas 2003, 475–76; see also Chenoweth and Lawrence 2010; Justino, Brück, and Verwimp 2013). In my research I found that nonstate armed groups in Myanmar are often internally fragmented into rival factions. Hence individual rebel leaders not only contest the incumbent state but also fight against each other for leadership of their respective movements, something others have described with respect to rebel groups in other countries (see Pearlman 2009; Cunningham, Bakke, and Seymour 2012; Berti 2013; Staniland 2014). Internal contention and fragmentation can undermine a group's capacity for collective action, redirect violence away from outside adversaries to inside competitors, and eventually lead to attrition and organizational demise (see Staniland 2014; Bakke, Cunningham, and Seymour 2012). They can also drive the strategies of armed movements in ways that are not consistent with the interests of the collective as a whole but instead benefit particular interests within the movement (see Pearlman 2009; Cunningham, Bakke, and Seymour 2012, 69).

The institutional approach of Paul Staniland is particularly helpful in conceptualizing organizational fragmentation and coherence in nonstate armed groups. Comparing rebel groups in Afghanistan, Kashmir, and Sri Lanka, he suggests that fragmentation unfolds along two dimensions: (a) horizontal ties between different rebel elites, affecting information flows, trust, contestation, and cooperation among the group's leadership; and (b) vertical ties between elites and grassroots of rebellion, which are crucial for building and maintaining stable support networks among local communities (Staniland 2014, 1–24). Horizontal fragmentation makes the leadership of armed groups prone to factional infighting and coups. Vertical fragmentation makes it difficult to sustain asymmetric warfare against a militarily superior enemy because it erodes a movement's support network. Knowing that fragmentation, particularly if it affects both of these dimensions, can lead to rapid decay and defeat, rebel leaders attempt to build and sustain both types of links whereas counterinsurgency planners attempt to break them (Staniland 2014, 1–24).

Scholars have mostly focused on horizontal ties between rival rebel leaders and their factions over vertical ties between competing rebel leaders and their rank and file. However, vertical ties drive internal contention and thus external strategies. As Scott emphasized, they bridge the gap between popular aspirations among a movement's base and the strategizing calculus among its higher echelons. Elite–grassroots relations are key to questions about organizational coherence and fragmentation within armed groups (see Scott 1979). The stability of rebel movements whose political motives are aimed at the state, such as secession or defeating the incumbent regime, depends on these vertical ties. Such groups often control pockets of state territory. Like the KIO and the KNU, they establish statelike structures through which they govern local communities. This increases their reliance on mass mobilization and popular support, as sustaining resistance against the militarily superior state depends on strong local support networks.

While little is known about elite–grassroots relations within rebel movements, scholars of rebel governance have highlighted the importance of vertical support networks (Wickham-Crowley 1987; Mampilly 2011; Arjona, Kasfir, and Mampilly 2015). A consistent finding of this literature is that rebel groups provide public goods in areas they control (or "liberate") in order to build stable support networks among local communities. Thus the pronounced efforts of the Kachin and Karen movements in this regard are typical. Linking this insight with the discussion of internal contestation among rival rebel factions suggests that rival rebel leaders also need to draw on strong support networks in order to compete against internal rivals. The fundamental challenge confronting leaders of rebellion, then, is how to ensure either active support for or at least passive compliance with their specific faction as they struggle against the incumbent state as well as other rebel leaders. This argument might seem contradictory to contemporary orthodoxies that associate rebel groups primarily with greed and predation, but it is in line with one of the common denominators in political and social thought. Students of the latter have argued for generations that "naked power" alone does not create sustainable systems of compliance, obedience, and support (see Zelditch 2001). Rather than wielding power within their movements on the basis of pure violence, rebel leaders need to establish some degree of legitimate authority among their grassroots.

If internal contestation drives the strategic choices of rebel groups, and authority relations are central to understanding these intramural contestations, the dynamics of rebel authority become a central mechanism that needs to be addressed when accounting for the shifting strategies of rebel groups. To explain why Karen rebel leaders signed a cease-fire with Myanmar's government even as Kachin rebels went back to the battlefield, this book examines how the struggle over leadership authority within the two movements has driven their strategic choices with regard to negotiation and conflict vis-à-vis the state. In highlighting dynamics internal to rebel movements to explain their collective strategy, I do not mean to downplay the complex interactions between the wider environment of rebel movements and their internal politics. Indeed, I understand rebellion as being embedded in a wider social context. External forces that transform the social context within which political violence takes place thus shape the internal composition and politics of rebel movements. In light of the rapid political and economic change that rebels in Myanmar's borderlands face, my book also asks how the changing politico-economic environment affects the struggles over authority within the movements under comparison. To get to the core of these questions, I explain how rebel leaders capture and lose authority among the grassroots of their movements. In other words, this book can be read as a journey into the inner workings of power at the center of the clandestine world of rebel movements.

The few scholars who have conducted fieldwork on Myanmar's ethnic armed groups have long stressed the multifaceted character of these movements (Lintner and Linter 1990; Smith 1999; Dean 2012; Sadan 2013). This book builds on my predecessors' by comparing the internal politics of the Karen and Kachin rebellions and their underlying social fabric, specifically the vertical relations between rebel leaders and their grassroots. In a guest column for *Irrawaddy* magazine in 2014, Aung Naing Oo, a peace negotiator for the Myanmar government and former resistance fighter himself, admitted how little is known about the complex internal dynamics of armed groups in Myanmar and their implications for war and peace. After holding negotiations with several Karen armed groups, he wrote,

> for two days and two nights, we listened to various officials from rival groups, local authorities and local commanders of the Myanmar armed forces. By the second night of listening to these various accusations, counter-accusations, local situations and history of these local conflicts, my notebook was almost full. But most importantly, I could no longer take notes. So I just wrote one word "Tha-book-oo," which is the name of a fruit. It has a labyrinth of fabric inside so intricate that no one knows the beginning, the middle or the end. Put differently, I thought I knew the protagonists and conflict situation in Karen State since I once worked with the Karen National Union. But my trip proved that I was wrong. Even within groups that broke away from the mainstream Karen armed movement, there were many layers of relationships, feuds, history of conflicts, friendships and camaraderie. (Aung Naing Oo, June 5, 2014)

In investigating the labyrinth of rebel politics in Myanmar's borderlands, I want to explain the puzzling dynamics of conflict and explore how to engage with armed resistance in constructive ways. From the outside, the strategies of the Kachin and Karen rebellions contrast with each other. But shifting the perspective to the inside of the movements reveals striking parallels. I argue that the respective strategic choices of Karen and Kachin rebel leaders to engage in negotiations or return to the battlefield were the outcome of a social process between differently situated and interdependent elite and nonelite actors. Their struggles over authority within their respective movements drove their strategies. Both cease-fires involved the partial co-optation of rebel leaderships by granting them stakes in destructive cease-fire economies surrounding large-scale resource extraction. This development aggravated existing local grievances and heightened internal conflict, which led to organizational fragmentation and contention. In the case of the KIO, it led to renewed resistance from within. Mounting internal opposition within the KNU over similar grievances highlights the danger of history repeating itself.

My discussion is not meant to argue that the state bears no blame for ongoing armed conflict in Myanmar. On the contrary, decades of authoritarian and ethnocratic rule have produced political grievances surrounding ethnic discrimination, marginalization, and brutal oppression (Smith 1999; Sadan 2013; Walton 2013). While democratic reforms have improved the plight of the Bamar ethnic majority in the country's center, the Myanmar military continues to violently abuse ethnic minorities in the border regions. Nonetheless, if the external environment explained the dynamics of conflict and the strategic choices of Myanmar's rebel groups, the KNU and the KIO would not behave that differently under substantially similar circumstances. To find solutions to the protracted conflict in Myanmar, I will also need to focus on the internal politics of rebel movements and the complex social fabric within which they are woven. Focusing on the vertical relations between leaders and grassroots of rebellion, I suggest that the fight for recognition is key to understanding rebel politics. In ways analogous to how the struggle for recognition forms the motivational bedrock of collective resistance against the state, it can shape the moral context for the grassroots within a rebel movement to rebel against their own rebel leaders. If rebel leaders manage to satisfy their grassroots' claim for recognition, their social and political orders are stable. If they do not, their authority erodes and faces challenges from below.

This book explains how the changing political economies of Myanmar's borderlands affected internal struggles over authority within the Karen and Kachin movements. As well, it analyzes how these internal contestations drove their respective external conflict and negotiation strategies. The book also explores how legitimate authority relations between differently situated rebel leaders and their movements' grassroots are built and maintained as well as the circumstances that cause them to erode.

Chapter 1 develops a conceptual understanding of rebellion that explains how shifting authority relations interact with dynamics of internal contestation in driving the wider trajectories of rebel movements, including their collective conflict and negotiation strategies. The chapter engages with the literature on the internal politics of nonstate armed groups and rebel governance through the lens of the relational sociologies of Norbert Elias and Pierre Bourdieu, drawing on a coconstructed and interdependent triad of core concepts: figuration/field, power, and habitus. Building on this, it identifies reciprocal exchange relations, social identification, and the struggle for recognition as the core drivers of the building and erosion of leadership authority within rebel movements.

Chapter 2 traces the genealogy of Myanmar's rebellious borderlands. This serves to explain the roots and development of the country's protracted ethnic conflict. It provides an introduction to the Kachin and Karen rebellions and their sociopolitical context. The chapter analyzes the emergence of both ethnonational projects within larger geopolitical conflicts and a wider, transnational borderworld between India, China, and Thailand. I discuss how geopolitical shifts since the end of the Cold War have worked hand in hand with a changed counterinsurgency strategy to increase commercialization and state consolidation in Myanmar's restive border areas. Taking this long view helps to contextualize both the structural changes in the politico-economic environments of both rebellions and the changing everyday lifeworlds of Kachin and Karen rebels.

Chapter 3 focuses on the KNU and delves into why this oldest of Myanmar's rebel movements, historically the one least willing to compromise with the state, signed a cease-fire in 2012 and has championed the country's nationwide peace process ever since. The answer lies in military and geopolitical pressures on the Thai–Myanmar border that sparked group fragmentation and internal contention within the Karen movement. The chapter demonstrates how shifting authority relations between rival leaders and the movement's grassroots have driven and accentuated these dynamics as well as how they have furthered internal contestation since the cease-fire. What emerges from this discussion is that what looked from the outside like a stable settlement has been highly contested inside the movement.

Chapter 4 examines why the KIO's seventeen-year cease-fire with the government broke down in 2011 and how the organization's willingness and ability to wage war increased so dramatically despite its faltering capacities and waning revolutionary agendas during the cease-fire years. The analysis reveals that eroding authority relations between rebel leaders and the movement's grassroots, which the modalities of the cease-fire had precipitated, propelled the movement's trajectory. This erosion gave rise to increased group fragmentation and ultimately to a rival faction that managed to rebuild authority relations with their grassroots, recruit a new generation of rebels, and take over leadership, actions that ultimately changed the organization's strategy from collaboration to confrontation.

I conclude in chapter 5 by comparing the findings in the case of the two movements, recapturing the main arguments, and drawing out their implications. The discussion highlights four stages in the trajectories of both the Karen and Kachin rebellions: partial leadership co-optation, group fragmentation, internal contention, and renewed resistance from within. It applies these arguments to a clarification of the social process that has driven the dynamics, in both instances, surrounding the practices of rebellion and the struggle for recognition among rebel grassroots. Building on this, I elaborate on the implications of engaging with rebel movements in Myanmar and elsewhere, with particular regard to the fragmentation of violence and the pitfalls of economistic approaches to counterinsurgency, conflict resolution, and peace building. Finally, I evaluate the most recent developments in Myanmar in light of these findings.

CHAPTER ONE

REBELLION AS A SOCIAL PROCESS

> Society does not consist of individuals, but expresses the sum of interrelations, the relations within which these individuals stand.
>
> Karl Marx

Rebellion can be understood as a social process between differently situated but interdependent elite and nonelite actors whose interactions drive the strategies of nonstate armed groups. This book takes a relational approach to studying this process of rebellion as ontologically embedded in its social environment. From this perspective, the landscape of interdependent rebel actors is multifaceted and dynamic, as their mutual interactions and ties with their social surroundings suggest. Fragmentation and factional contention are important driving forces behind the collective conduct of armed groups. Rebel leaders rely on the grassroots of the movement to create stable support networks for their rebel social order—or at least willing compliance with their opposition to the incumbent state. As I argue here, the key to understanding these internal struggles within armed groups, therefore, lies in whether the grassroots of a movement perceives their rebel elites as having legitimate authority. Such legitimate authority depends on two interlaced processes: reciprocal exchange relations between rebel rulers and local communities; and elites' display of respect for nonelites through interactions that satisfy nonelites' need to derive a positive social identity from affiliation with the rebellion.

A RELATIONAL APPROACH

Rebel movements are embedded in particular socio-temporal spaces. The elite and nonelite actors of rebellion are differently situated within these contexts. Understanding the environment of rebellion is therefore important to understanding why and how political violence takes places. While these social structures and processes do not dictate behavior, they play a significant role in it, especially at the group level.

Relationalism is the analytical focus on relations between social entities. It constitutes an ontological handle for reconciling structure and agency. Charles Tilly summarizes this approach as "the doctrine that transactions, interactions, social ties, and conversations constitute the central stuff of social life" (2008b, 7). Relationalism contrasts with substantialism, which infers motivations and behavior from the properties of social entities, including individual or collective actors as well as social structures. Methodological individualism, for instance, is a prominent substantialist approach. It posits that self-contained individuals act independently of their environment, whether they seek rational gains, as rational-choice models suggest, or follow internalized norms, as more sociological-inspired theories would predict. In a similar vein, structural theories frequently locate the source of action within self-subsistent, coherent social structures, including organization, class, and nation. From the perspective of a relational approach, individual motivations, including that to take up arms, are not the product of presumably self-propelled individuals who intentionally and purposefully act on a set of clear preferences. Indeed, individual motivations do not stem from within social actors themselves but emerge from the interactions between them (for an extended discussion, see Emirbayer 1997).

Relationalism has hitherto had limited impact on the study of armed groups and political violence, much of which remains grounded in methodological individualism. However, the work of the political sociology scholars Klaus Schlichte (2009a) and Jutta Bakonyi and Berit Bliesemann de Guevara (2014b) has demonstrated its usefulness in the study of political violence and rebellion. This book follows in their footsteps by looking to the sociologies of Norbert Elias and Pierre Bourdieu. The ontological embeddedness of actors in their transactional environment is central to the thinking of both of these scholars, whose work has created a complementary heuristic device that focuses its inquiry on the dialectic nature of social structures and individuals (Paulle, van Heerikhuizen, and Emirbayer 2012). While they worked separately, Elias and Bourdieu have a common understanding and deployment of a coconstructed and interdependent triad of core concepts: social space (which Elias terms figuration and Bourdieu terms fields), power, and habitus (Paulle, van Heerikhuizen, and Emirbayer 2012, 70).

FIGURATION

Societies are made up of intertwined structures and processes of interacting, interdependent actors whose identity, cognition, and behavior are mutually contingent (Elias 1978, 103). These interdependencies tend to stabilize social orders, including the range from family to the nation-state itself, in spite of the fact that some of their members might be treated unfairly and suffer. This, however, does not preclude change. In fact, the change of one actor entails changes in other parts of a figuration along chains of interdependencies, which ultimately changes the whole figuration (Elias 1978, 133–44). Hence social interactions unfold a multiplicity of simultaneous but interlaced processes without clear casual primacies, which create a momentum of their own that drives social processes. As Elias points out, this explains why an event can emerge from "the interweaving of countless individual interests and intentions" that none of the individuals intend, whether or not they were allied or opposed to one another in their actions. As he says, "really this is the whole secret of social figurations, their compelling dynamics, their structural regularities, their process character, and their development; this is the secret of sociogenesis and of relational dynamics" (Elias 1994, 389).

A relational perspective suggests that self-contained, nonsocial actors whose interests emerge from within themselves—the figures at the center of substantialist views—do not exist. Instead, Elias posits that "[because] people are more or less dependent on each other first by nature and then through social learning, through education, socialization, and socially generated reciprocal needs, they exist, one might venture to say, only as pluralities, only in figurations" (Elias 1994, 213–14). I argue that this understanding explains the actions of both elite and nonelite actors of rebellion: their embeddedness in different positions of the wider social environment plays a key role in their identities, interests, and behavior. This social environment—and with it the rebel figuration—is shaped by forces on various levels, including, for instance, external political and economic forces that transform the context within which rebellion is taking place.

POWER

Uneven but constantly shifting power relations between actors play a major role in determining societal figurations. Elias notes that dynamic power balances are indeed "at the very hub of the figuration process" (1978, 131). Using the term *field* instead of *figuration* to depict the social space under investigation, Bourdieu also highlights the role of "people who dominate and people who are dominated." To him, power "defines [every actor's] position in the field and, as a result, their strategies" (Bourdieu 1998, 40–41). In the thinking of Bourdieu and Elias, actors do not themselves have power; rather, their relationships confer power through their interactions. While power balances are skewed in most societal figurations, power does not flow only from above to below. Even where power differentials are at their greatest, the ruled fulfill certain needs and functions of the rulers. This exerts figurational pressures on the rulers. In fact, all parts within a figuration influence each other, and this includes the influence of the least powerful on the most powerful. This relational understanding of power sheds light on the reciprocity of power: the more powerful actor depends on the less powerful actor, in spite of the former's dominance (Elias 1983).

Authority thus becomes an inherently relational concept. The behavior of any social actor is not the result of self-propelled agents purposefully acting on their transcendental individual interests and powers. It is the outcome of figurational pressures that result from fluctuating power constellations within a particular social figuration (Paulle, van Heerikhuizen, and Emirbayer 2012, 75–78). Rebel movements have strict military hierarchies that entail stark cases of domination and obedience. Yet foot soldiers and other low-ranking rebels possess their own motivations and agency, which can both make for an uneasy relationship with elites and shape the dynamics of the overall movement.

HABITUS

From a relational perspective, identity, interests, and behavior all flow from the individual's internalization of the social. Bourdieu as well as Elias have conceptualized this phenomenon as habitus: evolving systems of dispositions that structure one's ways of perceiving, feeling, thinking, and acting. This understanding conceptualizes human behavior not as the outcome of calculated response to the individual's externalities but as the routinized practices of what he or she considers to be appropriate within a relational context. Past and present conditions, which occur within a certain social figuration, structure the habitus, ordering individuals' perception and actions in routinized practices (Bourdieu 1990, 53). History thus produces the habitus, and individual perceptions then rely on it (Bourdieu 1990, 54). Social actors essentially become the *"product of history"* (Bourdieu, as cited in Bourdieu and Wacquant 1992, 136).

Despite its structural qualities, habitus is not a deterministic concept. Comparing life to sport, Bourdieu also calls habitus "the feel for the game" (as cited in Maton 2014, 54), stressing the inventive, active side of habitual practices. Actors, indeed, strategize in order to improve their position within the power balance that lies at the core of every relational figuration (Maton 2014, 54). This turns figurations into sites of ongoing renegotiation and contestation between differently situated and empowered actors. In contrast to rational-choice theory, however, Bourdieu describes actors as being limited by their current position in the figuration. This affords them only a particular set of abilities and limited paths in which to maneuver. As habitus is also the basis of the actors' perception of themselves and their situation, not all of these options might be visible or seem to be feasible (Maton 2014, 52). Choices made will in turn impact future perceptions of their interests and options as the habitus evolves. This leads to the emergence of strategic schemes or repertoires which actors resort to in their everyday practices.[1] Applying this understanding to rebel movements reveals that rebellion is a dynamic social process.

REBELLION AND SOCIETY

In contrast to approaches that analyze rebel movements as being separate from society, the conceptualizing of rebellion as a social process involves analyzing it as a movement that is ontologically embedded in its social environment. Change in the social environment entails change in the rebel figuration. While zooming in on the internal politics of rebellion, my relational approach remains attentive to the ways in which powerful external forces—including, for instance, wider transitions in the political and economic landscape—shape not only the social context within which political violence takes place but also rebellion itself. In fact, my framework allows for asking how external forces impact the social figurations of rebel movements. These are not only organizations or groups but figurations that entail rebel soldiers as well as more loosely affiliated members and supporters like students, activists, and community leaders. Differently situated actors in these networks can have distinct ideas and motivations, which complicates the dynamic and reciprocal power relations between them. These tensions are especially pronounced between rebel leaders and the grassroots, such as rank-and-file soldiers or local communities. The fundamental challenge rebel leaders need to overcome to build a cohesive, capable political and military counterproject to the incumbent state is that of ensuring compliance and support with their rebel social order among local communities as well as the rank and file of a movement. Since sheer force cannot ensure compliance, rebel leaders need to promote a perception of legitimacy among rebel grassroots. Similar processes of legitimacy are as much at stake when rebel leaders compete with rival factions within their own movement as when they struggle against the state. Understanding this social process of rebellion involves answering the key question of how a movement's grassroots come to view differently situated elites as more or less legitimate in relation to one another.

Conventional theories of civil war have not been concerned with the internal politics of nonstate armed groups. This is also why they often failed to account for the empirically observed behavior of rebel movements, which often seem to employ violence in a suboptimal way when measured against their presumed strategic objectives vis-à-vis the state they are fighting against. Students of armed conflict have therefore started to question the assumption that rebel movements are unitary actors whose behavior is the result of purposive strategies in reaction to their external environment (Pearlman 2009; Cunningham, Bakke, and Seymour 2012; Staniland 2014). These scholars have generally explored the causes, dynamics, and effects of group fragmentation and factional contestation within rebellion. Wendy Pearlman's (2009) work, for instance, shows that these processes can lead to negotiation or spoiling strategies that, while suboptimal from an external utility perspective, can be rational for forwarding internal power interests. Cunningham et al. (2012, 69) agree that individual rebel factions struggle for leadership against each other even as they vie with the state, in which they seek to gain benefits for the movement as a whole. Their findings support the argument that conflict behavior of individual rebel factions that seems at odds with their preferences in the wider opposition toward the state is often perfectly consistent with their internal struggle for power.

My book builds on this body of literature. It understands rebel groups as heterogeneous movements in which differently situated actors form malleable alliances, fragment into factions along various fault lines, and wield different sources of authority corresponding to their location within a fluid network of power embedded in wider society. These internal cleavages entail contention for leadership between rival factions, which in turn develops a momentum of its own in driving armed group behavior. The interactions between both elite and nonelite actors play a vital role in these dynamics. Rather than being the outcome of elite strategizing, armed group behavior reflects a multifaceted and evolving social process between differently situated actors. The bulk of recent analysis has focused on strategic decision making at the level of factional elites based on new understandings of the impact of the social process. In fact, it focuses on factional elite politics to the exclusion of paying attention to mass participation.

Successful popular rebellion, unlike forms of nonstate political violence such as small-cell urban terrorism, is primarily sustained by mass participation. Leaders of popular rebellion rely on the grassroots of a movement for the intelligence, recruits, food, taxes, and shelter they need to challenge a militarily superior state army (Staniland 2014, 1–24). Generations of political theorists—from Machiavelli to Max Weber—have agreed that pure coercion is unstable and ultimately impotent for creating sustainable systems of compliance, obedience, and support (Zelditch 2001). Popular rebellion, therefore, depends on nonelites' granting of legitimacy to rebel elites in their authority over them and their struggle against the state (Wickham-Crowley 1987; Mampilly 2011; Staniland 2014). Rival rebel elites therefore must seek such legitimacy in their internal factional contestation with each other. A gap between the motivating ideas at the elite and nonelite levels of mass movements often makes their relationship an uneasy one. Thus, as James Scott wrote in his studies on communist and nationalist insurrections, "Doing justice to radical movements requires not only the analysis of the ideas and activities of radical elites but also the recovery of the popular aspirations which made them possible" (1979, 98). This book will seek to do justice to the rebel movements I study in this way.

I characterize the actors within rebel social networks as incumbent leaders, aspirant elites, and a movement's grassroots. The first two categories align with what Pearlman (2010) calls rebel leaders and aspirants. Incumbent leaders are the official political and military leaders of rebel groups. They wield the most power and have the greatest say in decision making. They might be fighting against the state, but they are also interested in maintaining the status quo within their movement. Aspirant elites are also elite actors. In contrast to incumbent leaders they are not in direct control and lack access to institutional resources. Yet they have political skills and ambition. They also command some power and authority within the movement, for instance, as junior leaders or commanders of regional units. Some aspirant elites wish to gain a leadership position for personal gain. Others vie for leadership because their aims for the collective or their preferred means to achieve shared aims differ from those of incumbent leaders. Incumbent and aspiring leaders conflict with each other in ways that can cause group fragmentation and power struggles within a movement.

Rebellion is a network that spans different nodes within wider society and can include such social elites as community leaders, activists, religious authorities, and businesspeople. Literature on rebellion has generally overlooked these actors, as they often have not taken up arms as part of the rebellion. Yet they may have close working relations with rebel leaders for whom they fulfill crucial functions, including mobilization, funding, and intelligence. They can legitimize or delegitimize incumbent rebel leaders by endorsing or opposing their cause among local communities. In fact, their loyalty to rebel leaders may be easily disrupted. Further, they can become rebel leaders or aspire to such positions. As they wield power with the rebel grassroots, they are an integral part of the rebel landscape.

Rebel grassroots are crucial to understanding rebel groups. They can, for instance, be the foot soldiers of guerrilla armies or administrators of a rebellion's political wing. They can include supporters from local communities who have no official role in the rebel movement but support it. As Schlichte (2009a, 19) pointed out, these multiple forms of participation create fuzzy in-group and out-group boundaries. Fluid overlapping between combatants and civilians is, in fact, a defining criterion of most nonstate armed groups. There are various reasons for this. It provides an essential advantage in fighting asymmetric warfare against a militarily superior state (Schlichte 2012, 722). In addition to complicating the state's task of combating actors of unclear status, blurriness arises from the creation of parallel governance structures and the provision of services, a key mechanism whereby rebel groups mobilize and build legitimacy (Mampilly 2011, 12). Moreover, popular rebellion is often embedded in the everyday meshing of society through kinship and other social ties between civilians and rebels (Shah 2013, 494). This can generate strong networks of support and loyalty in families of fighters (Kalyvas 2006, 125). In places of protracted social conflict rebel social networks can be widespread in society, comprising civil society actors like agricultural cooperatives, churches, student associations, social activist groups, and other community-based organizations and institutions, all of whose members may join without being active supporters of a particular rebel movement (Wood 2003, 190).

A researcher finds that active membership in and passive support of rebellion are difficult to distinguish. Civilians might support the rebel cause not by joining ranks on the front line but by providing intelligence or food to rebel soldiers or simply by not giving them away to state agents. Furthermore, participation in rebel governance structures need not involve conscious conviction and outright support of the rebels' political cause. Indeed, teachers and students in rebel-operated schools may simply lack alternatives. Similarly, local communities might support rebel groups that can provide effective security in times of war without necessarily sharing their ideologies. Still, their participation and support shape their views and values as well as strengthen and legitimize the rebel figuration. Membership and support are not fixed but fluctuate over time as people join and leave the rebellion or decide to support a rebellion at one time but not another. Local communities might support a rebel movement at one point in time, but their support can wane. A guerrilla might engage in combat during part of the year and then remove to his or her home community in harvest season to work in the fields. (Wood 2003).

Notwithstanding the manifold forms of participation, rebel grassroots have their motivations for backing the rebellion as well as opinions regarding the movement and its elites. They may not consciously direct or intend to direct the conduct of the collective, yet their importance in sustaining popular rebellion makes rebel elites dependent on them. Rebel leaders need to ensure their active support or at least their passive compliance.

AUTHORITY IN REBEL MOVEMENTS

Contrary to contemporary orthodoxies in Western scholarship, policy, and media that associate rebellion foremost with terrorism, "warlordism," and predation upon civilians, most rebels are political actors with complex relationships to local communities. Their principal aim is to seize power from the state and consolidate it (Wickham-Crowley 1987; Schlichte 2009a). Militarily, rebels depend on local community resources. Politically, rebels must create legitimate authority and voluntary obedience among local communities. Therefore they depend on stable support from the grassroots of their movement (Mampilly 2011; Staniland 2014). Given that coercion is not sufficient to create such stability, elites need to turn "naked power" into authority, which, in Weber's words, is "ein Sonderfall von Macht" (1980, 541)—a "special kind of power"—because it relies on some degree of voluntary compliance (Uphoff 1989, 295). Coercion is transformed into authority by processes of legitimation (Weber 1947, 324; Zelditch 2001). Thus legitimacy is quite literally the most important part of holding political power (Jost and Major 2001).

While this conceptual link between power, legitimacy, and authority is well established in theories of state–society relations, it is uncommon to ponder the legitimacy of violent nonstate actors. On the one hand, this is because normative theories about legitimacy, which ask what legitimate rule ought to be, and descriptive theories about legitimacy, which ask when the ruled accept a political order as legitimate, are often conflated. On the other hand, rebel groups by definition pose a threat to the established international system made up of sovereign nation-states. As Zacharia Mampilly points out, many political scientists in general and students of international relations in particular have therefore come to understand rebel groups above all as warlords, considering them "ahistorical, economically minded actors" who have no right to exist in the Westphalian state system (2011, 28). Empirical investigation has shown, however, that nonstate armed groups can contest state legitimacy. At the onset of a civil war, for instance, civilians' support is rarely decided and often depends on how they are treated by the warring factions (Kalyvas 2006, 101–3). To analyze empirically when the grassroots of rebellion accept or reject different rebel social orders as legitimate, it is necessary to adopt a subjective definition of legitimacy, one which stresses the perception of the actors themselves.[2] For this purpose I rely on the sociologist Morris Zelditch: Something is legitimate "if it is in accord with the norms, values, beliefs, practices, and procedures accepted by a group" (2001, 33).

The importance of building legitimate authority relations with local communities has featured heavily in the manifestos of left-wing rebel leaders, including Mao

Zedong, Ernesto "Che" Guevara, and Ho Chi Minh (Mampilly 2011, 11–13). Despite this earlier consensus, security and conflict studies have only just begun to investigate questions of rebel legitimacy and authority. A notable exception is the scholarship on rebel governance (Mampilly 2011; Arjona, Kasfir, and Mampilly 2015).

RECIPROCAL EXCHANGE RELATIONS

I conceptualize rebellion as a social process by drawing attention to the workings of authority within the rebel figuration, that is, between elite actors and the movement's grassroots. This allows one to analyze dynamics of legitimacy in both of the dual struggles in which rebel elites are engaged, namely, the struggle against the incumbent state and the internal contestation among rival factions. To do so, this framework proposes the following two interlaced processes that seem central to the building or erosion of legitimate authority between differently situated rebel elites and their movement's grassroots: (1) reciprocal exchange relations between the elites and grassroots of a movement and (2) experiences of recognition that enable rebel grassroots to derive a positive self-perceived social identity from affiliation to the rebel movement.

Mampilly's (2011) observations as well as my own suggest that leaders of popular rebellion recognize the need to build and maintain legitimacy among local communities. In fact, historic leaders of successful peasant revolutions attributed their success first and foremost to the building of legitimate authority by way of mass mobilization that integrated local communities into the structures of rebellion through the establishment of parallel governance systems (Mampilly 2011, 11–13). In his handbook *Guerrilla Warfare*, Guevara stressed the necessity of establishing administrative arrangements that local communities view as legitimate:

> In view of the importance of relations with the peasants, it is necessary to create organizations that make regulations for them, organizations that exist not only within the liberated area, but also have connections in the adjacent areas. Precisely through these connections it is possible to penetrate a zone for a future enlargement of the guerrilla front. The peasants will sow the seed with oral and written propaganda, with accounts of life in the other zone, of the laws that have already been issued for the protection of the small peasant, of the spirit of sacrifice of the rebel army; in a word, they are creating the necessary atmosphere for helping the rebel troops. (Guevara, as cited in Mampilly 2011, 13)

Rebel leaders of every stripe around the world have long studied these organizational ideas (Mampilly 2011, 11). The leaders of the Karen and Kachin rebellions have done so also (Smith 1999, 93–94). Scholars who study rebel governance, moreover, agree that the measures Guevara describes, including administrative capacities and services, effectively create legitimacy and gain support for rebel movements (Wickham-Crowley 1987; Mampilly 2011).

In his research on authority relations between rebel groups and local communities across Latin America, Timothy Wickham-Crowley (1987, 477) identifies an "implicit social contract" between rebels and local communities living in their controlled territories similar to the one Barrington Moore (1978, 17–31) identifies in peasant–landlord relations. On the one hand, civilians in rebel territories are to support rebel rule or at least not resist it. On the other hand, rebels are expected to defend the local populace from external enemies, maintain internal order, and improve the population's welfare, for instance, by providing basic health and education services. Local communities may not enter into such contracts consciously, but when rebels fail to meet their obligations under the contract, their legitimacy will erode (Wickham-Crowley 1987). As Wickham-Crowley points out, "guerrilla authority" is fragile (1987, 492).

The framework of my argument builds on the idea of an implicit social contract between rebel leaders and a movement's grassroots by stressing the reciprocal, noncoercive nature of authority relations within rebellion. I seek to account for a variety of factors that lead to such contractual relationships mindful of the legitimate criticism leveled against examinations of strongman authority which argue that local communities purposefully sell their allegiance to the highest bidder among local authorities (Barth 1959). Such strategic notions ignore constraining and motivating factors, most importantly dynamics of power and domination (Asad 1972). Weber's theories support the understanding that a variety of motivations work simultaneously to create rebel authority. Speaking about the person subjected to authority, Weber points out that the motives underlying obedience "can rest on considerations varying over a wide range from case to case, all the way from simple habituation to the most purely rational calculation of advantage" (1947, 324).

Joining or supporting a rebel movement rarely brings short-term payoff to anyone who is not elite within the movement, and it typically carries significant risk, including risk of death. Thus it seems likely that grassroots assistance does not reflect strategic calculations over distributional outcomes. Kalyvas suggests that those who aid rebellion might sometimes consider it a "natural course of action" and not make conscious deliberations (2006, 125). Similarly, Kevin Toolis reflected on his encounters with a family of supporters of the Irish Republican Army (IRA) in the small Northern Ireland town of Coalisland in the 1970s: "At the kitchen table, I sat asking the same question over and over again—why had Tony joined the IRA? The logic of the question was unintelligible to the Doris family. In their minds the mere description of life in Coalisland was sufficient to explain why Tony had joined the IRA. My naïve question shook this natural assumption. They searched for ways to explain something that was so obvious it was inexplicable" (as cited in Kalyvas 2006, 125).

Toolis describes a set of routinized practices that depend on relationships and embodied social environments that structure individuals' ways of perceiving, feeling, thinking, and acting. A habitus such as this generally stabilizes social orders by imposing control on actors. As Bourdieu writes, the habitus produces an "ongoing dialectic of subjective hopes and objective chances" (as cited in Bourdieu and Wacquant 1992, 130). For some rebels the expectations of the people around them fit the opportunities their position within their social context provides. Habitus and figurational interdependencies work hand in hand to stabilize the social order, which, in the case of rebel movements, involves giving them support. Thus people enter into the implicit social contract rebel movements offer because they perceive social orders as natural and therefore do not question their underlying injustices, including structural violence engrained within a rebellion's social foundation.

While rebel leaders' deliberate efforts to craft legitimate authority relations with local communities by providing public goods may be an element in maintaining the support of the grassroots, the grassroots do not make a similarly straightforward decision. Their struggle for recognition might be more important in determining perceptions of legitimacy.

RECOGNITION AND SOCIAL IDENTITY

In his comparative historical analysis of feudal authority relations between landlords and peasants Moore notes that the peasantry often relied on services by the landed class but rose against it in cases of nondelivery. Yet he stressed that undelivered material promises alone did not lead to uprising: experiences of injustice, such as arbitrary punishment, abrogated the perceived moral obligation to obey traditional rulers and also led to revolt (Moore 1978). Axel Honneth (1996, 167) used Moore's observation to substantiate his formulation of recognition theory. Honneth argues that the struggle for recognition as a morally responsible person by the wider society significantly drives the behavior of each individual (Haacke 2005, 189). Subjective experiences of injustice and resulting moral claims motivate this struggle for recognition (Haacke 2005, 194). If others share similar experiences and claims, the striving to achieve recognition can emerge as the motivational foundation for collective action, including rebellion.

According to Honneth, three spheres of recognition exist: love, rights, and esteem. Love within intimate relationships based on emotional support builds self-confidence. Having rights, whether formal or informal, to take part in public life and participate in collective decisions effectuates cognitive self-respect. Finally, positive societal feedback that results from following social norms improves self-esteem, allowing individuals to feel they possess honor or prestige (Honneth 1996, 92–130). Honneth writes that when present in combination, these three forms of recognition allow humans to feel positively about themselves. That is, "the cumulative acquisition of basic self-confidence, of self-respect, and of self-esteem" allows "a person . . . to see himself or herself, unconditionally, as both an autonomous and an individuated being and to identify with his or her goals and desires" (Honneth 1996, 169).

By contrast, abuse, social exclusion, and perceptions of insult contravene feelings of recognition. Honneth argues that such feelings of disrespect can form the "moral context for societal conflict" and "become the motivational basis for collective resistance" if individuals can articulate them in ways that others can relate to (1996, 162–63). This conception posits that social conflicts contain a "moral grammar." The desire to overcome perceived sources of injustice thus drives conflict because, as Smith writes, "a demand for due or proper *recognition*" from society motivates people (2012, 5). Also building on Honneth's ideas, Jürgen Haacke points out that recognition, social conflict, and legitimacy are inherently intertwined as an individual's claim to recognition from wider society essentially becomes a "normative judgement about the legitimacy of social arrangements" (2005, 187). Social orders that satisfy this claim to recognition are stable. When they do not, a society may experience collective resistance.

Many rebel movements involve the struggle for recognition. Ethnonational rebels, for instance, explicitly make claims to acknowledgment of minority identities and rights in light of cultural and socioeconomic discrimination by ethnocratic states and societies. This is arguably true of other civil conflicts as well. Indeed, Edward Azar's concept of protracted social conflict rests on a similar premise, holding that social groups generally take up arms because they are denied a "separate identity" (1986, 30). Wood's work on the peasant insurrection against a feudal social order in

El Salvador shows how this plays out. She describes feelings of pride derived from partaking in a collective political project endowed with moral principles, the defiance of discrimination and violence perpetuated by the state, and the pleasure of experiencing agency by way of changing entrenched unjust societal structures as the main motivation among rebel grassroots (Wood 2003, 231–40). Members of other kinds of social protest movements also build communal identities of protest upon feelings of purpose and companionship. In cases of violence and injustice, participation can represent what Wood calls a basic "claim to dignity and personhood" (2003, 233). Wood describes this as the workings of an "insurgent identity": "An insurgent might act out of pride in acting as an insurgent, thereby expressing his insurgent identity and membership in the insurgent community. He might act on moral principles, to build a more just world or to express outrage, but also to experience pride in having the courage to have done so. He might act to assert his political efficacy, even his capacity to make history, capacities long denied by landlords or state authorities" (2003, 237).

Members or affiliates of the rebel community, therefore, derive their rebel identity from the association to the rebel collective. The basic tenets of social identity theory see identity as in part derived from group membership, including identity groups such as ethnicity and gender or organizational affiliations, for example, sports team fandom, universities, youth gangs, or revolutionary movements. Self-perceived positive social identity is derived from feeling recognized as a respected member of a group that is associated with high societal standing and moral principles (Tajfel 1978). Such an identity is important, as it leads to feelings of self-esteem and self-worth (Turner 1999, 6–8). Positive social identification can be threatened when out-group or in-group sources question the status and morality of the group. Having one's membership in a group questioned or refused causes social identity threat. These threats can undermine positive social identification and lead to feelings of being disrespected (Branscombe et al. 1999, 46–55). Expressed in terms of recognition theory, group membership, therefore, constitutes part of the social conditions that convey social recognition or misrecognition.

In the case of popular rebellion, the moral principles of the collective are normally formulated with regard to the aims of revolutionary struggle, for instance, the struggle against social injustice and ethnic discrimination (Schlichte 2009a, 99–106). In prolonged armed conflict these principles can give rise to an alternative political culture with particular beliefs, norms, and practices of its own that resemble the collective defiance of the incumbent political order. Wood has called this the "insurgent political culture," encompassing "norms of group solidarity, . . . practices such as rituals and symbols, and beliefs concerning the feasibility of social change and the potential efficacy of the group's collective efforts towards this change" (2003, 219). Group value models in social psychology suggest that the extent to which the grassroots associates a rebel movement with revolutionary values depends primarily on whether nonelites perceive elite behavior as being in accordance with these accepted beliefs, norms, and practices of proper conduct within a society or social group (Tyler 2001). Elite interaction with nonelites primarily determines this perception, as it provides status-relevant information to nonelites through elites' acceptance or rejection of nonelites as recognized group members (Tyler 2001, 421–22).

Alpa Shah's analysis of intimacy relations among Maoist rebels in local Naxalite communities in India supports this argument. She describes the everyday social interaction process between commissars and peasants as a core aspect of elite legitimacy among the grassroots of rebel movements. India's Maoist leaders, who mostly originated from urban elites, managed to build legitimacy for their struggle among marginalized rural communities principally by developing reciprocal, intimate social connections (Shah 2013). Shah attributes importance to manners, tone of voice, willingness to sit on the floor in the homes of rural people. By affording the grassroots dignity and respect, the Maoists won their favor, even though, like state officials, they were of high caste. By means of procedural justice they conveyed to the nonelites acknowledgment as valued members of their movement, which is associated with high societal standing and moral values. The reverse of this argument implies that if elite behavior, decision making, and interaction with a movement's grassroots are perceived as unjust and morally wrong, feelings of misrecognition among nonelites can lead to indignation about the group as a whole and ultimately to resistance against group authorities. For generating or eroding legitimacy within rebel movements the interactions between elite and nonelite actors of rebellion might, therefore, become more important than whether everyone actually receives what participants perceive as a fair share of material benefits.

An Ethnographic Bent

How we see shapes what we see. In order to study the social process of rebellion within the Kachin and the Karen movements, I sought to capture the perspectives of the people involved: elite and nonelite rebels and rebel supporters. Although rebels are central actors in civil wars, conflict, security, and peace studies rarely capture their perspectives. Ranajit Guha famously described how generations of historians have inferred the motivations and dynamics of peasant uprisings in colonial India from the "prose of counter-insurgency" (1988, 84): primary sources produced, processed, and archived by the British Raj. In the absence of firsthand accounts by the rebels themselves, it is impossible to produce an analysis separate from what Guha calls "the code of counter-insurgency" (1988, 70). Guha writes that the historiographic discourse on rebellion produced in colonial India therefore "amounts to an act of appropriation which excludes the rebel as the conscious subject of his own history and incorporates the latter as only a contingent element in another history with another subject. . . . And since the discourse is, in this particular instance, one about properties of the mind—about attitudes, beliefs, ideas, etc. rather than about externalities which are easier to identify and describe, the task of representation is made even more complicated than usual" (1988, 77).

Much of the academic knowledge produced on past and present rebellion in the field of conflict and peace studies suffers from the same problem, namely, the absence of firsthand accounts by rebels themselves. This seems to be the case for two reasons. First, it might often not be convenient for scholars to do fieldwork in conflict areas and listen to rebels. Second, some scholars view rebels as particularly untruthful sources of information (e.g., Collier 1999, 1–2). In fact, the study of political violence has mostly relied on presumably more objective sources, such as government statistics or journalist accounts, to infer the motivations of rebels. Insofar as scholarship has traditionally been interested in the rebel perspective, it has mostly analyzed the ideologies and interests of rebel elites.

My ethnographic approach, in which I embedded myself within both the Kachin and Karen rebellions for several months at a time, thus presents a departure from the norms in the field. Beyond my formal interviews of leaders of the two movements and other relevant elites, the manifold everyday interactions with rebels at every level of the movements opened a window into their internal politics and social fabric. "Deep hanging out"—as anthropologists refer to this ethnographic research practice—enabled me to develop friendly relationships with many of my interlocutors over the course of my fieldwork, and these interactions opened the way to an understanding of their social meaning contexts and lifeworlds, including their perspectives and analyses of their situation (Clifford 1996).[3] Little of their internal constitution is known to outsiders, and it was not initially clear which questions were the right ones. Joining in people's everyday lives allowed me to develop appropriate questions during my research while listening to people on their own terms. This forced me to unlearn and relearn as much as to learn about the two movements.

My observations cannot be divorced from the conditions under which I observed them or indeed from my own persona as a researcher who cares for the people under study (Schatz 2009, 5). Nevertheless, I aim to present what James Scott described as a "plausible account" that should be "judged by the standards of its logic, its economy, and its consistency with other social facts" (1985, 46–47). To do so, I employed self-critical reflexivity before, during, and after my fieldwork to account for my positionality as a researcher and the politics of knowledge production this entailed. While full disclosure of my research within the movements is not expedient due to persisting armed conflict and authoritarianism in Myanmar, the following reflections on my fieldwork will help readers assess the plausibility of my account.

Field research does not mean simply traveling to specific geographic sites. It is primarily about entering and navigating a social space (Clifford 1997). Finding an entry point to the rebel figuration of the KNU in the Thai–Myanmar borderlands was easier than getting initial access to the KIO along the Chinese–Myanmar border. The difficulty in accessing the KIO was owing to the fact that it operates from within Kachin State, most of which remains largely fenced off to Western observers by both the Myanmar and the Chinese governments. By contrast, the KNU, which operates on both sides of the Thai–Myanmar border, has long been relatively more exposed to Western journalists, researchers, and aid workers. Nevertheless, the main challenge to researching both clandestine movements was not necessarily getting initial access. Rather, access points and positionality were interconnected, which inevitably shaped the ways in which I could navigate both social spaces, and this ultimately affected my perspective. My entry points came as a result of certain social associations that opened doors and also shaped the ways in which my interlocutors perceived me and my research. John van Maanen refers to these societies as "webs of local associations" (1991, 39). He advises researchers to choose their associations wisely before entering the field. Timothy Pachirat's (2009) work demonstrates that after gaining access to a particular social space, researchers cannot always freely choose their webs of local association. Their positioning is often determined by others (Pachirat 2009). This was the case in my experience, at least partly.

As I mentioned, I assisted the education arm of the KNU with a large-scale needs assessment survey of their schooling system in the "liberated areas" in Karen State; in addition, I conducted seminars on conflict and peace studies with officers of the KIO in their capital of Laiza in Kachin State. While the webs of local association that came with both entry points were unproblematic in some instances, reflecting on their implications was often important. This was especially the case for my research inside the Karen rebellion. During my time with the KNU, the movement was highly fragmented, parts of its leadership negotiating with the government while others took a position against this conciliatory line. Factionalism and mistrust pervaded the movement when I was with its educational arm. While the education department was not central to this internal power struggle, its leader and staff generally opposed rapprochement with the government. On the one hand, my research benefited from this situation, as it gave me a connection to the internal opposition. On the other hand, it soon became obvious that those who supported rapprochement, especially some of the leaders negotiating with the government, were less willing to talk to me as a result. The KIO was much less fragmented into rival factions at the time of my research, so this was less of an issue in my work on the Kachin rebellion.

In both cases information sharing was rarely a neutral exercise. On the contrary, my position as a white, German researcher in one of the least reported civil wars made me part of the local "information economy" (Goodhand 2000, 12). That reality was accentuated by a situation that was charged with instability, violence, fear, and trauma. This does not mean my interlocutors shared information only with the intention of distorting and distracting. Some people I talked with, those on the elite level especially, have surely presented events in particular narratives that serve their own purposes—such as self-legitimization or mobilization. Yet many others cited different reasons for speaking to me. Most Karen and Kachin rebels as well as other people affected by the armed conflict expressed an eagerness to convey their opinions and experiences to the outside world, which they felt had forgotten about them or formed opinions about the politics in Myanmar without listening to their marginalized perspective. Thus I believe that the main reason for the potential inaccuracies in the accounts I heard is that social processes of memory formation always affect testimonies about past events. Personal experiences, particularly losses, societal norms in grieving cultures, and subsequent political events such as the formation of new alliances all affect which memories are retained or accentuated and which are forgotten or muted (see Wood 2009, 123–24). Another important caveat about the information collected in the clandestine environment of rebel groups and their internal politics is that it was not always possible to discern facts from gossip and rumor, especially if my interlocutor took a rumor for a fact. However, rumors, true or not, were important sources of information in and of themselves for my research on the internal contestation over authority. For example, rumors about Lamborghinis being shipped across the Moei River to buy off rebel leaders are more central to my understanding of judgments about leadership legitimacy among KNU grassroots than whether such deals actually occurred. Rumors offer insights into the beliefs people hold about their leaders and the power relations affecting them in their lives (see Mazurana, Gale, and Jacobsen 2013, 13).

Nonetheless, triangulation of data was pivotal in my project in order to avoid misrepresenting actual events and mitigating potential bias. Independent information was difficult to obtain, but the writings of other academic and nonacademic researchers (Lintner and Lintner 1990; Smith 1999; Kramer 2009; Woods 2011; Dean 2012; Sadan 2013) as well as in-person discussions were invaluable. I also sought to verify information with local journalists, aid workers, and members of civil society. As might be expected, outside accounts did not verify much of the information I obtained on the internal politics of the two movements. Hence I also opted to triangulate information among differently placed members of the rebellions. To do so, I sought several alternative points of entry to different nodes of both rebel social figurations. The geographical spread of my field sites aided me in this regard. When traveling from one region to another, I could often disentangle from previous webs of local associations and embed myself in new ones. People in northern Karen State are, for instance, often more closely networked with individuals in Thailand's Chiang Mai than with people in southern Karen State. This enabled me not only to embed myself within the KNU educational arm but also to establish various other Karen organizations in different regions of Thailand and Myanmar. In the case of the KIO, which was geographically and organizationally less fragmented than the KNU, I triangulated information with KIO insiders from affiliated organizations, including local church leaders, community elders, members of Kachin civil society in rebel and government-held areas, and the diaspora community in the UK.

The various organizations and societal nodes linked to the wider Kachin and Karen rebel figurations also constitute a form of public sphere. While local elders or civil society activists would, for instance, not publicly criticize the rebel leaders and their movements, they critically reflected on their politics and were often willing to share their opinions anonymously. Finding these multiple access points became easier as my research progressed and I gradually broadened my knowledge of and built networks to various stakeholders. My gradual progression throughout both figurations also shaped the way in which my interlocutors perceived me; many would ask where I had been and whom I had spoken to. The KIO and the KNU have historically been allies and were theoretically still allied within the ethnic armed umbrella organization of the United Nationalities Federal Council (UNFC) at the time of my field research. While the movements' differing trajectories with regard to cease-fire negotiations with the government have created tensions and disagreements between some of their leaders, most KNU and KIO members still feel sympathetic toward each other. Therefore it was generally unproblematic to mention that I was speaking to both groups. Some of my interviewees even welcomed my comparative approach explicitly. A KNU insider in Chiang Mai said to me during a formal interview, "You are doing the right thing to compare the KIA and the KNU, or the Kachin case and the Karen. For us, we are trying to use the Kachin as a precedent, as a kind of example that we need to learn from: the dynamics, the pattern, the sequence."[4] These comments are among many that illustrate that local informants engage in sophisticated analyses of the questions I sought to study. They analyze and evaluate the rapidly changing world around them, including Naypyidaw's political transition, the ways in which the changing geopolitics affect local situations, the dynamics of rebellion and counterinsurgency, the ongoing negotiations between armed groups and the government, and, not least, the internal politics in their own movements.

To interpret the wealth of contextual data gathered during long-term fieldwork, the analytical framework used here draws inspiration from recent scholarship on the internal politics of nonstate armed groups. Yet it moves away from the orthodoxy of methodological individualism that focuses exclusively on the strategic decision making of self-propelled rebel leaders. This is because the changing strategies of the two rebel movements under comparison cannot be inferred either by judging from external utilities of supposedly unitary actors or by simply lowering the level of analysis to rival rebel elites. Thus I highlight the social dynamics of rebellion by adopting relational heuristics, as the sociologies of Elias and Bourdieu propose. By focusing on social interdependencies, reciprocal power relations, and embodied practices, this perspective reveals intertwined, multicausal social forces that operate at different levels within the wider networks of rebel movements and develop a momentum of their own in driving collective conduct.

Instead of analyzing rebels as self-propelled individuals, I understand them as being ontologically embedded in a rebel social figuration, which itself is inextricably rooted within a wider socio-temporal space and has indefinite in-group and out-group boundaries. Changes in the environment of rebellion thus entail shifts in the rebel figuration itself. From a relational understanding, external forces such as shifting geopolitics or political economies that transform the social context of political violence also have an effect on the differently placed elite and grassroots actors of rebellion and their relations with each other. Their interactions can lead to the formation of malleable alliances but can also fragment movements into various rival factions that struggle against not only the state but also each other for the movement's leadership. The fundamental challenge for rebel leaders in both of these contests is how to ensure active support or at least voluntary submission among their movement's grassroots. Building legitimate authority relations to the grassroots of a movement, therefore, becomes a pivotal process in the internal contestation of nonstate armed groups and shapes collective willingness and ability to engage in either fighting or negotiating with the state. Two interlaced processes seem to be at play in the building or erosion of authority between differently situated rebel elites across the rebel social network.

First, rebel governance arrangements, particularly the provision of public goods, including welfare and security, can establish reciprocal exchange relations between rebel rulers and local communities in their territory. This relationship can be conceived of as an informal social contract. It entails implicit obligations on both sides. Communities might trade taxes for security. Nonfulfillment can threaten the legitimacy of rebel social orders. Yet the motivations to support rebellion in situations of prolonged armed conflict might often revolve around routinized practices rather than conscious deliberations. Thus rebel authority does not depend solely on the distributional outcome of governance arrangements.

Second, following recognition and social identity theories, rebel authority seems dependent on whether the grassroots of rebellion derives a self-perceived positive social identity from affiliation to the collective. In other words, the struggle for recognition by the wider society motivates the participation and support of nonelite rebels. Rebel grassroots perceive rebel elites as being legitimate if their interaction provides them with feelings of self-respect and self-esteem that the incumbent political order has denied them. I suggest that if the grassroots regards elite behavior as being in line with the dominant beliefs, norms, and practices of the rebel project, they are likely to gain such feelings of self-respect and self-esteem. Elites communicate their dedication to the grassroots through everyday interactions, mainly by way of fair and dignifying treatment that conveys to the latter acknowledgment as valued group members. But if grassroots actors experience collective misrecognition they will question the morality of elites as well as of the rebellion as a social order. Such misrecognition occurs if their interaction with rebel elites involves abuse, social exclusion, or perceptions of insult. This can threaten the positive social identity derived from affiliation with the rebel movement and ultimately result in the erosion of rebel authority and resistance from within.

CHAPTER TWO

NONSTATE BORDERWORLDS

After riding on a small motorbike for almost half a day down a muddy track from the sleepy provincial capital of Dawei in southeastern Myanmar, I reached the site of a proposed deep-sea port midst white sand. The site had been designated for development into one of the largest industrial estates of the country as a special economic zone, including petrochemical facilities, automobile assemblage, a steel mill, and light industries. However, the Thai–Myanmar business conglomerate tasked with developing the special economic zone was encountering financial difficulties, and construction was temporarily suspended. Although no workers were in sight, a young government official was eagerly explaining the company's plans to a small group of potential private investors from across the country.

I introduced myself to the official and told him what my university affiliation was. While the sight of a sweaty foreigner in the middle of nowhere seemed to puzzle the official initially, he quickly warmed to the idea of sharing his developmental aspirations with a European researcher from a university that, after all, goes by the name of the London School of Economics. Overlooking a half-finished highway that connects the site to Kanchanaburi in Thailand by slicing through dense forests, the government official explained that Myanmar's location makes it a natural geopolitical partner for regional development. From his point of view, the only thing needed to transform the country's far-flung, inaccessible borderlands into prosperous hubs of connectivity for the ever-increasing cross-border commerce was the construction of physical infrastructure.

The official's narrative fits well with a currently popular understanding of Myanmar that portrays the impoverished country as Southeast Asia's so-called last frontier economy. Among the country's most valuable assets, this narrative holds, is its strategic location, sandwiched as it is between the region's affluent economies of China, India, and Thailand. The historian and grandson of the former UN general secretary U Thant, Thant Myint-U, for instance, stresses the transformative powers of these "geo-economics" in his 2011 book *Where China Meets India: Burma and the New Crossroads of Asia* thus: "When geography changes, old patterns of contact may disappear and new ones take hold, turning strangers into neighbors, and transforming backwaters into zones of strategic significance" (2011, 3).

Politicians' grand visions recall long-standing historic imaginings of Myanmar's geostrategic relevance, such as the Burma Road, built by the Allies during the Second World War as the "gateway to China" to supply Chinese nationalist troops fighting the Japanese (Deignan 1943). Such visions dovetail with current geopolitical strategies and worldviews in the region, including China's "look south" strategy, India's "look east" policy, and the Thai strategy toward its western neighbor as well as development policies of regional organizations like the Asian Development Bank. All of these aim at fostering commerce and regional economic integration by increasing connectivity through infrastructure construction to develop the Myanmar "land bridge" (Florento and Corpuz 2016, 215).

These plans rarely mention the fact that Myanmar's borderlands are far from stable. Indeed, the highway connecting the Dawei industrial project to Thailand passes through territory in which units of the Karen rebellion remain active. And while the heyday of ethnic rebellion in Myanmar has certainly passed, a small disruption in the safety of a highway may be fatal. Large parts of the country's borderlands contain an impressive array of nonstate armed groups, some of whom maintain relatively sophisticated statelike structures in the pockets of territory under their control. Since 2011 large-scale violence between the state and the Kachin rebellion and other ethnic armies has broken out in the country's north. This happened despite the fact that economic development coupled with bilateral cease-fire agreements had previously provided unprecedented stability and an inroad for the state to continually expand its presence. The escalation of conflict in Myanmar's Kachin State suggests that forces of state consolidation driven by powerful economic interests may not be the key to pacifying Myanmar's borderlands. Indeed, geopolitical and geoeconomic formations impact local conflict dynamics in Myanmar in more multifaceted ways.

In order to understand these contemporary dynamics, this chapter will take the long view to explain the roots and development of Myanmar's protracted ethnic conflict and the social contexts of rebellion, both of which emerged within a wider, transnational landscape of interconnected, nonstate borderlands, or what Mandy Sadan called the "borderworlds of Burma" (2013). It also contextualizes the politico-economic transformations in these erstwhile far-flung regions, which have enabled the state to consolidate its presence to an unprecedented, if still patchy, extent. These historical developments are crucial to understanding the situation Myanmar's rebels face today: overlapping and constantly shifting political orders that encompass a variety of state and nonstate authorities.

Nonstate Histories

The mountains that separate Myanmar from India, China, Laos, and Thailand have long interested students of borderlands in diverse disciplines. This is not least because they are among the last vestiges of an extensive zone of limited statehood, straddling the fringes of strong state centers across Asia, a region that has come to be known by the name of Zomia. This entity consists of approximately 2.5 million square kilometers of remote, inaccessible upland regions surrounding the outliers of the Himalayas, all of which encompass area borderlands outside of the traditional spatial compartments of South, Southeast, Central, and East Asia. *Zomi* means "highlander" in various languages spoken across the upland regions of Bangladesh, India, and Myanmar. In calling the area Zomia, Willem van Schendel (2002) stressed the distinctive historical development of highland political orders among the hundreds of "hill tribes" in these areas, located far from the various lowland centers of power.

The analytical distinction in Asia between the political orders of highlanders and lowlanders, or hill tribes and valley peoples, has a long tradition. The region that now comprises the polity of Myanmar has played a prominent role in forwarding this binary understanding. The colonial administrator of British Burma, James George Scott, for instance, stressed the distinctiveness of Burma's lowland plains from its highlands. He described the extremely remote gorge of the N'Mai River in the northern mountains, which "seem to be as wild and unengaging as the inhabitants"

(Scott 1900, 4). These inhabitants, the Kachin, were "essentially a hill people" characterized by ethnic fluidity and martial traditions (Scott 1900, 360). The multitude of "tribes, sub-tribes, and clans" was a symptom of "the isolating character of their abrupt hills and valleys and still more . . . their combativeness and their maintenance of blood feuds"; he compared the Kachin to the Karens (Scott 1900, 369–70).

Academic scholarship on Myanmar and Zomia more generally has reiterated the basic tenets of Scott's assessment, both in terms of the divided political orders between lowlands and highlands and the fluid, anarchic characteristics of highland societies. Most prominently, one of the founding fathers of modern political anthropology, Edmund Leach, noted that the historical development of state orders in the region led to the divide between highland and lowland societies, driven by their different agricultural practices. He refers to "Hill People" and "Valley People," attributing to the highlanders a more egalitarian form of social order. Their large-scale paddy rice farming in the more densely populated valleys necessitated higher degrees of organization and hierarchy than the small-scale, shifting cultivation practices in the sparsely populated mountain ranges (Leach 1960, 51). In his foundational work *Political Systems of Highland Burma: A Study of Kachin Social Structure* Leach (1954, 234) argues that Kachins stay in the hills because they value political independence over the economic advantage of migrating to a more prosperous valley area. Leach had served as an officer in the colonial British Burma Army, and he stressed that many Kachin social orders were not always nonhierarchical but oscillated between egalitarian and hierarchical modes of ordering, *Gumlao* and *Gumsa,* respectively. The Kachin's opposition to central rule, which created regular resistance to chiefs who might dominate a hill area, naturally placed them in opposition to the hierarchic orders of lowlands kingdom as well.

Leach's maybe romanticized idea that the Kachin, and by extension other highland societies in the area, preferred "independence above everything else" (1954, 234), influenced James Scott's take on Zomia. In *The Art of Not Being Governed: An Anarchist History of Upland Southeast Asia* Scott (2009, 283) seeks to explain why this area has been a hotbed of armed insurrection. Rather than viewing upland societies as historically separate from the region's centers of power, he explains that relations to lowland state development inherently shaped their evolution. In Scott's reading, swidden agriculture, dispersed modes of settlement, and decentralized political organization were not a sign of backwardness and separateness but instead reflected conscious state evasion, practiced by people who sought refuge from the authoritarian modes of extraction, control, and slavery that the political economy of lowland kingdoms was based on. While concentrating on present-day Myanmar, Scott contends that similar contentious relationships existed between the hills and other imperial cores, including the Siam, Khmer, and Han empires. This essentially turned Zomia into "a zone of refuge or 'shatter zone'" (Scott 2009, 7). While scholars have criticized the historical accuracy and evidence of Scott's claim that Zomia constituted itself through active state flight, the basic thrust behind the concept of Zomia as a region whose fluid political orders have defied the projection of power by nearby lowland states for centuries remains useful (for a critical engagement with Scott's work, see Lieberman 2010; Formoso 2010).

Other borderlands in the Global South evidence center–periphery conflicts between nonstate borderlands and state centers. Many of these conflicts date back to colonial powers' mapping of borders onto preexisting social, cultural, and political entities. In order to redraw such boundaries, colonial states and their postcolonial successors have therefore often engaged internal colonization, which turned many borderlands into militarized frontiers of exception and resistance, as they remain today (Goodhand 2008; Korf and Raeymaekers 2013). Nevertheless, the territorial expansion of Asian states since the early twentieth century has shrunk Zomia. State expansion, however, has not always translated into the linear consolidation of statehood in the region's far-flung borderlands. Attempts to incorporate these areas into colonial and postcolonial state-building projects have instead transformed and added additional layers to the uneasy relationship between centers and peripheries. In Burma colonial state making has solidified once-fluid social identities and given rise to competing and militarized ethnonational forces.

EMERGING ETHNONATIONALISM

After the third Anglo–Burmese War in 1885 the British Empire conquered the territory that today comprises the polity of Myanmar. Compared to neighboring India, British Burma remained peripheral to imperial core interests. Britain sought to rule it with minimal effort and cost. Burma's remote, inaccessible highlands interested colonial rulers even less than the central plains, whose timber, oil, and rice industries were soon booming. The British divided Burma into Burma Proper and the Frontier Areas. While the country's Burman ethnic majority was governed directly in Burma Proper, the colonial governors for the most part ignored the ethnic minorities who populated the Frontier Areas. As in other such supposedly unprofitable peripheries of the empire, for instance, southern Sudan, the minimal administration of the Frontier Areas largely occurred through local intermediaries. Colonial administrators mapped the diverse, fluid ethnic structures of society in ways that made them intelligible to the bureaucratic colonizing state (Smith 1999, 40–48).

Administrative standardization turned multifaceted identities and malleable social orders into fixed categories. The hereditary chieftain system, for instance, which the colonial government co-opted in order to maintain order in the Frontier Areas, became little more than a colonial invention, much like what has been described in other colonial contexts (see Ranger 1983). Rather than ruling the highlands benevo-lently through traditional institutions, the colonial government displaced fluid social orders that had often incorporated ample possibilities for ousting overarching rulers. Instead, it sanctioned the despotism of local strongmen (Smith 1999, 47). Moreover, the colonial state's reordering of society planted the seeds of ethnic conflict, again in a way similar to that in other colonial settings (see Mamdani 1996). While ethnic self-identification was traditionally fluid and often of secondary importance to other axes of identity—such as one's place in the tributary hierarchy (Gravers 1999, 19)—bureaucratic classification schemes created and entrenched ethnic identities and differences, usually along linguistic boundaries that had not previously existed. As Robert Taylor explains, Burma's political elite has accepted these boundaries, and "politicized ethnicity" has become the driving force of politics in Burma: "The politi-cally neutral Burmese word lu-myō literally meaning 'kind of man' came to be trans-lated as the emotive term for race or nation." Taylor writes that this has led to a situation in which "[it is] impossible to avoid the use of broad ethnic labels even while attempting to demystify them" (1982, 7–8).

Ethnic minorities in Burma had a relationship to colonial invaders different from that of the ethnic majority. Most had never been integrated into the precolonial king-doms in Burma and felt no allegiance to it. Some had historic grievances against

Burman domination and rule. A series of violent wars between Burmese, Mon, and Siamese courts that killed many Karen preceded British colonial rule. Many Karen thus viewed the British as liberators from decades of oppression and aided in the British conquest of Burma in the nineteenth century as guides and porters (Smith 1999, 44). Missionaries found greater success in highland areas than in the valleys, and many ethnic minority communities there—particularly the ones that are known today as Karen, Kachin, and Chin—converted to Christianity and were educated in Christian schools, which made them amenable to Western rule (Taylor 1982, 12). Coupled with the stereotype of naturally martial ethnic groups, these factors made the colonial armed service favor ethnic minority soldiers. Furthering their efforts, enlistment became one of the few career options leading to status and economic benefits for young men in remote villages (Sadan 2013, 198–253). On the eve of the Second World War, the British Burma Army had 472 Burman soldiers and 1,448 Karen, 886 Chin, and 881 Kachin soldiers (Smith 1999, 44). Preferential recruitment hardened the distinctions between ethnic groups, and the colonial government put the army to work in ways that increased their animosity.

The main purpose of the British Burma Army before the Second World War was to quell majority dissent and growing Burman nationalism. The deployment of ethnic minority units to violently suppress Burman uprisings, such as the Saya San rebellion of 1930–31, unsurprisingly led Burma's ethnic majority to resent minority collaboration with imperial rule (Taylor 2006). The effect of such ill will was that nationalism in Burma Proper developed in opposition to its ethnic minorities as well as to British colonial rule. As Matthew Walton notes, emerging nationalism in lowland Burma was ethnically exclusive, equating "elements of Burman culture and Burman history with a presumably broader 'Burmese' heritage" (2013, 8).

Societal rifts deepened when the geopolitics of the Second World War further pitted Burma's population groups against each other. Many ethnic minorities remained loyal to the British and their allies and proved instrumental in repulsing the Japanese forces that overran Burma in 1943. US Department 101 of the American Office of Strategic Services, the forerunner of the CIA, for instance, recruited almost eleven thousand Kachin soldiers for its war effort in Burma (Sadan 2013, 262–63). Burman elites sided with the Japanese Imperial Army; they trained in Japan and established the Burma Independence Army (BIA) that drove the British out of Burma along with the Japanese. During this campaign independent units of the BIA and adjunct local militias committed reprisal attacks on ethnic minority communities, including several massacres in Karen and Kachin villages (Callahan 2003, 75; Sadan 2013, 257). These violent interactions drove mutual antagonism and fear between Burma's ethnic majority and its minorities to an unprecedented level. The director of the colonial Frontier Areas Administration, H. N. C. Stevenson, expressed his worries about this situation in a letter he wrote toward the end of the Second World War. He observed that the way in which the war had set Burma's ethnic groups against each other "increased a hundredfold the ancient animosities between the hills and the plains" (Stevenson, as cited in Smith 1999, 48).

Rising tensions during the Second World War in fact served as a catalyst for the emergence of competing ethnonationalist agendas and organizations in the country's borderlands. Scholars have sometimes viewed this minority ethnonationalism in Burma as a merely reactive and somewhat less authentic phenomenon than the emerging Burman nationalism in Burma Proper (Taylor 2006). But Sadan argues persuasively that Kachin nationalism should be viewed as part of "the region-wide anti-colonial zeitgeist" (2013, 261). Smith states that ethnic minority regions in particular witnessed an "extraordinary political awakening" during these years (1999, 63). Central to the creation of ethnonationalist projects in both Kachin and Karen States were two kinds of local elites: veterans of the imperial service and Christian missionaries.

Imperial service often enabled young men from peripheral ethnic communities to travel across British Burma and across the globe. This exposure led them to appreciate the wider workings of power within which they were serving and opened them as well to new political ideas, including the anticolonialism and nationalism emerging across the region. Kachin soldiers, for instance, trained and fought alongside British Gurkha forces as part of the Mesopotamian campaign of the First World War and often returned as highly distinguished war veterans. Britain sent them to crush Indian colonial troops in the Singapore mutiny of 1915. Witnessing and taking part in this global political struggle in turn sharpened returning veterans' identity as Kachin and therefore their desire to create a space for their own community within the reordering political landscape of Asia (Sadan 2013, 230–37). Analogously, global exposure shaped the ideas of Karen elites serving in the imperial service. The Karen district medical officer San C. Po, for instance, visited London to study in the 1920s. There he published his pamphlet "Burma and the Karens," which compared Burma to Great Britain and the Karen State to Wales, predicting it might become an autonomous entity under the central government (Smith 1999, 51).

Po had attended an American-run Christian missionary school in the Irrawaddy Delta. The school's head, Charles Nichols, was so impressed by the fourteen-year-old boy that he sent him to live with his own family in New York so he could pursue further education. After graduating from Albany Medical College in 1893, Po returned to Burma, where he worked in the imperial civil service as a medical officer and developed a strong interest in the Karen nationalist cause. In addition to fueling ethnic differences by supporting preferential recruitment in the colonial administration and military service, Christianity helped create ethnic disparities in Burma in other ways. In the context of neglect by the colonial state, Christian missionaries provided public services in the Frontier Areas. In contrast to their limited success in proselytizing the Buddhist peoples of the central plains—including the Karen who lived in the Irrawaddy Delta—the animist Kachin, Karen, and Chin communities living in the hills were much more inclined to accept the Gospel and converted in large numbers. In order to translate the Bible into local languages, Western missionaries like Jonathan Wade in Karen State and Olaf Hanson in Kachin State developed the first orthographies for Sgaw Karen and Jinghpaw, respectively. They established an extensive network of mission schools to instill Western-style education as well as tertiary education facilities, including the Kachin Theological College in Myitkyina and the Baptist College, also known by its nickname, Karen College, in Yangon. These colleges trained local elites and quickly turned into hotbeds of their emerging ethnonationalist projects (Sadan 2013, 381–82; Smith 1999, 44–45).

On a broader level, Christian primary and secondary schooling was crucial to overriding parochial self-affiliations with local communities and tribes, which fostered the development of transcending social identity categories such as Kachin and Karen. Besides building the infrastructure that enabled minority ethnonationalisms to emerge, Christianity thus became an intrinsic part of these projects. It served as the ideological vehicle for the imagining of national communities and, indeed, modernity by formulating new meanings and symbols that furthered cohesion in otherwise loosely connected social orders. Lian Hmung Sakhong, who is an academic as well as a nationalist leader of the Chin minority, writes, "Christianity itself became a new creative force of national identity" (2003, xvi). Charles Keyes, who conducted anthropological research on the Karen, argues that Christianity "created 'Karen' identity in Burma" (2004, 212). The same can be argued in the case of the Kachin (Sadan 2013, 35). While non-Christian people self-identify as Karen or Kachin in Myanmar, Christianity has certainly shaped their ethnonational projects in important ways.

In addition to promoting ethnonationalist agendas by exacerbating intercommunal differences and fostering intracommunal cohesion, Christian missionaries actively encouraged local minority leaders in their nationalist quest. Such inspiration was most pronounced in the case of the Karen, which is why subsequent governments of independent Burma commonly accused Christian missionaries of having sown the seeds of ethnic hatred and conflict. One American missionary, for instance, reportedly praised the role of Karen levies in the violent suppression of a Burman-led uprising in 1886 as follows: "I never saw the Karen so anxious for a *fight*. This is just welding the Karens into a nation, not an aggregate of clans. The heathen Karens to a man are brigading themselves under the Christians. The whole thing is doing good for the Karen. This will put virility into our Christianity. . . . From a loose aggregation of clans we shall weld them into a nation yet" (Vinton, quoted in Smith 1999, 45). The "weld[ing]" of Burma's ethnic minorities into nations would lead to civil war when Burma gained its independence in 1948.

Descent into Civil War

Instilled with nationalistic ideas, alienated by the preceding communal violence, and afraid of Burman reprisal for their collaboration with colonial rulers, many ethnic minority leaders demanded substantial provisions of regional autonomy or even outright secession from Burma as the British prepared to cede control of the country. Christian Sgaw Karen elites had organized the Karen National Association, the only sizable ethnic minority party in British Burma and the forerunner of the KNU. Relying on promises that local British officers fighting with Karen units behind Japanese lines had made during the Second World War, Karen leaders believed they had the right to self-determination in principle and that therefore there was little need to negotiate with Burman independence leaders (Smith 1999, 72–76; Walton 2008, 896).

As a matter of fact, ethnic minorities had prominent advocates among the British colonial administration, above all, Stevenson, the director of the Frontier Areas Administration, who had said that the Second World War had worsened tensions between ethnic minorities and the Burman majority. He told the British government in June 1946 that a war for an independent "Karenistan" by the Karen was inevitable. The Karen, he said, "have the guts, the skill, and the allies (the northern tribes) necessary to wrest them [the Karen] from the Burmese by force" (Stevenson, as cited in Smith 1999, 75), and, indeed, they had fought a guerrilla war alongside British forces for four years. Stevenson recognized the demands of the Karen forces, saying that war had not yet started only because they expected that Britain would "giv[e] them a homeland" in compensation for their loyalty (as cited in Smith 1999, 75).

Karen leaders were, in fact, preparing for secession as early as 1945. But other ethnic minorities, including the Kachin, Shan, and Chin, were more inclined to negotiate their potential whereabouts in the future state with Burman elites (Smith 1999,

75–77; Walton 2008, 900). Maj. Gen. Aung San and the Anti-Fascist People's Freedom League (AFPFL), which grew out of a united front of anticolonial political actors resisting both Japanese and British occupation, led the Burman elites. At the first conference at Panglong in 1946 Kachin elders expressed their hopes as follows: "For the hill peoples the safeguarding of their hereditary rights, customs and religions are the most important factors. When the Burmese leaders are ready to see this is done and can prove that they genuinely regard the hill peoples as real brothers equal in every respect to themselves shall we be ready to consider the question of our entry into close relations with Burma as a free dominion" (as cited in Smith 1999, 75).

The Frontier Areas Administration under Stevenson supported these demands for autonomy, for instance, in his proposal, made at the same conference, for the creation of a United Frontier Union encompassing Kachin, Chin, Shan, Karen, and Karenni territories (Walton 2008, 895). Despite a general dislike of the proposal among large segments of the AFPFL, Aung San was open to negotiating autonomy provisions and went to great lengths to convince Burma's ethnic minorities to stay within a future federal polity. Touring Kachin, Chin, and Shan communities, the charismatic leader relentlessly lobbied for a joint national future, stressing the common struggle to achieve the independence of a country that would be based on equal rights for all its citizens. Shortly before the historic second conference at Panglong in 1947 he articulated this vision before a gathering of delegates: "As for the people of the Frontier Areas, they must decide their own future. If they wish to come in with us we will welcome them on equal terms" (Aung San, as cited in Walton 2008, 896). At the conference the Kachin, Chin, and Shan delegates indeed came to an amicable conclusion with Aung San in what has become known as the Panglong Agreement. The positions of the Kachin, Chin, and Shan negotiators were far from homogeneous, but their general posture was to negotiate considerable autonomy provisions within a wider federal union. The Karen were not present; the Mon and the Arakan were counted as belonging to Burma Proper and hence had no representation; and the smaller minorities, including the Naga and Wa, were excluded on the premises of their "primitive nature" (Walton 2008, 903).

Signed on 12 February 1947, the Panglong Agreement states that the parties agree to form a new state together, "believing that freedom will be more speedily achieved by the Shans, the Kachins and the Chins by their immediate co-operation with the Interim Burmese Government," under certain provisions. Among these were that the "citizens of the Frontier Areas shall enjoy right and privileges which are regarded as fundamental in democratic countries" as well as the potential future creation of autonomous ethnic states (Panglong Agreement 1947). The agreement tasked the Constituent Assembly with drafting the new state's constitution. Burman paramilitaries assassinated Aung San in July. The constitution adopted on 24 September 1947, therefore, did not incorporate any of the federal provisions included in the Panglong Agreement. The fact that by then the Karen National Association and various other Karen organizations had reorganized into the much more militant KNU also complicated efforts to resolve the Karen question. Burma refused to create a separate Karen State or to maintain exclusively Karen units in Burma's armed forces, as the KNU, which boycotted the Constitutional Assembly, had demanded (Smith 1999, 83–84). The KNU started to train its first armed wing, the movement's local defense village militia named the Karen National Defence Organisation (KNDO); a larger military wing called the Karen National Liberation Army (KNLA) was formed, but the KNDO endured.

When the British left Burma on 4 January 1948 the new government was already confronting various rebel movements, not least the Communist Party of Burma (CPB). Aung San's assassination had fragmented the AFPFL (Smith 1999, 102–10). Burma's army, the Tatmadaw, was established by drawing on the disparate remainders of these anticolonial forces and the British Burma Army. The Tatmadaw was initially preoccupied with fighting the CPB, despite the fact that Karen units of the KNDO had already taken control of the cities of Thaton and Moulmein in eastern Burma. However, the anticommunist counterinsurgency campaign soon heightened tensions within the multiethnic armed forces. Burman officers grew increasingly distrustful of the loyalties among the many Karen soldiers and officers in the Tatmadaw. They raised Burman levy units, the so-called Sitwundan, in order to fight the CPB. Soon, however, these militias began to attack Karen communities and committed massacres on a large scale. The Tatmadaw's Karen Rifles responded by deserting and joining the ranks of the KNDO (Callahan 2003, 127–32). By the beginning of 1949 the Karen rebellion was in full swing. While the Kachin rebellion was established in 1961, the First Kachin Rifles refused to retake the city of Toungoo from Karen rebels and instead joined their insurrection in February 1949 (Callahan 2003, 134). Trained and experienced from fighting the Japanese, the Karen rebellion quickly took control of most parts of eastern Burma. Various other rebel groups, above all the CPB, conquered large swathes of territory, including most major cities. One year after independence, all-encompassing civil war had torn Burma apart (Callahan 2003, 134–35). The Karen and Kachin rebel social orders developed within this escalating civil war as well as within a wider, violent transnational borderworld that emerged across the region during the Cold War.

Rebel Borderworlds

The Karen and Kachin movements have been the two most powerful ethnic rebellions in Burma for decades, holding large areas of the borderlands. Both have established relatively sophisticated quasi states in their extensive "liberated territories" that have come to be known as Kawthoolei and Kachinland, respectively.

In the official province of Kachin State in the 1980s, for instance, Burma government operations were limited to the major towns and railway corridors in the south. Along the twenty-one-hundred-kilometer Chinese–Burma border, the Burma state was almost nonexistent, as the Tatmadaw controlled only sixty kilometers of the boundary (Smith 1999, 360). But the KIO controlled almost half of Kachin State, governing over forty thousand square kilometers in which more than thirty thousand people lived. Besides fielding more than eight thousand regular troops, organized into four brigades and aided by adjunct village defense militias, the rebel movement operated an extensive governance apparatus. They provided 119 primary schools, 10 middle schools, and 5 high schools. They delivered health care via various medical stations and two hospitals fully equipped with X-ray facilities and operating theaters. Although the KIO-controlled territory has since diminished to about one-fifth its original size, along the Chinese border around the rebel-held towns of Laiza and Maijayang and in the lesser-populated parts of northern Kachin State the KIO has both maintained an extensive nonstate bureaucracy and continues to provide public services in areas under its control (Dean 2012, 121).

Analogously, the KNU once controlled most parts of Burma's officially designated eastern province of Karen State, spanning from Shan State in the north to the

Tenasserim Region in the south, an area much more densely populated than Kachin State. They too established statelike structures in their rebel state of Kawthoolei, including schools and health facilities as well as several departments that functioned much like government ministries. While authoritative numbers are hard to come by, the rebellion's operating territory likely encompassed a population of more than two million people during its peak in the early 1990s. The KNU has lost most of this territory to counterinsurgency campaigns, but it fields up to five thousand regular troops and maintains a partly functioning administrative skeleton (South 2008, 55). Rebellion has become a way of life in both Kachinland and Kawthoolei. Generations of people have relied on governance apparatuses the KIO and KNU provide and have enlisted in the rebel movements.

The international dimensions of Burma's civil war have long been inseparable from the dynamics of regionwide conflict. China, India, Laos, and Thailand have all experienced interstate or intrastate conflicts or both. This transnational network of conflicts emerged in the wake of decolonization and the geopolitics of the Cold War. As in Burma, British and French colonial rule fortified ethnic identification and differences across South and Southeast Asia. Many postcolonial nation builders heightened these tensions by drawing on ethnically exclusive narratives of the national community, equating national heritage with the culture and history of the ethnic majority. Government policies across the region tried, with mixed success, to assimilate indigenous minority groups, most of which live on the fringes of the state, into the larger nation-body by way of social and economic development programs (Duncan 2004). This worked for some minorities but sparked fierce resistance among others. Between 1956 and 1992 several ethnic minorities in Vietnam mobilized armed resistance against the Kinh-dominated South and North Vietnamese governments (McElwee 2004). Ethnic Malays have fought against the Thai State in Thailand's southern borderlands touching Malaysia since 1948. In each of India's northeastern border provinces, the so-called Seven Sisters, an ethnonational insurrection seeks autonomy or secession from India. Some of these conflicts have become intertwined with the rebel movements in Burma. The Naga rebellion fighting the Indian government in Nagaland, for example, operates cross-border from within Myanmar, where it also claims territory (Egreteau 2006, 91–147).

The peripheral location of the social spaces of the Karen and Kachin rebel movements vis-à-vis the state exists simultaneously with their central location within Zomia, where postcolonial remnants have transformed into a transnational rebel landscape of unremitting violence (Sadan 2013, 347). The relations between these manifold rebel movements are multifaceted, involving varying degrees of conflict and cooperation. On the one hand, historical tensions and rivalries fuel resentments among communities, for example, among the Wa, Shan, and Kachin (Scott 2009, 150–53). On the other hand, pragmatic working relations and strategic alliances have fostered cooperation among these various movements, which ignore country boundaries and professed ideological differences when it is expedient. Some groups that have cooperated formally sided with opposing sides of the Cold War. Some even fought alongside each other, as when they adopted so-called united front tactics, which happened, for instance, when the CPB and KNU joined forces in the late 1950s against Burma's government. Rebels also travel frequently within Zomia, trading intelligence and weapons and training each other's cadres (Smith 1999, 183–85, 329–31). In the 1980s it was common for Kachin officers to use their ties to the Assam and Naga rebel movements in order to enter India's higher education system and then return in the service of the Kachin rebellion as doctors and engineers (Sadan 2013, 1–3). The far-flung, rugged mountains and forests allowed little state penetration and constituted an ideal geography for this rebellious, transnational borderworld.

States, too, have affected the politics of Zomia, especially during the Cold War. Maoist China's support of the CPB, which operated mostly from border areas in Shan State, for example, vastly increased the organization's strength. While both the KNU and KIO identify with capitalism, Mao's writings on how to organize guerrilla warfare have inspired and shaped many rebel movements in Burma and beyond, including the Karen and Kachin rebellions. Both movements organize the peasantry by embedding the rebel organization within local communities, and they have elaborated the decision-making structure of their organizations and the institutional makeup of their rebel quasi states on the basis of Mao's *On Guerrilla Warfare* (Smith 1999, 150–51; Smith 2007, 16).

Both rebellions use an intertwined structure of political cadres and military officials that reaches all the way down to the village level. They have adopted the politburo system of communist parties: executive committees head central committees, which are in turn recruited from central and local leaders in the political and military wings. Both the executive and central committees hold periodic meetings reminiscent of regular party congresses. In the KNU's organization a district chairman heads each of the seven districts in Kawthoolei, and each has representation in congress. Until the mid-1990s the Kawthoolei government had a designated prime minister to lead the political apparatus and a defense minister to lead the military apparatus. The KIO's organization is more centralized but substantially similar. Both movements provide services to the peasantry and encourage them to participate in mass-mobilizing organizations, including youth wings and organizations for women. David Taw (2005), who from the mid-1980s until his death in 2012 acted in various leadership positions in the KNU, including as head of its justice department, openly compared the organization's structures to a one-party state.

The Kachin and Karen rebellions' nominal commitment to capitalism brought them into conflict with the CPB at times, but that did not prevent them from forging strategic alliances with the party until its collapse in 1989 (Lintner 2015, 171–203). The KNU's staunchly anticommunist rhetoric won the support of Thailand during the Cold War. The Karen rebellion functioned as a proxy force against communists as well as against the rapidly expanding "narco-armies," most notably the forces of the legendary drug kingpin Chang Shi-Fu alias Khun Sa, dubbed the Opium King of the Golden Triangle. Thai support encompassed material goods, including arms, as well as offers of sanctuary on the Thai side of the border. While these relations have cooled since the end of the Cold War, the KNU maintains close relationships with elements of the Thai security establishment even today. For example, many KNU leaders have lived in Thailand since the fall of their headquarters in the village of Manerplaw in the mid-1990s. Further, Thailand has long hosted liaison offices of the KNU, the KIO, and other Burma rebel groups, which provide a platform for coordinating activities (Sadan 2013, 358; Smith 1999, 293–300).

In addition to the outright backing of neighboring states, the existence of extensive illicit border economies has sustained Burma's conflict by enabling rebels to fund their military campaigns and quasi states. The smuggling of drugs, timber, and gemstones has become a lucrative trade in that regard (Jones 2014a, 791). For many years, however, the most important source of rebel revenues was Burma's isolationist economic policy itself. Under Prime Minister Ne Win's Burmese Way to Socialism, in force between 1962 and 1988, Burma suffered from an immense shortage of everyday goods, from medicine to petrol and textiles. Smuggling these goods into the country proved to be highly profitable, and traders paid for them with raw products like teak, gemstones, rice, cattle, and opium. The annual volume of illicit border trade in 1988 was an estimated US$3 billion, equivalent to 40 percent of the country's gross national product at the time (Smith 1999, 25). For many years the rebel movements funded their rebellions primarily by levying 5–10 percent taxes on smugglers (Smith 1999, 99). According to KNU officials, the Karen rebellion earned up to 500 million Burmese kyat per year during the mid-1980s—at the time £50 million at the official exchange rate—by controlling the most strategic smuggling points along the Thai border (Smith 1999, 283).

This figure may well be overstated, yet these border economies empowered entire rebel movements, including the KNU and the KIO. The main border crossings for smugglers at the Thai border, for instance, were located at Shwe Hser at Phalu and Wangkha by Kawmoorah. These were located, respectively, just south and north of Myawaddy, the only government stronghold on the Thai–Burma border at the time. In the mid-1980s up to one thousand head of cattle moved into Thailand through these points every day, and several tons of manufactured small commodities crossed back into Burma. Smuggling once produced up to one hundred thousand kyat per day at the hands of the KNLA's Brigades 6 and 7 (Smith 1999, 283–84). As of 2013 the only goods that cannot be imported into Myanmar are beer and palm oil, a situation that reduces the former opportunities to make money by smuggling to a mere shadow of their former selves. Since the 1990s the changing geopolitics of Southeast Asia have enabled Myanmar's state to reverse these economic flows and as a result consolidate its presence over large parts of its restive borderlands for the first time.

FROM BATTLEFIELD TO MARKETPLACE

When the Cold War ended in 1991 the state in Burma—by then renamed Myanmar—began to gain power in relation to the various rebel armies. It has since managed to territorialize its restive borderlands to an unprecedented extent. The crucial driving force behind this development was a wider rearrangement of regional geopolitics, owing primarily to changing interests in China and Thailand. Dropping Cold War–era policies that gave covert backing to various nonstate armies, Beijing and Bangkok became increasingly interested in profiting from their neighbor's economic potential by developing their own landlocked and marginalized peripheries. Myanmar's vast but largely untapped natural riches, comparatively large but undeveloped export market, and strategic location for the construction of trade and energy infrastructure presented ideal opportunities for regional development interests. In 1988 Prime Minister Chatichai Choonhavan of Thailand famously pledged to direct Indochina from "battlefield to marketplace," reflecting this interest (Jones 2014a, 791).

Myanmar has seen a rapid influx of foreign direct investment (FDI), mostly from China and to a lesser degree Thailand. The bulk of official incoming FDI, US$38 billion between 1988 and 2012, went into large infrastructure projects, such as gas and oil pipelines and hydropower stations (Buchanan, Kramer, and Woods 2013, 28). These created export rents for the state, empowering it vis-à-vis the borderlands. The steep decline in border smuggling, whose estimated ratio to official trade fell from 85 to 50 percent between 1990 and 2005, also weakened the rebel movements (Jones 2014a, 794). However, two-thirds of the official incoming FDI in 1988–2012 was invested in the country's borderlands, 25 percent of it in Kachin State alone (Buchanan, Kramer, and Woods 2013, 28). These funds support infrastructure projects, above all, hydro-electric dams and pipelines, which were constructed partly or entirely in the country's border provinces, and the extraction of natural resources, including gemstones, precious metals, and timber, which are located above all in the border regions.

With regard to natural resources in the borderlands, official trade and investment figures capture only the tip of the iceberg. The actual investment and trade volumes in these border provinces are much higher, as most money in this sector flows through illicit channels. The country's jade industry is a case in point. Located mainly in Kachin State, jade mining and smuggling have fueled the Kachin conflict for decades. Global Witness, an organization specializing in the study of war economies, concluded in a 2015 report that Myanmar's jade industry "may well be the biggest natural resource heist in modern history" (2015, 95). It is controlled by a network of hidden actors composed of Tatmadaw generals, crony businesspeople, rebel leaders, and the Chinese mafia. According to Global Witness, the main profiteers include the families of the former dictator Than Shwe, the former general secretary of the Union Solidarity and Development Party and retired army general Maung Maung Thein, and a former regional army commander in Kachin State, Ohn Myint, who was minister for livestock, fisheries, and rural development in the U Thein Sein administration. Others profiting from jade mining in Kachin State include drug lords with links to nonstate armed groups, such as the ethnic Kokang Lo Hsing-Han, and Wei Hsueh Kang, a narcotics kingpin and longtime supporter of the United Wa State Army (UWSA) who has a US$2 million US government bounty on his head. Kang and the drug lords are invested through crony business corporations like the Asia World and Ever Winner groups (Global Witness 2015, 10–12).

Some of the KIO's leaders amassed personal riches by collaborating in the expanding jade business during the cease-fire period, but the Tatmadaw has increasingly squeezed both the rebel leaders and their Kachin cronies out of the most lucrative parts of the industry. Indeed, the Tatmadaw has taken control of the main mining sites in Hpakant since the 1994 cease-fire, which mostly left the KIO to tax smuggling operations at the Chinese border (Global Witness 2015, 87–91). The high amount of cross-border smuggling further complicates the estimation of the jade sector's actual value. Myanmar officially bans the sale of high-quality jade outside of the annual Myanmar Gems Emporium in Naypyidaw, but industry insiders report that between 50 and 80 percent of jade stones are smuggled directly across the border to China, the key market for jade gemstones, to avoid taxation and tariffs in both countries (Global Witness 2015, 36). There are no standard rules to determine the value of jade per kilogram. Prices at the 2014 emporium ranged from about US$2 per kilogram for low-quality jade to over US$2.89 million per kilogram for the highest-valued stones, which are known as Imperial jade. Unsurprisingly, available figures of the jade sector diverge widely. The official 2014 Myanmar Gems Emporium reported the total value of jade sales as US$3.5 billion. By contrast, Chinese official import data for the same year recorded an overall import value of precious and semiprecious stones from Myanmar, the vast majority of which was jade, at US$12.3 billion. Figuring in the rampant smuggling activities, Global Witness (2015, 98–106) estimates that the sector's actual value in 2014 was at least US$31 billion, the equivalent of almost half the country's total GDP.

State elites were able to divert a large part of these economic flows from rebel leaders to themselves as well as to consolidate their presence in Myanmar's borderlands to an unprecedented extent because a shift in counterinsurgency strategy accompanied the newly incoming economic interests. This happened at a time when, after the crackdown on the nationwide prodemocracy protests in 1988, Myanmar's regime struggled to prevent ethnic armed groups and militarized democracy activists from uniting. Under the auspices of the newly formed State Law and Order Restoration Council (SLORC), the Tatmadaw reversed its previous strategy of all-out war. The head of Myanmar's infamous military intelligence at the time, Maj. Gen. Khin Nyunt, sought instead to create individual cease-fires with ethnic armed groups. This policy proved to be successful, appeasing the remainder of the CPB, which emerged as various ethnic splinter armies. The communist rebellion had disintegrated after its ethnic rank and file mutinied against a predominantly Burman leadership in 1989. By 2004 almost all nonstate armed groups in Myanmar, including the KIO (but not the KNU), entered into bilateral cease-fires with the state and renounced separatism (Jones 2014a, 795). In 2004 the KNU was the only sizable rebel group still fighting the Myanmar government. Smaller groups included the Karenni National Progressive Party, the militarized prodemocracy activists that trained in ethnic territories post-1988 and formed a movement known as the All Burma Students' Democratic Front; and the geographically isolated National Socialist Council of Nagaland–Khaplang on the Indian border, which operates in Myanmar territory but has mostly fought the Indian military and other nonstate armed groups in northeast India's Nagaland Province.

While these cease-fires did not lead to substantial political dialogue, they allowed rebels to retain their arms and govern pockets of territory (Smith 1999, 421–41). Moreover, the pacts encouraged the involvement of nonstate armed groups in what has since been referred to as the country's "cease-fire capitalism": the collaborative exploitation of the area's natural riches by army generals, rebel leaders, and Chinese businesspeople (Woods 2011). Indeed, political economy scholars have attributed the success of Myanmar's cease-fire politics in the 1990s chiefly to the economic benefits they yielded to elites on all sides. According to this argument, Myanmar's cease-fires challenge he common "resource curse" narrative, showing that natural resources can lead to peace instead of fueling violent conflict (Sherman 2003, 225; Snyder 2006). The longtime observer Martin Smith hints at the importance of these economic dimensions for understanding the deescalation of conflict along the Chinese border since the early 1990s. He notes that turning rebel leaders into business partners accomplished what twenty-six years of fighting had failed to do (Smith 1999, 441). As the veteran Myanmar journalist Bertil Lintner notes, "Rebel commanders who have entered into cease-fire agreements with the government have invariably got, in return, profitable business opportunities—once they have stopped fighting" (2015).

A report titled the *Economics of Peace and Conflict* by the Myanmar Peace Monitor platform makes the argument that economic interests not only were an important force behind the cease-fire politics of the 1990s but also have buttressed the cease-fires U Thein Sein's semicivilian government has concluded with several armed groups since 2012. The platform encapsulated its position in a cartoon that depicts Thein Sein as a teacher-like figure lecturing the leaders of various cease-fire groups, including Sai Leun aka Lin Mingxian, on the "Burma Government Peace Process" (figure 1). Sai Leun leads the National Democratic Alliance Army, a splinter group of the former CPB that was the first nonstate armed group to sign a cease-fire in 1989. The ethnic Shan rules over Mong La, a small town on the Chinese border that has become one of the most well known symbols of cease-fire capitalism because of its thriving prostitution, gambling, and narcotics industries as well as its role as a hub in the global trade in endangered animals. Together with his "teacher" Thein Sein, the "model student" Sai Leun explains to the other "students" how the "Burma Government Peace Process" plan works by dint of a blackboard. The chart on the board illustrates how cease-fires lead to a nexus of economic projects, including resource exploitation and infra-structure development. While this generates money for the cease-fire leaders, political negotiations fade away and legal safeguards such as land rights are denied. The other depicted students, leaders of the rebel groups that signed a cease-fire with Thein Sein's government in 2012, appear to be listening intently. They include Pu Zing Cung of the Chin National Front, Nai Htaw Mon of the New Mon State Party, and General Mutu Say Poe, the Karen leader who led the KNU to accept the movement's historic cease-fire of 2012.

While economic benefits have long played a pivotal role in forging and sustaining the country's extensive cease-fire politics and continue to do so, it would be wrong to reduce the motivation of rebel groups to sign cease-fire agreements to economic inter-ests only. Lee Jones (2014a, 792) points out that battle fatigue, humanitarian consid-erations, a desire for socioeconomic development that would benefit the grassroots, and the genuine belief in political negotiations over the root causes of conflict also played a role. But he does not dispute the role of co-optation of borderland elites since the early 1990s. Co-optation in this context can be understood as the state's attempt to negotiate control in a situation of fragmented state authority. That is, the state projects power indirectly, as scholarship on the "mediated state" and public authority

Figure 1 Cartoon about the new wave of cease-fires in 2012.
Source: Burma News International 2013b, 26.

has shown (Menkhaus 2007). In contrast to such concepts as domination and imposition, co-optation involves a degree of interdependency and constant renegotiation between state and nonstate actors, despite power balances skewed in some direction or other. Co-optation is a well-established practice of government in contexts of fragmented statehood around the world, including the borderlands of Myanmar, from the precolonial era to the present (Scott 2009). Selective co-optation of warring factions is common practice in peace negotiations around the world and has frequently entailed accommodating the economic interests of rebel groups (Le Billon and Nicholls 2007; Wennmann 2009; Driscoll 2012).

In the wake of increased business interests, a securitized development agenda further enabled state territorialization in previously off-limits territories starting in the 1990s. The main vehicle for this has been the Program for the Progress of the Border Areas and National Races Development, introduced in 1989 and later upgraded to the Ministry of Border Affairs. The program is locally known as Na Ta La. Its stated objective is to develop ethnic minority regions, mainly through the expansion of physical infrastructure and the state bureaucracy itself. The frontline commanders of the Tatmadaw have been directly responsible for carrying out this agenda (Lambrecht 2004). Indeed, bureaucratic reform established the military's regional commands as the de facto governments in border provinces. Regional Tatmadaw units have since engaged in local governance, including policing and economic development. The army's overall troop size has increased dramatically from 200,000 troops in 1988 to 320,000 in 1995 (Smith 1999, 426–27). Most of these units were stationed in the country's border areas and were outfitted with US$2 billion worth of modern Chinese weaponry (Jones 2014a, 792). According to local sources, the Tatmadaw presence in Kachin State increased from twenty-six battalions at the time it signed a cease-fire with the KIO in 1994 to over one hundred battalions by the time the accord broke down in 2011 (Burma News International 2013b, 3). A military buildup has also been reported in Karen State since the signing of the KNU cease-fire in 2012 (Karen Human Rights Group 2014, 106–18).

Despite the Tatmadaw's substantial expansion in terms of troop size and mission since 1989, the central government has allocated only meager funds to support regional commands. Between 1989 and 1998 the reported expenditure for borderland development was a modest US$79 million, disregarding the money siphoned off by corrupt officials. Regional commands have been tasked with becoming self-sufficient (Meehan 2015, 269), and this has translated into a reliance on extortion. A large portion of development funding during the 1990s and early 2000s was extorted from local communities as so-called people's contributions in the form of labor, cash, and material (Lambrecht 2004, 156–58). To feed the troops and maintain operational viability, local army units have levied informal taxes on the commodities and assets of local communities, including their land, crops, livestock, and small businesses (Meehan 2015, 2270).

These developments transformed the Tatmadaw into Myanmar's most powerful economic actor, controlling access to the country's most lucrative assets by setting up its own company conglomerates, the Union of Myanmar Economic Holdings Limited (UMEHL) in 1990 and the Myanmar Economic Corporation (MEC) in 1997. While the MEC is mostly invested in heavy industry and commodities, UMEHL controls most of the lucrative gemstone industry in Myanmar's borderlands, including jade mines in Kachin State and ruby mines in Shan State (Maung Aung Myoe 2009, 175–87). The military holding companies tie private entrepreneurs to officials who are in charge of granting trade licenses, joint venture deals, and other business concessions. MEC and UMEHL have squeezed armed groups out of the most lucrative businesses, breaking the KIO's decades-long hold on the jade industry. They also gifted regional commanders of the Tatmadaw with substantial sources of wealth and power on which they could establish personal fiefdoms (Jones 2014b, 149). SLORC's successor, the State Peace and Development Council government, attempted to curtail this emergence of independent power bases by appointing regional commanders to union-level positions (Jones 2014a, 794). Moreover, administrative reforms under President Thein Sein transferred local administrative powers back to the chief ministers of the states and regions. The extent to which these changes have been effective remains unclear. The escalation of conflicts with various ethnic armed groups in Myanmar's north since 2011 and the Tatmadaw's repeated violation of Thein Sein's executive orders to cease fire point toward ongoing fragmentation of military authority in Myanmar's borderlands.

While the changing regional geopolitics and domestic counterinsurgency strategies have worked hand in hand to drive state territorialization in Myanmar's borderlands, state consolidation is far from complete. The empirical analysis in chapters 3 and 4 disputes the idea that economic growth has led to a teleological progression that will culminate in peace and a consolidated state in Myanmar's borderlands. As my research shows, patchy and often overlapping landscapes of political authority that involve the state, semi-autonomous army commands, armed groups, business actors, and informal institutions have risen to varying degrees. Exploring the same phenomenon in the 2000s, Callahan (2007) proposed a good way of conceptualizing this fluid, multifaceted web of power. Drawing on Mark Duffield's concept of an "emerging political complex" (2001, 156), she describes "a set of flexible and adaptive networks that link state and other political authorities to domestic and foreign business concerns (some legal, others illegal), traditional indigenous leaders, religious authorities, overseas refugee and diaspora communities, political party leaders, and NGOs" that "exist in a competitive, yet often complicit and complementary, milieu that varies across geographical space and time" (Callahan 2007, 4–5).

The socio-temporal space of the Kachin and Karen rebellions is indeed not part of a nation-state-like entity akin to the Westphalian nation-state. Applying Duffield's notion of an emerging political complex, one can see the existence of fluid political and social orders in the country's borderlands. Large parts of central Myanmar have undeniably witnessed a remarkable political and economic liberalization since 2011, yet the borderlands have been left to follow their own logic, and the notions of cease-fire capitalism and emerging political complexes continue to be useful for analyzing dynamics of conflict and accommodation. Nevertheless, a focus on material interests alone cannot explain either why the Kachin movement remobilized despite mutual business collaboration with the government or why its cease-fire ultimately broke down. Neither can it account for the increased contestation that surfaced within the Karen movement in the wake of its cease-fire. As Sherman points out, economic incentives alone do not address the root causes of conflict, and they therefore do not in and of themselves create sustainable peace. Myanmar's cease-fire deals have led to an uptick in corruption and criminality, which are destabilizing (Sherman 2003, 246–47). The breakdown of the Kachin cease-fire and subsequent reescalation of conflict with other cease-fire groups along large swathes of the Myanmar–Chinese border proved him right. To understand this return to violence it is important to trace how the politico-economic transformations of Myanmar's borderlands have affected dynamics of authority and contestation within the KIO. Focusing on the intramural relations between differently situated elite and nonelite rebels also reveals how similar challenges are destabilizing the KNU cease-fire in Myanmar's eastern borderlands. This perspective shows how internal, figurational pressures have developed a momentum of their own in driving the conflict and negotiation strategies of both movements.

Back at the deep-sea port construction site in Dawei in southeastern Myanmar, one is inclined to brush aside the existence of continued ethnic armed conflict, including that by units of the Karen rebellion's 4th Brigade that operate not far from there. From here, Myanmar seems merely like a latecomer to the regionwide trend of state consolidation. It appears as though the last unruly corners of a bygone Zomian borderworld will soon disappear. In addition to the state's growing power vis-à-vis rebel movements in the country, increased economic interaction between Myanmar and its neighbors has made inroads by which the state can consolidate its presence in territories once off-limits by turning rebels into business partners. Even though state territorialization and consolidation in the country's restive borderlands are far from complete, observers generally expect this trend to continue. Ashley South, a prominent policy consultant in Myanmar, argues that rebel movements must demonstrate to the international community and especially to foreign investors that they are "part of the solution to developing a modern, equitable and sustainable economy" by participating in peace if they are to benefit their ethnic minority constituencies (2011, 22). Even James Scott wrote Zomia's obituary some years ago. He calls state territorialization and economic development in Southeast Asia "the world's last great enclosure" (Scott 2009, 282). As I will argue, however, the powerful structural forces at work in Myanmar do not override deep-rooted ethnnonationalisms and rebel identities.

CHAPTER THREE

KAREN REBELLION: CEASING FIRE

On 12 January 2012 Myanmar's oldest ethnic armed group, the KNU, signed a cease-fire agreement with Naypyidaw. The truce received much international praise, not least because the KNU was the only sizable rebel movement that continued to battle Myanmar's government during the 1990s and 2000s. Most other ethnic armed groups entered bilateral cease-fire agreements. Commentators expressed the hope that the Karen agreement could lead to lasting peace because of Myanmar's wider political transition. At a time of remarkable democratization, the Karen cease-fire seemed like a direct result of political reforms. While applauding the release of political prisoners in an official statement heralding the restoration of full diplomatic ties between the United States and Myanmar, US president Barack Obama mentioned the "important cease-fire agreement" as yet another milestone on the country's winding road to democracy and peace (2012). At the signing ceremony the late KNU leader Saw David Taw also referred to the altered political landscape as the main game changer.[1] He said that the agreement would garner broad popular support among Karen people: "According to the changing situation everywhere, peace talks are unavoidable now; this is something we have to pass through without fail. The people have experienced the horrors of war [for] a long time. I'm sure they'll be very glad to hear this news. I hope they'll be able to fully enjoy the sweet taste of peace this time" (Taw, cited in Mydans 2012).

Beginning in 2012 a friendship seemed to grow between Naypyidaw and the KNU leadership. The decidedly uncompromising armed group, indeed, became one of the country's main peace advocates. The new pacifist leanings of the organization culminated in October 2015, when it became the only sizable rebel group to sign the Nationwide Cease-Fire Agreement (NCA). At the NCA summit a joint statement by the government's chief peace negotiator, U Aung Min, and general secretary Padoh Kwe Htoo Win of the KNU declared that the agreement was the means to "lasting and sustainable peace in Myanmar."[2] Addressing the public after President U Thein Sein as the second keynote speaker at the cease-fire summit, Gen. Mutu Say Poe called the signing of the NCA "a new page in history. . . . [T]he first step on the important road towards the establishment of a federal and democratic Union" (2015).

Yet some representatives of the wider Karen society seemed less supportive of the conciliatory line of the KNU. Most prominently, forty-one Karen civil society organizations (CSOs), including groups advocating human rights and social and environmental justice, condemned the NCA as deeply flawed days before Mutu Say Poe's delegation signed it. They denounced the KNU leaders who supported the signing of the agreement as a small clique of corrupt elites who represented neither the Karen revolution nor the local communities. In a joint letter they wrote,

We, Karen CSOs, are alarmed by the fact that:

> Currently, the small group of KNU leaders has demonstrated a chronic lack of transparency and accountability to the Karen people and to their own organization by making the undemocratic and non-inclusive decision to rush to sign the NCA. . . .
>
> Currently this group of KNU leaders is in Yangon with the expectation of signing [the] NCA. They do this in violation of KNU . . . official procedures and without properly informing or receiving the majority's consent from members of the KNU's Central Executive Committee or the Central Standing Committee.
>
> These senior KNU leaders refuse to heed the concerns and voices of other Karen leaders, of civil society organizations, of community groups and the local people whom they claim to represent. (41 Karen Civil Society Organizations 2015)

In fact, Mutu Say Poe and his faction took power at the KNU's 15th Congress in December 2012 among heated internal power struggles within the group. These divisions lingered. A focus on the contention over legitimacy and authority within the Karen rebellion helps explain why the grassroots of the movement and local communities support KNU leaders who oppose the country's peace process; and this despite their having suffered most during decades of civil war. What's more, zooming in on the KNU's internal relations challenges the common assumption that the country's wider political reform process was the only factor in producing the cease-fire. As I will demonstrate, the agreement resulted from internal contention among rival rebel factions and has given rise to an increased struggle over authority within the movement. To understand this struggle it is vital to acknowledge the conflicting relationships between the brigades of the KNU's armed wing, the KNLA.

SHIFTING POWER RELATIONS

En route to the KNLA 5th Brigade stronghold in northern Karen State, I rode with a KNU official in a Japanese utility truck. The rebel leader was speeding along the Thai side of the Myanmar border. The roads in Thailand are good, and they are often the quickest route from one rebel-held area in Karen State to another, particularly to regions where roads and cars do not exist and dense forests take over completely. Chewing betel nut, the KNU officer cursed at the sight of the Thai border police who appeared at regular checkpoints. They search for narcotics smuggled from the neighboring Golden Triangle and also extort bribes from undocumented Myanmar migrants and refugees. As the KNU official explained, "You know, we [meaning the KNU] don't really have a problem with them. I mean, they know us well, and we had good relations for a long time. In fact, the Thai relied on us to control this border for a long time. *We* used to be in control here, *we* used to be *the* police. All that"—he waved his arm wide to encompass the lush green forest that surrounded us—"is Karen land: Kawthoolei. I still remember when we could roam around here freely."[3]

His words describe the extent to which the power and territorial control of the once-mighty rebel rulers have deteriorated since the early 1990s. The KNU, which had more than ten thousand well-trained rebel soldiers, was a distinct threat to Myanmar's government for half a century. During the 1980s the movement ruled over vast parts of eastern Burma, spanning territory from the border to Shan State in the north all the way to the Tenasserim Region in the south, which it administered as a quasi state, known as Kawthoolei (map 2). The KNU still operates across the whole of Karen State with about five thousand soldiers, but the balance of power now decidedly favors the state. The KNU lost ground to the Tatmadaw's counterinsurgency and to rival nonstate armed groups that emerged from the increased fragmentation of the main movement. Geopolitically, the changing bilateral relations between Thailand and Myanmar brought powerful outside economic interests from the two countries to the former periphery.

These pressures have shifted not only the power balance in favor of Myanmar's government but also power relations within the movement. The strain led to the fragmentation of the KNU, which in turn has driven power struggles between internal rival factions who compete against the state as well as against each other. The origins of internal divisions and contention are crucial to explaining the movement's negotiation and conflict strategies vis-à-vis the state. They are also essential to understanding the growth of rival factions within the KNU, which are critical to grasping why Karen grassroots community members feel so alienated by the conciliatory actions of the KNU leaders and why many of them oppose rapprochement between their leadership and the Myanmar government.

The Karen rebellion has always been a highly heterogeneous movement, comprised as it is of members from diverse political, religious, geographic, economic, and educational backgrounds. In fact, the ethnic category Karen is inherently fluid and incorporates diverse linguistic and cultural heritages. Most important are the distinctions between Sgaw Karen and Pwo Karen as well as between the so-called Hill Karen in the rugged forests of eastern Myanmar and the so-called Delta Karen from central Myanmar. Karen on the Thai border often speak more than one of the three main Karen languages; Karen from central Myanmar often speak only Myanmar. As explained in chapter 2, the colonial state, missionaries, and the emerging rebel political culture under an ethnonational agenda advanced by Karen elites played key roles both in generating a relatively coherent sense of identity and cohesive organizational structures and in unifying the "liberated territories" of Kawthoolei (Smith 1999, 390–91).

In addition to claiming representation over the diverse Karen people, the multifaceted nature of the KNU is owing to its organization: it is divided into seven geographic districts, each of which is under the control of a KNLA Brigade: Thaton District (Brigade 1), Toungoo District (Brigade 2), Nyaunglebin District (Brigade 3), Mergui-Tavoy District (Brigade 4), Papun District (Brigade 5), Duplaya District (Brigade 6), and Pa'an District (Brigade 7). These districts do not correspond to official administrative demarcations. Officially the government calls Karen State Kayin State and divides it up into seven townships: Pa'an, Kawkareik, Kya-In, Seik-Gyi, Myawaddy, Papun, Thandaung, and Hlaingbwe.

Power imbalances among the movement's brigades and their administered areas have existed since the movement's inception, above all in terms of troop strength and prosperity. Finance flows and mobilization processes within the KNU are centralized on paper, but in practice each brigade recruits and finances itself. For this reason Brigades 6 and 7 emerged as the strongest forces in the movement during the heyday of the Karen revolution in the 1970s and 1980s, when they controlled the main smuggling routes to Thailand. By comparison, the much smaller Brigades 1 and 2 in Nyaunglebin and Toungoo have long been struggling to make ends meet (Smith 1999, 395).

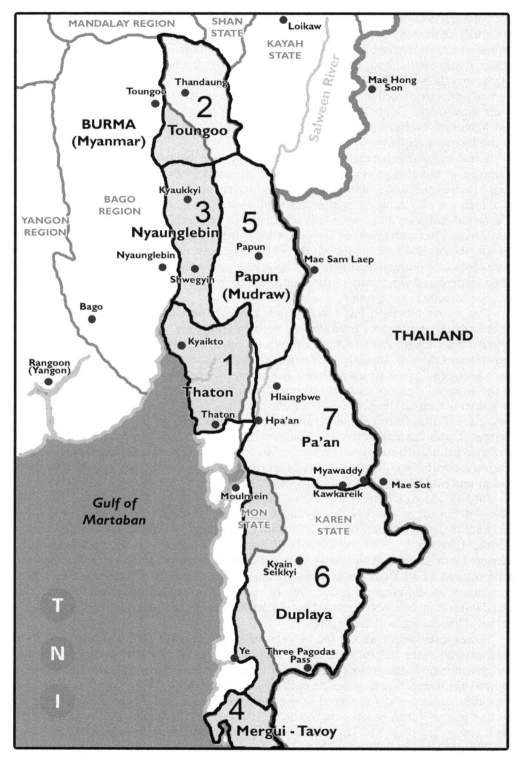

Map 2 KNU administrative districts and brigade area. *Source:* South 2011, 9.

The movement's current fragmented status, including the origins of its rival factions that hold differing opinions with regard to the 2012 cease-fire, strongly relates to how the military and geopolitical changes along the Thai–Myanmar border throughout the 1990s and 2000s have impacted this multifaceted power landscape within the KNU. Most important was the shifting internal power balance from central to northern units of the KNLA, particularly to Mutraw's Brigade 5. Various KNU members, elite and grassroots, have told me that the divergent stances regarding the cease-fire emerged from this shifting power balance. A leader from the central KNU district of Duplaya, in which the movement's struggling Brigade 6 operates, put it this way: "The Burman [the government] activity is different from places to places. And so we have to make different moves as well. So we also have different opinions in different brigades."[4] Changing military and geopolitical dynamics have impacted the movement's brigade territories in vastly unequal ways, producing disparate outcomes.

BATTLEFIELD: FROM KAWTHOOLEI TO LOST GROUND

Between the 1980s and the 2012 cease-fire the KNU had been hard-pressed to fight off military offensives by the government. It suffered gravely after the breakdown of cease-fire negotiations in 1994. Because most other ethnic rebel groups signed truces with the government at the time, the Tatmadaw was able to concentrate its firepower on the Karen rebels in Myanmar's eastern borderlands.

According to the longtime KNU leader Saw David Taw, a "younger, middle-level section of the KNU leadership" recognized "that the burden of the conflict had become unbearable for the Karen population in the conflict area" (2005, 41). Many KNU members wished to conclude a cease-fire along the lines of that made with the KIO and other northern groups, which granted territorial pockets—as well as the right to engage in business and economic development—to armed groups. However, after several rounds of negotiations the KNU leadership rejected the proposed cease-fire owing to pressure from its ally the National Coalition Government of the Union of Burma, a formerly powerful exiled NLD grouping that emerged after the violent crackdown of the 1988 prodemocracy demonstrations. The National Coalition Government group asked the KNU not to sign a cease-fire because it felt that would undermine its efforts at the UN "to win decisive international action against the SLORC" by the UN (Taw 2005, 42). Similar alliance pressures exerted by the Myanmar democratic diaspora movement prevented the conclusion of a cease-fire again in 1997 and in 2005 (South 2011, 16–17).

The decision to continue fighting came with heavy costs for the KNU, as the Tatmadaw made large, rapid advances in eastern Myanmar. Myanmar's generals also invested heavily in the modernization and enlargement of their armed forces by way of large-scale recruiting and, with the help of China, the purchase and production of modern weaponry. By the mid-1990s Myanmar's armed forces had expanded to over 400,000 soldiers, up from 180,000 in 1988 (Callahan 2007, 36). In addition, internal tensions within the Karen movement played into the hands of the state's counterinsurgency campaigns.

Just after the breakdown of the 1994 cease-fire negotiations, the KNU experienced a mutiny by Buddhist elements of the KNU from which it never fully recovered. Years of grievances among Buddhist Karen soldiers against the Christian-dominated KNU leadership came to a head when the followers of the influential Buddhist Karen monk U Thuzana sought to build pagodas near the KNU headquarters at Mannerplaw.[5]

Citing a concern that the brightly painted structures might turn the site into an easy target of Tatmadaw air attacks, the leadership declined to allow them. In December 1994 Sgt. Maj. Kyaw Than defected and founded the Democratic Karen Buddhist Army (DKBA). He quickly recruited some three thousand disillusioned Buddhist soldiers from the KNLA and the KNDO. The Tatmadaw soon courted the DKBA with logistical and military support. The DKBA started to fight alongside its former foe against its ethnic brethren and former comrades. The insider intelligence and additional troops that DKBA provided were instrumental in the counterinsurgency's success at overrunning the Mannerplaw headquarters of the KNU in 1995, a defeat that marked a turning point in the history of the Karen rebellion.

The joint military and DKBA offensives of the mid-1990s were concentrated in central Karen State and dealt a serious blow to the once-mighty KNLA "mother brigade" (South 2008, 55), Brigade 7, which formed the military and logistical backbone of the movement in the 1980s. Located in Pa'an District, Brigade 7 used to preside over the KNU headquarters at Mannerplaw and oversaw the area's main trade and smuggling routes, including the strategic border crossing between Myawaddy and Mae Sot in Thailand. The loss of territory to the Tatmadaw and the DKBA meant a major loss of KNU revenue in general and Brigade 7 in particular. Fragmentation has increased in the movement since the 1990s, and there are now even more armed organizations making territorial claims in central Karen State's Pa'an District. In 2007 the so-called KNU/KNLA Peace Council (KPC) splinter group emerged with five hundred soldiers in a government-supported militia after the Brigade 7 commander, Maj. Gen. Htein Maung, negotiated an individual cease-fire with Naypyidaw. In addition to military pressure in the area, personal motivations were said to have played a role in bringing about Maung's move, as he saw his political influence within the KNU decline after his patron, the long-term KNU strongman Gen. Bo Mya, died in 2006. The individual cease-fire awarded the splinter group with government aid, a small pocket of territory, and business opportunities (Core 2009, 98–99). Complicating the situation in Pa'an even further, the 5th Brigade of the DKBA split from its main organization after deciding not to follow its transformation into a formal Tatmadaw-controlled government militia, a so-called Border Guard Force (BGF). This group of about fifteen hundred soldiers calls itself the DKBA-5, or Democratic Karen Benevolent Army. They are once again fighting Myanmar's armed forces, formally acting in a loose alliance with the KNU.

Geopolitics: From Periphery to Border Hub

In addition to the military and territorial losses that have weakened the KNU in Kawthoolei, changing geopolitics along the Thai–Myanmar border at the end of the Cold War sapped the movement even more. The impacts of this were, again, especially severe in the territories of central and southern brigades. This development tipped the internal power balance within the movement further toward its northern units.

As we have seen, the Thai military supported the KNU for many years, not least because the Karen rebellion operated as a proxy border guard for Thailand against real and perceived threats posed by narco-armies and communist forces. This situation changed in the early 1990s when Thailand embarked on a "constructive engagement policy" with Myanmar to promote bilateral trade and investment in order to develop its marginalized and landlocked western provinces. Initially, Thai businesses invested in Myanmar's timber sector when the Thai government implemented a logging ban in Thailand after flooding there caused by heavy deforestation (South 2008, 73–74). Since then Thai logging companies have decimated the dense forests of Karen State to an unprecedented extent. Cash-strapped and unable to oppose the economic interests of their erstwhile benefactors, the KNU quickly became part of this destructive industry by way of receiving compensation from logging companies and by granting their own logging concessions. At the same time, Thai companies have started to mine for tin, wolfram, and lead in Karen State (South 2008, 75). The Thai government, moreover, set out to tap into its neighbor's energy resources, including hydropower and natural gas. As a result, Thai authorities soon lost interest in supporting the Karen rebellion as a strategic buffer force and began to consider the movement a "nuisance impeding investment in the borderlands" (South 2011, 20). While the Thai security establishment has not entirely cut its ties with the KNU, and individuals continue to turn a blind eye to its transborder operations, the rebels nevertheless had to give way to Thai economic interests.[6]

That relations between Bangkok and the Karen rebellion had cooled became most visible when Thailand and Myanmar constructed the Yadana gas pipeline in the late 1990s. Myanmar had effectively weakened the Karen rebellion by liberalizing trade policy, which dismantled the KNU's smuggling operation and therefore cut off its major revenue source. At the time, the improved relations between Thailand and Myanmar enabled the bilateral exploitation of natural gas in the Gulf of Martaban. A consortium composed of French Total, US American UNOCAL, Thai PTT-EP, and Myanmar MOGE started to transport sufficient natural gas to meet 15 to 20 percent of Thailand's needs. The gas travels via a sixty-three-kilometer-long onshore pipeline through southern Karen State to the Thai border (Kolås 2007, 628). This area, known locally as Mergui-Tavoy District, used to be the stronghold of the KNLA's 4th Brigade. In 1997 and 1998 the Karen rebels came under heavy pressure from both the Tatmadaw and KNU's former allies in the Thai security establishment to allow construction of the pipeline. Heavily outnumbered and careful not to displease the Thais, local rebel leaders negotiated their strategic withdrawal into demarcated areas with Tatmadaw frontline commanders. Ignoring this informal deal, a Tatmadaw offensive of twenty-one thousand army soldiers advanced well beyond the pipeline's corridor and drove the KNU further into the jungle.[7] Reliable evidence shows that advancing government troops displaced local communities to make room for the construction of the pipeline and forcibly conscripted villagers as slave labor for the project.[8] Brigade 4's inability to protect the people from these and other human rights abuses accelerated its demise by eroding its legitimacy among local communities. Hundreds of Karen villagers calling themselves God's Army confronted the advancing Tatmadaw after the KNLA had retreated (Human Rights Watch 2002, 157). A popular legend that holds that the leaders of God's Army were nine-year-old twin brothers implies the villagers' anger and sense of abandonment.

FRAGMENTING AUTHORITY

The changing economic conditions of the various factions of the KNU helped precipitate the growing factionalism of its increasingly parochial regional brigades in the 1990s and beyond. To be sure, power and wealth disparities always existed among the seven KNLA brigades, and the territory they ruled over was never homogeneous in terms of physical geography or population. But the KNU was a relatively coherent movement prior to the fall of its headquarters at Mannerplaw in 1995. While local units

wielded considerable autonomy over day-to-day administrative and military operations, the movement's central command was the undisputed decision-making organ
responsible for the movement's overall political direction. The organization retains
the same structure it had before 1995: the KNU district chairpersons and the KNLA
brigade generals are jointly responsible for, respectively, the movement's administrative and military operations in their region. Each administrative KNU department, for
example, the Education or Forestry Department, has a regional branch. At the same
time, the movement operates a central command that encompasses a similar double
structure between KNU administrative departments and the central command of the
KNLA (Taw 2005, 41).

KNU central leadership organs have only limited means to raise revenues of their
own. They mostly depend on resources from district level administrators and brigade
generals who relied on taxing smuggling operators and mining and logging businesses
in their territory as well as taxing the local population for revenue. While there was
never a set quota of revenue sharing, wealthier brigades, such as Brigades 6 and 7, traditionally surrendered up to 40 percent of their incomes to the central revenue department, which then allocated these funds to its central command structure as well as
to finance regional operations where leadership deemed necessary.[9] Together with
the district chairmen and brigade commanders and their deputies, the central KNU
department heads form the Central Committee of the KNU. The Central Committee
elects the movement's top ten leaders, who comprise the KNU Executive Committee,
the head decision-making organ (Taw 2005, 41). In theory, elections occur every four
years, but in practice individual strongmen have always dominated both committees,
demoting them to little more than consultative organs and sometimes even suspending elections. Gen. Bo Mya ruled the movement in staunchly authoritarian fashion
from 1976 to 2000, when he stepped down as chairman due to poor health. He per-
mitted little dissent and held no Executive Committee elections from 1976 to 1991
(Smith 1999, 390–92).

Notwithstanding the decentralized mobilization and funding structures of the
KNU, the movement's political leadership has thus been centralized for many years.
Until the mid-1990s this enabled the Karen rebellion to maintain a cohesive organization despite internal heterogeneity and power imbalances. More recent military
and geopolitical developments have fragmented and decentralized the movement
considerably and uprooted its central leadership from its power base. Severe military
defeats sent large contingents of the KNU fleeing to Thailand. Many rebels, together
with tens of thousands of civilian refugees, found refuge in the ever-growing camps
along the border. The lower rebel ranks increasingly blended in with other refugees
in what were to become permanent forest settlements along the Thai border. The
organization's top leaders mostly settled in urban centers along the Thai–Myanmar
border, particularly in and around the border town of Mae Sot. Many KNU leaders
were thus detached from the everyday realities of their organization's grassroots in
the refugee camps as well as those left fighting in the Karen forests. A KNU officer
who grew up in Mae La refugee camp put it this way: "The Burmese government
should be thankful to the Thai government for welcoming [the KNU] in Thailand,
because now we are too busy going shopping and to the cinema, which distracts us
from fighting."[10]

Geographic fragmentation created a continually widening cleavage between
the individual brigades and districts that now lack the support of a central organization. This break led to an increasingly parochial outlook on the part of different

organizational segments. Discussing the central leadership's stance on the increasing collaboration between individual brigade leaders, Tatmadaw generals, and Thai and Myanmar businesspeople in cease-fire Karen State, a retired officer of the KNLA central command explained as follows:

> Power today lies with the district level. It does not depend on the KNLA headquarters anymore. You see, Pa'an District is 7th Brigade territory. The KNLA headquarters has no land, no territory. Like the German High Command, hahaha, they are only in a building and give orders. But the district commissioner and brigade commander have the full authority within their territory. Today they do a lot of things, like warlords, like kings. But they have to feed their troops, you see. People sometimes don't like it and think they are crazy. But this also depends on the population.[11]

According to this officer, increasing warlordism has eroded the support of the local population. He explained that the degree to which local KNU leaders relied on extortion and coercion, however, depended on the relationships between local brigade units and local communities. In fact, these vertical relations differ considerably.

In the 1980s Pa'an was home to the most powerful and wealthiest district of Kawthoolei. Far more than in the northern areas, in Pa'an territorial loss and increased commercialization have disembedded the KNU units from local communities. Much the same thing happened in other central and southern brigade areas. This disrupted the implicit social contract between southern and central rebel units and local communities, which eroded the legitimacy of regional rebel leaders among their grassroots. Comparative territorial control and isolation from wider geopolitical change have left the implicit social contract in northern areas relatively intact. Local rebel units in these regions continue to rule as a quasi government, delivering social services and security in return for taxes and recruits, and in effect they maintain reciprocal exchange relations to local communities. Thus whereas regions like Pa'an were rebel strongholds before the 1990s, since then northern areas have become the strongest areas of support. Throughout Kawthoolei shifting degrees of rebel embeddedness shape the social context and, in effect, the habitual practices of local communities to back or take part in the rebellion.

BRIGADE 7: AT THE CROSSROADS OF GLOBALIZATION

The vast transformations along the Thai–Myanmar border are most visible in the two border towns of Mae Sot and Myawaddy, located opposite each other on the Moei River. For many years Mae Sot, in Thailand's Tak Province, has been home to an eclectic mix of people connected in one way or another to the Karen conflict and other Myanmar ethnic conflicts. Among the residents of Mae Sot are humanitarian workers who provide aid in nearby refugee camps, KNU rebels who relocated their unofficial headquarters after the fall of Mannerplaw, smugglers carrying out their illicit business, soldiers of fortune from around the world seeking to join various rebel armies in Myanmar, and spies from all sides who exchange intelligence at the local night market. According to KNU district demarcation, the town of Myawaddy in Karen State's Myawaddy Township belongs to the 7th Brigade area of Pa'an. Since the fall of Mannerplaw it has been one of the rare outposts of Myanmar statehood in an area that nonstate armed groups otherwise dominated. The Tatmadaw and progovernment

BGF militias secure the corridor to Myawaddy via Hpa'an, the government-held capital of the official Karen State, along the Asian Highway 1, a road that used to be a winding dirt track until 2015. Today, Mae Sot and Myawaddy form the backbone of the thriving border trade between the neighboring countries. They are the main crossing point for goods shipped across the Thai–Myanmar border as well as Myanmar's second-busiest official border-trading route after Muse on the Chinese–Myanmar border. In Mae Sot sporadic gunfire has given way to the noise of construction works and busy traders filling the streets of this new boomtown with modern shopping malls and droves of Myanmar migrant workers. According to official trade figures, the formal import–export volume rose from US$27.32 million in 2001 to US$156.09 million in 2006 (Kudo 2013, 194).

Within earshot of the loud rattling of jackhammers being used in the building of a hotel, I interviewed three Thai businessmen in December 2013. We met at the Tak chamber of commerce in Mae Sot. All three men were sensitive to the new geopolitics and prosperity of the region. Two of them have non-Thai family backgrounds—one is from a family of ethnic Chinese, and the other comes from a family that immigrated to Thailand from India. Seated on bright pink sofas and surrounded by trophies made of rubies and other precious stones sourced in Myanmar, they spoke enthusiastically of a new government plan to create a special economic zone to further liberalize trade, investment, and labor markets in the transborder region. They considered the armed conflict an issue of the distant past. They explained that the biggest impediment to greater development was the dire state of physical infrastructure, including bad road conditions on the Myanmar side and the crumbling Thai–Myanmar friendship bridge that large trucks (those carrying more than twenty-five tons) cannot cross. Hopes were high for the Asian Highway 1 under construction at the time, which would connect Da Nang on the Vietnamese coast to Mawlamyine on Myanmar's Gulf of Martaban through Lao PDR and Thailand. The highway is meant to become the Greater Mekong Subregion East–West Economic Corridor. The section from Mawlamyine to Myawaddy—some of which, in 2013, was a dusty road that could be traveled only in one direction on alternate days—is financed with the support of the Thai government and the Asian Development Bank (Asian Development Bank 2010). The businessmen were aware that smuggling had strengthened the Karen rebellion and that drying up the Karen war chest had been a main motivation behind the Myanmar government's decision to liberalize its border trade with Thailand. As one of the men explained to me, this process had begun in the early 1990s: "So they changed the policy and opened the Myawaddy side for official trade. First, this was only twice a month, than once a week, and then regularly every day. Initially they needed to protect the road from the Karen because there was a lot of fighting about this road. Then step by step they developed everything." He concluded, "And now there is peace." With business-minded optimism he explained that the rebels pose little viable threat to trade, crediting both the 2012 cease-fire and the fact that rebels "can do legal business now" and that they do not pay taxes or duties to bring goods across the border.[12]

The businessman's depiction of rebels-turned-businesspeople materialized as I crossed to Myawaddy and drove on to Hpa'an. On the other side of the river, in Myawaddy, the KNU had indeed opened its first legally registered companies in 2013: Moe Ko San Travel and Tour Company Limited and Trading Company Limited. In a public statement the manager of the two businesses declared that Moe Ko San was the KNU 7th Brigade's economic office and his aim was to engage in business in order to raise revenue for the brigade (KNU official, as cited in S' PhanShaung 2013).

As I traveled further in the direction of Hpa'an, various nonstate armed groups, including the BGF, DKBA, and the KNU, were extorting fees from passenger and commercial vehicles along the road, despite official reports that the route is under government control. Reports from 2015 indicate that extortion has continued along the newly built Asian Highway 1 (Lawi Weng 2015c). Karen who live between Myawaddy and Hpa'an or who frequently travel back and forth from Thailand say they often have problems distinguishing among the various armed groups. They usually associate demeaning behavior at road checkpoints and unofficial border gates with units of Karen BGF militias operating on behalf of the Myanmar government. The local KNU has provided only very limited social services and protection in this area since it lost most of its territory to the counterinsurgency since the mid-1990s. The Tatmadaw has taken advantage of the cease-fire and the fact that it does not specify demarcation of territory, buffer zones, or troop demobilization. The KNU cannot stop the military advancement throughout Karen State without breaking the truce.[13] One education worker from the Karen Education Department (KED), the KNU's educational arm, who trains KED teachers in rebel-operated primary and secondary schools throughout Karen State explained the situation as follows: "Before the cease-fire it was difficult for the Tatmadaw to send reinforcements and supplies to the frontline areas because we attacked them. Now they can bring everything easily. So they send much more support and reinforce their military bases. Today there are much more government soldiers in our areas. This is a great concern to us and the local villagers. They also don't feel safe. They had to run away from [Tatmadaw] soldiers for all their life. How can you expect them to feel safe now?"[14]

The counterinsurgency has in fact historically committed human rights violations on a much larger scale than the rebellion and continues to do so. Targeting and displacing civilians has for many years been an instrumental component of the Tatmadaw's "Four-Cuts" strategy, a plan to divide rebels from nonrebels in order to cut off four vital resources, food, revenue, recruits, and information, to rebel groups (Human Rights Watch 2005, 8). Lacking protection from the KNU, many people in Karen State feel they are in more danger of violence than they were in before the cease-fire, even though active fighting has ceased. Even as local KNU units in Pa'an no longer offer social services or protection, many continue to collect taxes from villagers informally. A Karen English teacher who works in a school for Myanmar migrants and refugees in Mae Sot told me he had sympathized with the KNU in his youth when he attended a rebel-operated school in the late 1980s. He still has family in Pa'an whom he visits regularly. Now he viewed the KNU as no different from the Tatmadaw or the DKBA. "In the end it does not matter who they are," he said, "they just come into your village and demand money. But they do not give anything in return. They just make our lives more difficult."[15]

BRIGADE 5: THE LAST STRONGHOLD

Mutraw District of northern Kawthoolei stands in stark contrast to the rapid transformations witnessed further south on the border. Its rugged hills make it one of the most remote and underdeveloped regions of Southeast Asia. Mutraw, which mostly overlaps with the official Hpapun District in northern Karen State, spans twenty-six hundred square miles, making it bigger than the Palestinian territories. Despite its size, Mutraw is among the least populated areas of Myanmar, having only about thirty-five thousand inhabitants (compared to five million in the Palestinian territories).[16] Hpapun Township, the official district capital, is controlled by the government and hosts the Tatmadaw's Southeastern Regional Command. The dense forests outside Hpapun belong to the Karen rebellion, or, more precisely, to the movement's 5th Brigade.

A trip to KNU-held parts of Mutraw feels like going back in time. As very few roads exist, people must travel by boat along the Salween or Moei Rivers to some parts of the region. Most villages are located in the hills and are accessible only via long, difficult hikes on small footpaths through the dense rain forest. Whereas mobile phones are widely available in most parts of Myanmar's border areas today, in Mutraw District villagers often share a radio and satellite phone to communicate with the outside world or other parts of the district. Their settlements consist of simple bamboo huts constructed on stilts. Shared generators produce sporadic electricity, but the settlements frequently run out of fuel to operate them. The overwhelming majority of people are farmers practicing small-scale agriculture or breeding small animals like chickens and toads. Most parts of the local economy do not use money. People commonly conduct barter trade or produce basic goods communally. Items of daily need are produced locally, and the area is still largely detached from the rapid development taking place further south along the border. Constantly growing infrastructure, booming investment and commerce, and state consolidation all seem far away in this part of Karen State.

Mutraw District has not changed much since Karen rebels were the uncontested ruler of Kawthoolei. Much less affected by the army offensives of the 1990s and 2000s and by the emergence of rival armed groups, the 5th Brigade is still in firm control of large pockets of territory in Mutraw and maintains an extensive, remarkably well-functioning rebel state. Most children go to school in KNU-operated primary and middle schools, where students learn Sgaw Karen as their first language and Myanmar as their second. The history curriculum portrays the Karen as the first settlers of Myanmar and includes an extensive narrative of the KNU and its decades-long armed struggle complete with biographies of legendary martyrs and meticulous accounts of historical battles. Teachers must complete a two-year course at the local Karen Teacher Training College (figure 2). Small health stations in the larger villages offer health care, and disciplined KNLA units, together with local village defense militias organized under the KNDO, provide security. Villagers pay taxes in kind and must send one son per family to serve in the KNLA. The conscripts usually serve for up to seven years in the most meager conditions. They are given food, shelter, and some supposed luxuries, such as cheroot cigarettes but receive no significant money compensation. Similarly, KNU bureaucrats, teachers, and nurses are housed and fed by the KNU but earn negligible wages.

This arrangement between the KNU and its rank and file works only because KNU staff and soldiers in Mutraw are deeply embedded in the local communities, and most receive additional support from their families. The majority of them return to their home villages at least once a year to help their communities with harvesting. These practices have constructed a tightly knit social network in which the social identities of rebels and nonrebels alike commonly overlap. They have also established a functional informal social contract between the KNU and local communities, and many local Karen refer to the Karen State as "our government." A local KNU administrator who served the Karen movement for almost his entire life in various roles but never traveled outside of Mutraw described the workings of this implicit social contract as follows: "We all earn our living as farmers here. As KNU members we also have our

Figure 2 The Karen Teacher Training College. The college is located deep inside the
KNU stronghold of Mutraw in Kawthoolei. It is operated by the Karen
Education Department (KED), the KNU's education arm, and trains teachers
to staff the extensive network of KED schools. Photograph by the author.

farms. Even if we are in the army, we come back to help our families with the harvest
if we have the time. We do not say: 'Give me money and then I will serve in the army!'
It's not like that. We fight to protect our people, ourselves. Our soldiers are all very
motivated. . . . Most people understand that civilians have to feed the government,
and in return, the government will have to look after its people. So people try to pay
tax to the best of their ability."[17]

He explained that the local KNU administration has a formula to calculate taxes
based on acreage and if some people could not pay in money they paid in food, which
the KNU uses to feed its soldiers. Under the implicit social contract the administrator described, working reciprocal relations have left the rebellion enmeshed in local
communities to an extent that conflates the social identities of local communities and
the Karen revolution. While military and geopolitical forces have uprooted central and
southern KNU brigades (as occurred, for instance, with Brigade 7 in Pa'an), the units
of Brigade 5 remain deeply embedded in the remote villages of Mutraw.

The regional fragmentation of power and authority among different brigades of
the KNU has translated into the emergence of two rival factions within the movement. At the time of my research, Chairman Gen. Mutu Say Poe and General Secretary Kwe Htoo Win were the movement's top leaders. This faction had pushed for
the 2012 cease-fire and has professed a conciliatory stance toward Naypyidaw ever
since. It was supported by central and southern units of the KNU, most notably by
Brigades 4, 6, and 7. General Mutu and Hkwe Htoo, as they are referred to within
the movement, had dominated the Karen rebellion ever since they gained positions

in the Executive Committee in 2012. Then vice chairperson Naw Zipporah Sein and the KNLA's vice chief of staff, Lt. Gen. Baw Kyaw Heh, known locally as Zipporah and Baw Kyaw, had the backing of the northern Brigades 5 and 2. They opposed General Mutu and Hkwe Htoo and their conciliatory policies. The internal contestation between these two groups is pivotal to understanding the Karen cease-fire and the internal contention that has riddled the movement since.

FACTIONS BENEATH THE CEASE-FIRE

Located on the Moei River, the new KNU "capital" at Law Khee Lar was a large, bulldozed clearing in the forest when I visited there in 2013. It consisted of a meeting hall surrounded by four sleeping barracks and one canteen. The place was meant for temporary meetings only. The various central departments of the KNU had mostly remained in Mae Sot.

In December 2013 I attended the annual strategy meeting in the organization's new headquarters in Law Khee Lar. The ten-member Executive Committee as well as the forty-five members of the Central Committee came together to discuss post-cease-fire developments. The meeting lasted for five days. The members' assistants brought office stationery, laptops, and printers; canteen workers shipped large quantities of vegetables, fish, and rice across the Moei River from Thailand; and heavily armed special units of the KNLA's 7th Brigade stood guard. During those five days the jungle clearing was a bustling hub of Karen rebel politics. During the meeting I stayed with a senior KNU Central Committee member I'll call Thara. Thara and I had met during my four-month stay while working with the KED, whose staff I assisted in their survey of students in the hundreds of rebel-operated schools across all regions of Kawthoolei. The discussions at the gathering were heated from the onset. During the official meetings the two rival factions openly and loudly disagreed with each other. The supporters of General Mutu and Hkwe Htoo not only proposed that the Karen rebellion could trust U Thein Sein's semicivilian government but also wanted to speed up the peace process. This group claimed the sleeping barracks above the meeting hall, and they did not sit down to eat with members of the other group. A much larger group opposed them. Vice Chief of Staff Baw Kyaw Heh, Vice Chairperson Naw Zipporah Sein, Joint Secretary Padoh Saw Thawthi Bwe, most administrative department heads, and many leaders from the northern areas of Brigades 5 and 2 expressed a deep mistrust of Naypyidaw (figure 3). They felt they had been ignored in the negotiating proceedings leading to the cease-fire. While at least outwardly suggesting they might support a better process for seeking peace, they attempted to slow it down. This group took the three lower barracks, and they ate together but not with members of the other group.

In official interviews KNU leaders generally tried to portray the rebellion's internal divisions as reflecting only diverging opinions on the movement's current strategy for reaching their shared goals (Karen News 2013; 2014). But in fact the strategy meeting reflected deep-seated tensions, mistrust, and divisions that had been growing for years.

THE UPHILL BARRACKS

General Mutu, who led the delegation that signed the cease-fire agreement without the approval of KNU leadership at the time, was the most powerful man in the

Figure 3 KNU leadership meeting in Law Khee Lar. General Secretary Kwe Htoo Win addresses the Central Standing Committee of the KNU at the meeting in the KNU headquarters in December 2013. Present on the panel is the KNU Executive Committee, including (*from left to right*) Padoh Mahn Mahn (joint secretary 2), Padoh Saw Thawthi Bwe (joint secretary 1), Padoh Saw Kwe Htoo Win (general secretary), Gen. Mutu Say Poe (chairman), and Naw Zipporah Sein (vice chairperson). Photograph by the author.

upper barrack. He had come to power at the December 2012 general leadership meeting to elect the movement's Executive Committee. The elections were controversial within the KNU. This started with choosing the venue of the electoral meeting. Both factions wanted the vote to take place in their own strongholds. Mutu eventually prevailed and the meeting was held in his home region, the 7th Brigade territory of Hpa'an, where Law Khee Lar is located, instead of in the 5th Brigade territory of Mutraw, as Zipporah Sein's faction desired. His ultimate victory in the election itself, which took two rounds of voting, was tainted: when backers of Zipporah demanded a recount, the electoral committee revealed it had burned the ballot box; some electoral observers felt that holding the meeting in the headquarters of Brigade 7, known as staunch supporters of General Mutu, had intimidated delegates; and Zipporah's faction had demanded open ballots. Many people I spoke with among Karen grassroots believe that the Executive Committee elections were rigged.[18]

　　Thara was obviously uncomfortable when I asked him to arrange an interview with the controversial leader, so I was not surprised to see that General Mutu looked unhappy when I was introduced to him. He was relaxing in a hammock while listening to the radio outside of the uphill barrack on the evening of the first day of the meeting. The sun had set an hour earlier, and the surrounding forests had disappeared in the darkness of a quiet, moonless night. When Thara introduced me to the general and told him I was a researcher at a university in London who wanted to interview him about the cease-fire developments, Mutu rebuked him in Sgaw Karen. To me, he said in English, "The British never helped us. In fact, they abandoned us. Why should I help you now?"[19]

I had heard that General Mutu is secretive and authoritarian. Many KNU members, both senior and grassroots, feel he does not allow any opposition to his conciliatory course of action with Naypyidaw. But he appeared to reconsider his objection to me when I explained that I was German. After a long, uncomfortable pause he switched to a more conciliatory tone and invited Thara and me to speak to one of his confidants inside the barrack, Padoh Mahn Nyein Maung. I knew Mahn Nyein Maung by reputation: he was one of Myanmar's long-term political prisoners during the military dictatorship. In the 1960s, when he was in his early thirties, Mahn Nyein Maung was imprisoned as a prodemocracy activist from the Delta region. His mysterious and extraordinary escape from the infamous high-security Coco Prison Island three hundred kilometers off the Myanmar coast in 1970 had earned him the nickname Burma's Papillon after the French author and prisoner Henri Charrière, who managed to escape from a French prison island in French Guiana. He joined the KNU soon after his escape and quickly rose through the ranks.

Burma's Papillon was far more welcoming than General Mutu. Having overheard my conversation with the general, the seventy-three-year-old leader explained that Mutu was frustrated over the divisions in the movement.[20] Pointing to his companions in the barrack, he said, "We here trust the president [U Thein Sein]. Every leader here today [in the upper barrack], they all trust in him." He went on to say why: "We can see that President U Thein Sein really wants to reform the country. We have met him three times already. He said he wants to end this civil war. He doesn't want to pass it [on] to the next generation. . . . For us, we have been suffering from the civil war for more than sixty years, so our people want peace, so we have decided to build peace, we must."

Mahn Nyein Maung described General Mutu as "a peace man" who believes in peaceful negotiation. He framed this as a matter of keeping up with the times: "The world today does not support resolving problems with violence." He suggested that this bound the Myanmar state as well: "They also don't have a choice but to reform."[21] As Thara listened quietly I spoke with Burma's Papillon about the cease-fire and his aspirations for a negotiated settlement. Padoh Kwe Htoo Win, the KNU general secretary, soon entered the barrack. Kwe Htoo was officially the second most powerful leader in the KNU. Many KNU insiders viewed him as the chief strategist of the movement. He extended a friendly greeting in fluent English. Kwe Htoo became general secretary in December 2012 and has been a driving force behind the 2012 cease-fire. Many KNU members consider him to be very pragmatic. He studied economics at Rangoon University in the early 1970s but left without getting his degree to "go underground" with the KNU in 1974. He rose to the position of district chairman in the southern KNU area of Mergui-Tavoy in 1990. In that position he negotiated the retreat of the KNLA's 4th Brigade when the Tatmadaw advanced along the corridor of the Yadana gas pipeline, which transported offshore gas from the Andaman Sea to Thailand, in the late 1990s.

Kwe Htoo invited me to his room, and Thara excused himself. We sat down on bamboo mats. The small, simple room was undecorated. In fact, the only objects present were a medium-sized backpack, a sleeping bag, and a rolled-up mosquito net. Kwe Htoo said, "You see, when [the government] want[s] to build a road, we cannot stop them. The problem is not only the Myanmar government. We are reliant on the Thai side. The problem started from the Thai side, the Thai companies supported by their government."

To Kwe Htoo, the shifting geopolitics of the border and the changing interests of Thailand in particular spelled doom for KNU's intention to hold on to areas where the powerful economic interests of Thailand and Myanmar wanted to appropriate land. As he said, "Both governments understand that they can benefit from each other here, so they make development projects like the Italian–Thai [the planned deep-sea port close to Dawei, affecting the KNLA 4th Brigade area in southern Karen State]. We cannot stop them. We could disturb them to delay the project but we cannot stop them." Kwe Htoo saw a future for the KNU in learning how to conduct business and promote economic development: "From the KNU, we are now forming an economic committee to find opportunities to train our people to get knowledge on how to do business. We invited some economic experts to train our people. So some people blame us and say: 'Hey, you revolutionary, you should not do any business!' But we have to do that. . . . The bigger countries are playing the tune. We have to dance to it."[22]

Kwe Htoo, joined by General Mutu and the group's late foreign minister, Saw David Taw, pushed for a cease-fire with Naypyidaw since the mid-2000s. Taw (2005) outlined the need for a cease-fire in a report he wrote for Conciliation Resources, a peacebuilding NGO engaged in third-party mediation, in 2005. A KNU leader who opposes the cease-fire called Taw the original "mastermind behind the cease-fire."[23] While this group has been officially directing the KNU's strategy and behavior since 2012, it is battling a powerful internal opposition.

THE DOWNHILL BARRACKS

The day after my encounter with Kwe Htoo in the upper barracks I met with a senior leader of the KNU at one of the downhill barracks, where I was staying. I'll call him Padoh Dar Poe. Dar Poe was among the top leadership at the time the cease-fire was signed and asked not to be identified. Seeking shelter from the relentless midday sun, we sat on bright blue plastic stools under the barrack, which was built on stilts.

Over a cup of green tea Dar Poe explained that he did not exactly oppose a cease-fire. Rather, he felt that the KNU had initially prioritized political issues, such as negotiating power-sharing arrangements, but that under pressure from the government leadership it had put economic concerns, including business and development projects, first. By his account, the government had claimed it was too difficult to sort out political issues—which require parliamentary action—and urged KNU leaders to focus instead on business and economic development. Dar Poe emphasized the role the Princess Dawei Company, a Yangon-based crony company, had played in funding the cease-fire negotiations and follow-up meetings. Princess Dawei had invested heavily in infrastructure and resource exploitation across Karen State under the auspices of a retired Tatmadaw major. He asserted that most of the members of the Executive Committee were working with the state on business opportunities and were just "pleasing the government."[24] According to Dar Poe, the KNU should have signed only a preliminary cease-fire. He consequently opposed further cooperation with the government until the underlying political issues, including federal arrangements and ethnic minority rights, were settled.

Dar Poe explained how the shakiness of the cease-fire was, in fact, built into its DNA. The KNU top leadership had not actually negotiated the cease-fire. In early 2012 Naw Zipporah Sein and David Tharckabaw were leading the KNU as chairwoman and vice chairman, respectively. Both were generally skeptical about the nature and extent of transition in Naypyidaw. The Myanmar government announced that a KNU delegation had signed the historic agreement in Hpa'an, but Zipporah and Tharckabaw had not been present. General Mutu, who at the time was the KNLA's chief of staff, had overstepped his authority. The KNU had sent a delegation under his leadership, but their mandate was to discuss controversial points. The chairwoman had not authorized General Mutu to sign an agreement. A former top KNU leader contended that she had grudgingly accepted the agreement for the sake of unity and because she was reluctant to displease the Western governments that were praising the agreement.[25]

Zipporah and Tharckabaw as well as the movement's chief of staff and former leader of the strong northern Brigade 5, Baw Kyaw Heh, refused to take part in the negotiations. The cease-fire delegation exceeded its authority nonetheless, organizing working groups, informing the government about internal KNU discussions, and setting up a liaison office for the movement in Karen State's capital, Hpa'an.[26] On 2 October 2012 these tensions escalated, leading the Executive Committee to dismiss General Mutu, Gen. Saw Johnny, and David Taw for "repeated violations of KNU rules and regulations" (KNU Executive Committee, as cited in Radio Free Asia 2012). Yet three weeks later, at a KNU Central Committee meeting, all three were reinstated. The committee's statement read as follows: "There will never be an end to the discussion on the leaders' dismissal because each side claims they are right. The Karen people do not want the KNU to be divided, and so, for the sake of unity, the KNU leaders have decided to forgive each other and move forward in their respective positions until the upcoming 15th congress" (Saw Yan Naing 2012).[27]

Despite the formal victory of the pro-cease-fire faction under General Mutu, internal opposition in the KNU was growing. This is so not least because Zipporah's group garners support among the movement's grassroots, particularly in comparison to the new incumbent leadership. Grassroots support for the internal opposition is prevalent across the social networks of the Karen rebellion, including individuals and community-based organizations in various regions on both sides of the Thai–Myanmar border and overseas.

ALIENATED GRASSROOTS AND INTERNAL CONTESTATION

In early October 2013 a series of bombs hit various sites frequented by foreigners in Yangon and Mandalay. The rumor mills in the country's teahouses began grinding wildly. Customers spun conspiracy theories and pointed fingers at the usual suspects, among them Myanmar's marginalized Muslim community and the Tatmadaw. Government investigators, however, soon presented a suspect believed to be linked to the KNU who was operating from the remote Mutraw region, deep inside Brigade 5 territory. They alleged that the suspect belonged to rogue elements of the movement, someone opposed to peace who also wanted to scare off foreign investors from the country's liberalizing economy. Top KNU leaders were quick to join Thein Sein's government in condemning the "terrorist acts" and promised to assist in the official investigations (Saw Yan Naing 2013b).

Shortly after the bombings I attended a meeting of the KNU's educational arm in the Mutraw region at a teacher training college. After a long day discussing the implementation of curriculum changes, the teachers and administrators, who had come together from throughout Karen State, gathered in one of the half-open bamboo barracks. About fifteen young men and women in their twenties and thirties listened to a multiband radio and heatedly discussed the news of the bombings. Most had never been to these distant cities in central Myanmar. Nobody knew whether the government's assertion, that KNU rebels from Mutraw, one or more of their own, had carried out the bombings, and no one knew the man they had arrested. One thing everyone agreed on was that the KNU leadership should not have promised full cooperation in the government investigations. If the perpetrator was a Karen revolutionary, the KNU should protect him or her.

The disillusionment of these educators seemed emblematic of a wider feeling. They were all part of the rank and file of the Karen rebellion. Most seemed to agree with a senior KNU education worker present at the meeting. The man, who looked to be about sixty years old and had served the KNU in one way or another for most of his life, condemned the cease-fire as "like a tree with cut roots. From the outside people think that this cease-fire is beautiful and that it benefits the Karen people. But from the inside the tree is already dead."[28]

Some weeks later I told a Karen political activist who is well networked within the KNU how frustrated low-ranking revolutionaries are with their leaders' response to the bombing incidents. He agreed, saying the current leadership was not steadfast. In his mind, they had committed the ultimate betrayal in promising to help the government investigate the incident. He brought up the overstepping by General Mutu's delegation in the matter of the cease-fire and the exclusion of some KNU leaders from the process, concluding, "This is absurd, you know, it's like discrediting your own organization. . . . We never accepted the government's law. We have our own system, our own laws. Don't they fight for all this anymore? So can you see now why we are frustrated with this kind of leadership these days?"[29]

It is not difficult to understand why General Mutu's leadership alienated much of the KNU grassroots, the people who actually bore the brunt of decades-long civil war. Social identity and recognition theories suggest why this might be the case: Claims to due and proper recognition as a fully accepted member of society primarily drive the motivation to support or take part in armed struggle, particularly in identity conflicts such as Myanmar's ethnic conflict. Becoming a valued member of a rebel movement that is associated with high social standing and moral principles—such as protecting the community and fighting against perceived injustices—can meet the rebel grassroots' demands for recognition that the dominant political order has denied. Joining or championing a rebellion can generate self-perceived positive social identities, which lead to feelings of self-esteem and self-worth and in turn render the rebel social order and its elites legitimate. Rebel leaders convey both—the moral principles of the movement as well as their recognition of others as valued group members—by way of using fair procedures and dignified treatment in their interactions with the grassroots. By contrast, elite interaction that the grassroots perceives as unjust and disrespectful conveys misrecognition, which threatens positive social identification with the rebel collective. This, in turn, undermines the legitimacy of rebel leaders and their rebel social orders, which can ultimately lead to resistance from within.

The incumbent leaders' legitimacy has eroded because the Karen grassroots see their leadership style as authoritarian and their negotiations with Naypyidaw as a corrupt selling out of decades of revolutionary struggle for independence. Against this background, collective perceptions of misrecognition have taken hold among the movement's rank and file, above all surrounding a sense of

Figure 4 A KNLA guerrilla guards a hill position in the morning mist of Mutraw. Photograph by the author.

disrespect. This impression, in turn, has threatened social rebel identities, leading to growing alienation among the lower ranks of the movement and its traditional supporters among wider Karen society (figure 4). In contrast, members of the rebel grassroots feel that the movement's internal opposition treats them with respect. Identifying with the internal opposition enables the grassroots to maintain a positive social identity from continued affiliation with the KNU. The result is a generation of authority for the group's internal opposition across the social network of the Karen rebellion.

Eroding Legitimacy

Since the 1990s the Tatmadaw has utilized economic incentives to build a counterinsurgency approach that focused on conflict containment. The country's generals have sought to contain and weaken the country's insurrections by negotiating separate cease-fire agreements with individual armed groups. While these accords did not lead to substantial political dialogue, they allowed rebels to retain their arms and govern pockets of territory. Moreover, these pacts encouraged the involvement of armed groups in the collaborative exploitation of the area's natural riches by army generals, rebel leaders, and foreign businesspeople. The co-optation of rebel leaders by economic means has led to a remarkably durable stability along the Myanmar–Chinese borderlands in the 1990s (Smith 1999, 421–41). On the other hand, the increasing involvement of rebel leaders in business ventures and the corruption this has sparked within the higher echelons of ethnic armed groups has posed serious challenges for relations between the leaders of cease-fire groups and their grassroots (Sherman 2003).

While the KNU remained locked in combat during the first cease-fire wave of the 1990s and early 2000s, what Kevin Woods (2011) has called, as noted earlier, "cease-fire capitalism" took hold Karen State in 2012. An uncontrolled influx of venture investments in the natural resources, agrobusinesses, and the construction of large infrastructure in Karen State has accompanied ongoing militarization (Karen Human Rights Group 2015). The longtime observers of Myanmar's civil war Bertil Lintner and Tom Kramer have pointed out that liberal land and foreign investment laws attracted business interests and made these developments possible (Lintner 2013).

The KNU grassroots sees its leadership as vulnerable to co-optation not least because some leaders have amassed personal fortunes, which they mostly invested in Thailand. The rapid expansion of border trade in the 1970s and 1980s and large-scale logging in the 1990s made this enrichment possible (Smith 1999, 395). Shortly before his death in 1982 the former KNU chairman and first commander of the KNDO, Mahn Ba Zan, warned that these developments could bring down the rebellion. The Karen, he said, could "survive poverty," but he doubted they could "withstand prosperity" (Mahn Ba Zan, as quoted in Smith 1999, 395). But local and outside accounts of life in Kawthoolei during this period suggest that Karen leaders focused on building social services in the quasi state, acts that generated legitimacy among local communities and the KNU grassroots (Smith 1999, 283; 395; 384–401).

KNU members are well aware that many of their leaders favor a luxurious lifestyle in Thailand over the hardships of armed struggle in the jungle. The local KNU admin-istrator in Mutraw contrasted the dedication of local rebels and working local rebel governance arrangements with Karen in other parts of the KNU. He worried that the current incumbent leadership surrounding General Mutu had pushed for the cease-fire agreement to advance its personal economic interests rather than revolutionary ideals, saying that "serv[ing] the revolution for money" would ultimately destroy it.[30] Many lower- and higher-ranking rebels I spoke to shared these concerns. A retired KNLA colonel averred that money had become everything after the 2010 elections. He said, "I warned my colleagues that the British army never really occupied Burma, only the British timber companies occupied Burma. So I told them to be aware of the companies. The Burmese are very clever. They approach low-level officials of our administration and low-level officers of our army to infiltrate our land area by area. After the cease-fire they can come freely. They don't carry guns, they don't carry bul-lets. They carry money."[31]

At a group interview with KNU education workers from various parts of Karen State, people expressed their outrage at Myanmar's chief peace negotiator, U Aung Min, who reportedly postulated after a meeting with KNU leaders that the Karen would "abandon their arms" if they became "rich" (U Aung Min, as cited in Phan 2013). One KNU teacher said angrily, "They know that our Karen people are thirsty for money and material goods because most of us local people and KNU members are poor. So they think that we will agree with them, once they give us a car or motorbike. But our main point is to get our country back. We have not fought for the last sixty years to get some cars." One of his colleagues responded, "We don't know exactly why [the KNU leadership] signed the cease-fire now. They keep everything top secret. But we see that they get nice cars. I think that the government also gives them money and positions."[32]

Another rebel educator said that the enemy (meaning the state) had "poisoned" the KNU leadership: "Their hearts have change[d], and they believe our enemies because of their gifts. That's why they don't stand firmly on our revolutionary principles. We feel bad about our organization because they deviated."[33]

In October 2013 in Chiang Mai I spoke about these matters with Saw Ko Nu, a popular, well-connected Karen political activist and founder of one of the forty-one CSOs that decried the NCA in a public letter.[34] He said that the behavior of the KNU leadership had made it difficult for the Karen grassroots to continue to identify with the movement. Ko Nu attributed the split between leaders and the grassroots to corruption among the KNU's higher echelons, citing the "moral self-destruction" in the movement.[35] These developments affected Karen community-based organizations and their work on social justice in Karen State because they made the KNU leadership that signed the cease-fire accord secretive and unresponsive to their demands. Ko Nu described a meeting he attended in 2013 as the point at which he realized that the relationship between the KNU and local communities had become severed. It was an annual gathering established in the mid-2000s to facilitate consultation between local civil society and the KNU. Representatives of the Karen civil society expressed their misgivings over social and environmental problems that had reportedly worsened in Karen State since the cease-fire, including land confiscation for economic use by companies and the military, adverse side effects of unsustainable natural resource extraction, and the growing problem of drug use among local youth. Ko Nu recalled that a senior KNU leader had become angry, responding "in the most inappropriate, crazy way you can imagine":

> He said that the KNU is not the savior of the Karen people. I mean if he would have said that they are not solely responsible for all this, okay, but he basically said that this is none of their concern. Many people were really upset and angry. This told us very clearly that [leadership does] not listen to our concerns. It is the complete opposite than what they have told us for years, I mean that the KNU represents the Karen as a political organization or even like a de facto government. Usually you tell your government if you have problems, and it should not answer that this is not its problem.[36]

Ko Nu recalled further that the previous KNU leadership, headed by Zipporah Sein, had consulted with the Karen civil society about the concerns of local communities. He stressed that her grouping continued to seek the opinion of CSOs such as his, despite the faction's marginalization to the ranks of the opposition. To him, this clearly marked Zipporah and her companions as the movement's legitimate leaders.

GROWING INTERNAL RESISTANCE

At the time of this writing, Lt. Gen. Baw Kyaw Heh was probably the most popular Karen rebel leader among the KNU grassroots. Despite his senior rank, the commando soldier Baw Kyaw Heh looks youthful, particularly compared to most other KNU leaders, many of whom are in their sixties or older. He has a reputation as a fierce fighter, staunch revolutionary, and caring leader. He was the commander of the 5th Brigade in Mutraw for many years before becoming the KNLA's vice chief of staff (VCS). Rank-and-file members of the KNU, who often refer to him as Baw Kyah or the VCS, told me that he lives among his soldiers in the dense forests of Mutraw, a contrast to the luxurious lifestyles of other high-ranking KNU leaders. Many grassroots members of the KNU regard him as the opposite of General Mutu.

Baw Kyaw's youthfulness endears him to the grassroots, especially to young members and supporters of the movement. By contrast, a KNDO sergeant described General Mutu as being "old now, very old and should retire but he wants to hold on to power like a dictator. You know, like the guy in North Korea or Ne Win, Pol Pot, Qaddafi, all these very old dictators."[37] An administrator in his early twenties at the KNU Department of Health and Welfare (KDHW) likewise complained about the authoritarian attitude of the movement's elderly chairman: "Sometimes we young people have too much respect for the old leaders. Actually it is not respect, but it is fear. Being afraid is different than having respect, no? It is like the military, where you have to listen. But you are not allowed to question. This is maybe the culture. But we have to wait when the young people come back from abroad, the US. Then they have a different culture. But for us from the inside it is different, really different."[38]

He spoke fondly of the "'strong and passionate VCS," whom he perceives as "listening closely to the people."[39] Many other KNU grassroots members expressed their trust in the young general and his factions, including Zipporah Sein. Like Zipporah Sein, Baw Kyaw has repeatedly and publicly talked about the preoccupations of the KNU grassroots, a sharp contrast from the leaders who signed the cease-fire. In public interviews Baw Kyaw and Zipporah Sein have criticized the cease-fire process for its lack of political dialogue on the underlying causes of conflict, the continued militarization of cease-fire territories, and a deficient military code of conduct. They condemn the cease-fire's lack of territorial demarcation, the territorialization of KNU-held areas by way of securitized economic development, and the detrimental social and environmental aftereffects of increased resource extraction and infrastructure construction.[40]

Leaders of the opposition suggest that pro-cease-fire KNU leaders have supported peace initiatives to serve their personal interests rather than the common interest of the movement or the Karen communities they claim to represent. A leader of the internal opposition pointed specifically to the inclusion of businesspeople in the cease-fire talks of 2012 as a sign of corruption.[41] Baw Kyaw publicly stated that economic incentives are the main drivers of cooperation between the incumbent leadership and Naypyidaw. He said they had "taken over the agenda" (Baw Kyaw Heh, as cited in Eh 2013).

When I met the VCS I could readily see why people consider him the antithesis of General Mutu. A soft-spoken man, he considered his answers to my questions very carefully. As his bodyguards prepared rice with pumpkin curry and fermented fish paste for the two of us for lunch he expressed grave concerns over what the increased commercialization of Karen State after the cease-fire agreement is doing to the Karen rebellion: "If we work together with all the businessmen coming here, we will turn into businessmen ourselves. I mean, we are members of the armed resistance. We shouldn't engage in business too much. But the Burmese government and some of our own leaders don't see it this way. You know, the cease-fire has largely been driven by business interests. This is our concern."[42]

Baw Kyah is aware that his outspokenness is popular among the KNU grassroots and local Karen communities. He also knows that the Myanmar government and Western donors who have supported cease-fire and peace negotiations since 2012 view him as an uncompromising hardliner. According to the VCS, Charles Petrie, a former UN diplomat in Myanmar and the head of the now-suspended Myanmar Peace Support Initiative (MPSI) founded by Norway, has begged him not to obstruct the cease-fire (Baw Kyaw Heh, as cited in Saw Yan Naing 2014a). In fact, Western donors in Myanmar accuse leaders like Baw Kyah and Zipporah Sein of not being pragmatic and contend that their motivations for opposing rapprochement with Naypyidaw were ideologically motivated.[43] One of Baw Kyah's confidants said, "Some people criticize that we are hardliners in the KNU who don't like peace and just want to continue fighting. I say that this is not true. We are no hardliners, we are steady. Maybe it is fair to say that we are hardliners in the right respects."[44] In other words, the internal KNU opposition might be uncompromising with regard to its principles, but this does not mean they are unreasonable.

Conscious of the detrimental effects of past internal divides, the leaders of all factions within the KNU asserted the need for unity. Despite such unanimity, the group has fragmented further, and the internal resistance to the incumbent leadership and its conciliatory cease-fire policies in relation to the government has grown. This unease surfaced most poignantly in mid-2014, when the incumbent leadership surrounding Chairman General Mutu attempted to leave the ethnic armed-group alliance organization United Nationalities Federal Council (UNFC). The KIO, KNU, and four other rebel groups founded the alliance in 2011 as a means of promoting the unity of ethnic armed groups. The reescalation of the Kachin conflict was looming at the time. Since then the new KNU leaders have grown increasingly uncomfortable with their movement's membership in the alliance, which they perceive as putting constraints on their bilateral negotiations with the government. Their attempt to withdraw from UNFC, however, led to stark disagreements with the internal KNU opposition. The opposition pressured the incumbent leaders to remain in the organization, fearing it would further speed their movement's rapprochement with the government (Karen News 2014a).

Three months later, in October 2014, Gen. Baw Kyaw Heh and the commander of the KNDO, Col. Ner Dah Mya, met with representatives of the DKBA and the KPC and signed an agreement that founded a new armed group, the Kawthoolei Armed Forces (KAF) (Saw Yan Naing 2014c). This time the incumbent KNU leadership was caught off guard; it renounced the KAF, which it rightly saw as a threat to its control. The two factions renegotiated both of these disagreements in an emergency meeting in October 2014 (Ei Ei Toe Lwin 2014b). The meeting ended with a declaration of compromise that stated, "Reunification of the Karen armed organizations under the political leadership of the KNU or the formation of Kawthoolei Armed Forces (KAF) is accepted, in principle," but it also declared that the "temporary suspension of [UNFC] membership will be sustained."[45]

While the KAF exists only on paper, the KNU's two rival factions have continued to drift further apart. The KNU's official leadership was the most important ethnic armed group that signed the NCA in October 2015. Indeed, a few days before the signing of the NCA, an alternative summit took place in Panghsang, the mountain headquarters of the United Wa State Army (UWSA) on the Chinese border. The meeting was attended by representatives of ten ethnic armed groups that objected to the NCA: the UWSA, the KIO, the Myanmar National Democratic Alliance Army, the Ta'ang National Liberation Army, the National Democratic Alliance Army, Shan State Army, New Mon State Party, Karenni National Progressive Party, Arakan Army, and Kayan Newland Party. According to the UWSA, the National Socialist Council of Nagaland-Kaplan was not able to attend the meeting because of the location (Sai Wansai 2015). In addition to these nonsignatories, some of whom remained locked in fierce battles with the Tatmadaw, the KNDO were not present at the meeting, but Zipporah Sein and Tharckabaw attended on their behalf. Tharckabaw publicly denounced Mutu and his allies, saying that "some leaders did not walk on the right path [but] we do not want to lose our path" (as cited in Lawi Weng 2015a).

The internal opposition lost the 2017 elections, and Zipporah Sein had to step down from the movement's executive committee. It has since rebranded itself as the KNU Concerned Group, an unofficial grouping within the KNU. Despite the faction's formal loss of leadership positions, actual power within the movement has shifted in its favor. This is because the opposition has not attempted to split the rebellion. Instead it successfully won over large parts of the movement's armed wing, beyond its traditional backbone in northern Karen State. It also managed to forge a new solidarity across the disparate brigades of the KNLA. It did so by leading an energetic internal campaign. One of the internal opposition leaders told me that Brigade 5 has, for instance, started to offer training for officers from all KNLA brigades. Sending personnel to Mutraw provides an effective way of military training for the movement's weaker brigades. While the main focus of these courses is on guerrilla warfare, KNU Concerned Group also organizes political seminars as part of this training program. In these seminars, senior leaders of the internal KNU opposition engage officers from across the KNLA on Karen revolutionary ideals and the flaws of the cease-fire and peace process.[46]

The effectiveness of the KNU Concerned Group's internal mobilization efforts showed in 2018 after fighting re-escalated in parts of Mutraw. In March 2018 the Tatmadaw intruded deep into the territory of Brigade 5 to construct a road with which it sought to connect two of its military bases in the region. The infrastructure project led to the heaviest fighting in eastern Myanmar since 2008. The army clashed with local village guards and KNLA units, who sought to defend the last stronghold of the Karen revolution (Karen Peace Support Network 2018). Northern and southern KNLA brigades rallied in support of Brigade 5 and threatened to withdraw from the NCA and peace process. The KNLA initially recommitted to the NCA after KNU Chairman General Mutu personally negotiated a pause in the road construction with the Tatmadaw's commander in chief Sr. Gen. Min Aung Hlaing. Yet the pressure from the KNLA eventually rose too far. In an emergency meeting in late October 2018 the KNU declared that it suspends its participation in the countrywide peace process and has to rethink its participation in the NCA. According to one internal opposition leader, this significant shift in policy was forced onto the top KNU leadership by the KNLA after it emerged that Kwe Htoo signed an agreement with the government earlier that month which stated that ethnic armed organizations should eventually integrate into one national army.[47]

At the time of writing, Mutu and Kwe Htoo officially remain KNU's chairperson and vice chairperson respectively (Kwe Htoo has become vice chairperson in the 16th KNU Congress after Zipporah lost this position). However, it appears that their power has hollowed out considerably. In fact, it seems that they lost authority over large parts of the movement's armed wing. New leaders have also risen in the ranks. The KNU's new general secretary Padoh Saw Tha Doh Moo has become particularly influential. A former leader of the KNU's youth wing, Tha Doh Moo has sought to reconnect the movement with its grassroots, for instance through utilizing social media. While he is not officially part of the KNU Concerned Group, he is sympathetic to the concerns of the movement's rank-and-file. In an official statement on the KNU's new Facebook presence he writes in support of suspending peace talks, stating that the "visions for peace [of the government and the KNU] are not the same."[48] It remains to be seen which faction of the KNU will ultimately gain the upper hand in their struggle over the right way forward, but it is clear that the movement's internal divisions are of fundamental importance to understanding the Karen cease-fire and Myanmar's wider peace process.

I have analyzed here the reasons the KNU signed its historic cease-fire in 2012 and the tensions that have boiled up within the movement since then. I have described how military and geopolitical pressures along the Thai–Myanmar border have left the once-powerful rulers of Kawthoolei fragmented into parochial brigades that face different individual circumstances. The Tatmadaw and other nonstate armed groups have challenged Karen rebels' control of central and southern areas of Karen State since the early 1990s. Changing regional geopolitics, moreover, have brought powerful commercial interests to southeastern Myanmar. In their wake, the legalization of border trade eroded the black market revenues of central KNU brigades while infrastructure construction eased state territorialization in the central and southern brigade areas. The movement's northern units, by contrast, maintain relatively strong control over a rugged territory that remains isolated from the military and geopolitical change. External changes on the Thai–Myanmar border have shifted the internal power balance of the movements from the central to the northern brigades.

Territorial loss and increased commercialization have led the southern and central KNU units to pull out of local communities. This disrupted the implicit social contract between southern and central rebel units and local Karen civilians, which in turn eroded the legitimacy of regional rebel leaders among their grassroots. By contrast, relative territorial control and comparative isolation from wider changes on the Thai–Myanmar border have left the reciprocal exchange relations in northern areas relatively intact. Local rebel units remain enmeshed in local communities to the extent that social identities between civilians and rebels are conflated. Rebellion in these parts of Karen State remains part of the social context and is embodied in habitual practices in ways that stabilize local rebel authority.

Such regional fragmentation has given rise to two factions with diverging views of negotiations with the government. The new incumbent leaders emerged from the movement's central and southern brigades, which continue to back them. Having lost military power and authority within local Karen communities, these commanders have sought to compromise with Naypyidaw, signed the 2012 cease-fire, and promoted the peace process with Myanmar's government. The previous top leaders, now demoted to second rank, have their stronghold in the relatively powerful northern units of the KNLA. This alliance has formed an internal resistance, which has faced off against the new incumbent leadership and their conciliatory policies. This internal opposition, often depicted as the group's hardliners, has attracted support from the movement's grassroots. This is the case elsewhere in the faction's northern stronghold, where the rebellion has remained comparatively well entrenched in wider society.

During the period I was conducting my research, many in the movement's grassroots viewed the leadership style of General Mutu as overly authoritarian. His increasing conciliation with Naypyidaw was seen as being driven by personal profiteering. Such complaints gave rise to collective perceptions of misrecognition, particularly surrounding feelings of disrespect. This, in turn, has threatened rebel social identities, leading to the growing alienation of the KNU's lower ranks and its traditional supporters from the rebel movement. By contrast, the rebel grassroots considered interactions with the movement's internal opposition as respectful and dignified, not least because of their outspoken criticism of the controversies surrounding the cease-fire, including personal business interests, increased militarization, and the detrimental social and environmental side effects of increased business investment affecting local communities. Identifying with the group's internal opposition, therefore, enabled the grassroots to maintain a positive social identity from continued affiliation to the KNU. This lent authority to the group's internal opposition across the social network of the Karen rebellion. By championing the peace process, the official KNU leadership has become increasingly isolated within its own movement and seems to command little authority over large parts of its armed wing.

What the future holds for the KNU and the prospects of Myanmar's fragile peace process is obviously unknowable. But it is clear that the internal tensions within the Karen rebellion have the potential to cause an organizational split or an internal reshuffling of power, which could jeopardize the group's cease-fire and the nationwide peace negotiations. Whether the cease-fire will hold depends on various factors. The most important is whether the current cease-fire framework and the ongoing peace process can accommodate the genuine grievances of the movement's grassroots as well as the claims to power of the internal opposition. Another important factor has to do with the ability of the KNU's internal opposition to use the authority it has garnered among the movement's grassroots to build alliances across the wider Karen rebel social network and bring about a more cohesive movement again. Such an eventuality would allow them to break with the main movement or retake leadership. Similar dynamics have, indeed, led to the remobilization of rebellion in Kachin State and to the breakdown of the country's most important cease-fire of the 1990s.

CHAPTER FOUR

KACHIN REBELLION:
CEASING CEASE-FIRE

Shortly after the KNU signed the NCA in Naypyidaw in October 2015 I was chatting with a Karen friend from the KNU on a social media platform, inquiring about his opinion on recent developments. He strongly disagreed with his leaders' decision to sign the accord at a time when government forces were battling various other ethnic armed groups, including Kachin, Kokang, Shan, and Palaung movements. That fighting has resulted in heavy losses on both sides and the displacement of more than 120,000 civilians along the Myanmar–Chinese border.[1] My friend felt more affinity at that point to the Kachin Independence Organization (KIO) than to the conciliatory leadership of his own KNU. Knowing that I had visited Laiza, the KIO's informal capital, the year before, he expressed a wish to travel there. In his imagination Laiza was the last symbol of ethnic armed struggle, and he longed to see it for himself.

The Kachin insurrection was founded on 5 February 1961, fourteen years after that of the KNU. A broad coalition, including Kachin university students in Yangon, intellectuals in Kachin State's capital of Myitkyina, and Kachin veterans of the Second World War, came together in reaction to repressive state policies that discriminated against ethnic minorities. The KIO quickly developed into one of the most powerful, best-organized ethnonationalist rebel movements in Burma. Bertil Lintner, one of the first foreign correspondents to visit KIO territory, noted that the movement was the "strongest ethnic rebel army in Burma" at the time (1990, 6). By the end of the 1980s it controlled vast parts of Kachin State and northern Shan State, administering them as a para-government (Smith 1999, 191–92). During these decades the KIO was at the forefront of Burma's ethnic minority struggle against the central state. It signed a cease-fire in 1994 but returned to battle in 2011. My Karen friend's sense of the superiority of the KIO focuses on its condition since 2011 rather than on the seventeen years that preceded the breaking of the cease-fire. Fighting between the Tatmadaw and the KIO's armed wing, the Kachin Independence Army (KIA), has been fierce.[2] Observers who had thought of the Kachin cease-fire as being stable and the KIO as being relatively weak and conciliatory have been surprised by the violence (Global Witness 2003, 117–18; International Crisis Group 2003). And in fact Kachin leaders established intimate ties with Tatmadaw commanders during the cease-fire and accommodated the government (Woods 2011, 761; International Crisis Group 2012, 5–6). Moreover, the revolutionary ambitions and military capacities of the KIO seemed to have withered away over the long cease-fire years, while its leaders profited from the spoils of a lucrative cease-fire economy. In 2003 a Global Witness report noted that the KIO had been weakened by "self-interest, opportunism, corruption and incompetence" among the KIO leadership and a resulting breakdown in its ability to provide social services since the cease-fire. The report also stressed that this led to a plunge in the morale of the KIO's rank and file. While it deemed a revitalization of the movement by a return to fighting unlikely, it acknowledged that breaking the cease-fire would have that effect (Global Witness 2003, 118). In a similar vein, an International Crisis Group (2003, 11) report of the same year described the movement's eroding power as a reason that the government would readily squelch any return to armed struggle in Kachin State. At the time, it did indeed seem unlikely that the KIO would have the ability to maintain a sustained and powerful resistance.

Eight years later things looked different: since 2011 the Kachin rebels have been making uncompromising political demands and displaying notable military strength, organizational discipline, endurance on the battlefield, and a vast popular support base among the wider Kachin public. Remobilization did not happen, however, after incumbent leaders returned to the battlefield in order to regain the loyalty of a disaffected grassroots, as suggested by the Global Witness analysis. I find that the co-optation of senior KIO leaders alienated young officers who had already started to remobilize the movement in opposition to a leadership they saw as being corrupted since the mid-2000s. Tracing the ways in which these leaders rebuilt the legitimacy of the movement among its grassroots explains why and how the KIO's ability to wage war against Myanmar's government increased so dramatically after years of eroding capacities.

CEASE-FIRE: LOSING THEIR WAY

The KIO capital of Laiza is a small town straddling the Myanmar–Chinese border. Before the KIO signed a cease-fire with the Tatmadaw in 1994, the settlement was a small village. After the truce was put in place it quickly grew into a bustling border town. At that point the KIO moved its quasi government, including so-called civilian departments, from its mountain fortress in Pa Jau to the valley settlement. Increased economic activities turned Laiza into a bustling border trading hub with China. In addition to the rapidly expanding resource economies, a buzzing entertainment industry opened its doors to Chinese customers. It included casinos, which reportedly featured dancers, transvestites, and prostitutes from as far away as Russia. Western diplomats had viewed the KIO in a positive light during the Cold War, but they now began to associate the movement with the "bad" armed groups running illicit businesses along the Myanmar–China border (Sherman 2003, 234). Today, Laiza is the Mecca of armed ethnic resistance that my Karen friend imagined. Rebel units dug into fortified hilltop positions protect the twenty thousand people who live there. Rebel policemen patrol the streets, tailors produce KIA uniforms, nurses are being trained to work in the KIO-operated hospital, and Kachin soldiers sing revolutionary songs in dingy karaoke bars, their self-manufactured AK-81 assault rifles beside them. Soldiers from various other allied rebel movements are regular visitors in town (figure 5).

When I visited Laiza in 2014, three and a half years after war had returned to Kachin State, the town's once-bustling central bus station lay deserted: normal traffic could not cross through the nearby front line to the rest of Myanmar. Yet the town's sheer size and modern facilities spoke of more prosperous days, as did its paved roads. Neighboring China's Yunnan Province had roads like this but most Myanmar towns did not. The spacious Laiza Hotel was the best in town, featuring hot running water and Chinese Wi-Fi internet. Receptionists were still at work there, but guests from China no longer came now that heavy fighting had resumed in the area. The small golf course on the outskirts of Laiza was generally deserted, although KIA officers used it occasionally to practice their swing. Lorries arrived sporadically at the border crossing with

Figure 5 KIA soldiers in Laiza. Since the breakdown of the Kachin cease-fire in 2011 many video gaming shops and gambling halls have closed down in Laiza. War has become a reality again in Kachin State. Photograph by the author.

China to be checked by the KIO's customs authority, and Chinese traders, hawking small commodities in the town's market, complained about declining profits. The most striking sign of the town's transformation was that the KIA had turned Laiza's largest casino into its operational headquarters. Locals proudly called the building complex "the Pentagon" or "the war room." They said the cease-fire entertainment industries were long gone. One KIA officer explained, "Laiza is not a town for businessmen anymore. This is a political town now."[3]

FRAGMENTATION AND INFIGHTING

Throughout most of the Cold War Myanmar's generals applied all-out military force to crush the KIO as well as other rebel armies, including the Karen rebellion, but the KIO only seemed to grow stronger as a result. Lintner reported after a visit to KIO-controlled areas in the 1980s that discipline in the movement's armed wing "was always impressive by any standards" (1990, 174). In the early 1990s the state changed to a strategy that sought to pacify these restive borderlands by granting rebel movements the right to hold on to pockets of territories, retain their arms, and pursue their own businesses. Welcoming these terms, many armed groups in Myanmar's north signed individual cease-fires before the KIO did. KIO leaders decided to sign a cease-fire for several reasons, among them the battle fatigue of their soldiers, humanitarian considerations for local communities, and a genuine belief that settling the conflict at the negotiating table was possible (Jones 2014a, 792). In addition, the KIO was weakened by two events. In 1991 a Tatmadaw offensive isolated the Kachin movement's strong southern brigade, which was fighting in neighboring northern Shan State. The KIO had no means of resupplying and reinforcing these units, and they formed an independent movement to sign an individual cease-fire with the government. Another, less-reported factor pushing the larger KIO to sign a cease-fire was that Chinese arms dealers had cheated the group, disappearing with almost all of its funds without delivering the promised weaponry.[4]

The KIO signed a cease-fire with Yangon on 24 February 1994. Nicholas Farrelly, who has conducted long-term research in Kachin State during the cease-fire period, describes the agreement as "integral to the security of northern Burma" during the seventeen years that followed (2012, 54). This conclusion was evidenced by the fact that the breakdown of the KIO cease-fire reignited conflict across large parts of Kachin and Shan States in northern Myanmar. The general secretary of the KIO told me that the movement was war weary at the time and that the state's willingness to allow rebels to retain their arms and to administer a sizable part of Kachin State was crucial in making the agreement possible.[5] This cease-fire territory, the so-called Kachin State Special Region-2, spanned approximately one-fifth of Kachin State, mainly along the Chinese border. In addition to Laiza it included the town of Maijayang and lesser populated parts of northeastern Kachin State. Militarily weakened at the time, KIO leaders decided that this deal was in their best interest. The government took control of approximately 70 percent of Kachin State, including the official provincial capital of Myitkyina (Dean 2005, 131). It gave Kachin State Special Region-1 to the New Democratic Army-Kachin (NDA-K), a group that split from KIO in 1968 and signed a cease-fire with the state in 1989. The NDA-K, made up mostly of non-Jinghpaw Kachin, split from the KIO in 1968 because of intra-ethnic grievances and ideological differences and joined the communist umbrella of the CPB. After the collapse of the CPB in 1989, the NDA-K concluded a cease-fire with the Myanmar government. It became a Tatmadaw-controlled BGF militia in 2009. The NDA-K was not overly strong, commanding about one thousand soldiers in a relatively large territory. The territorial expanse reflects the fact that the state generally rewarded groups that signed cease-fires earlier on more generously than those that signed them later. In contrast to the KIO, the NDA-K never exerted exclusive control over its assigned territory and did not attempt to create a state within a state. Observers agree that the group was focused on business rather than politics (Global Witness 2005, 54; South 2008, 153; Callahan 2007, 42–45).

Outside analysts claim that economic incentives have been a main motivation for rebel leaders of different movements in Myanmar to sign armistices since 1989 (Sherman 2003). The government indeed granted the KIO the right to exploit their area's vast natural resources by allowing it to set up its own legal corporations, to sell concessions to other companies, and to tax the continually growing transborder trade with China. The KIO became one of the most accommodating cease-fire groups. According to Global Witness (2003, 117–18), KIO leaders seemed more interested in plundering their territories together with Tatmadaw generals and Chinese businessmen than in looking out for the rights of Kachin people.

Elite economic interests alone might not be a negative in the estimation of a movement's grassroots. Joint–General Secretary U La Nan, a young leader in KIO who had not personally joined in the plunder, justified his predecessors' interest in economic development as benefiting the Kachin people as well as the leaders themselves. According to him, KIO leaders at the time genuinely believed that incoming business interests presented opportunities for the socioeconomic development of marginalized Kachin communities. He pointed out that other ethnic groups enjoyed such opportunities.[6] This rhetoric resembles that of the government itself. For example, trumpeting the alleged success of the Border Regions Development Program, in which it welcomed the KIO to take part, the regime's mouthpiece newspaper, the *New Light of Myanmar,* wrote in 1994, "Border regions of today are not like before. Education, public health, communications and agriculture have progressed and developed. The city of Yangon has now become more easily accessible to border regions. Post and telegraph services are already functioning. Electric lights have brightened the border regions. National races who had lived in darkness in the past are now enjoying the fruits of progress" (14 February 1994, as cited in Lambrecht 2000).

Many KIO grassroots did indeed welcome the idea of economic development.[7] But they were wary, as the construction of roads and bridges gave the state—mostly in the form of the Tatmadaw—the opportunity to tighten its grip over territory the KIO had once controlled.[8] In addition, Myanmar's military government argued that it could not decide political matters due to its status as an interim administration. Thus the Kachin had little hope of negotiating institutional arrangements for power sharing, including a federal constitution.

The KIO's formal authority to govern Kachin State Special Region-2 transformed the movement from a rebel army into a local para-government. Lacking the means to achieve its original political goals, it was left to focus on administration and economic development. A local leader in this region who commented for the International Crisis Group (2003, 10) report described political negotiations as hopeless. He argued that economic development was answering the need to "build for the future." While the KIO always had governing ambitions in its controlled territories and possessed rudimentary administrative structures, before 1994 it was primarily a guerrilla war-fighting organization (Lintner and Lintner 1990). With the cease-fire in place, its civilian components proliferated. The KIO established functional offices, including departments of health, education, agriculture, and women's affairs. In addition, it started to operate several civilian hospitals, facilities equipped with Chinese utensils and run by Chinese-educated doctors and technicians. Nurses that staff these hospitals have since been educated in a dedicated training school, much like KIO-trained teachers who work in the rebellion's school system (figure 6).

General Secretary Brig. Gen. La Ja of the KIO described the cease-fire years as a period of focus on the development of physical infrastructure.[9] Private companies handled the construction of roads in return for logging and mining concessions. For instance, Jadeland Company built the road from Myitkyina to Sumprabum and further on to Putao. The Kachin businessman Yup Zaw Hkawng, who had close connections with the KIO as well as the Tatmadaw, owned the company. The KIO sought to improve the deficient electricity supply in Kachin State by establishing the BUGA Corporation, which hired the Chinese company Jinxin to construct two hydropower plants on the Mali and the Dabak Rivers in return for extensive logging rights in the area (Global Witness 2009, 59–69). Since 2006 BUGA has provided electricity to the KIO-held towns of Laiza and Maijayang as well as to the government-held urban centers of Myitkyina, neighboring Waimaw Township, and Bamo.[10] Electrifying the previously unlit urban centers of Kachin State generated not only revenues but also legitimacy for the KIO.[11]

Besides creating revenues from KIO companies, the rapidly expanding cease-fire economy, fueled by Chinese hunger for the area's natural riches, was instrumental in funding the KIO and its developmental ambitions. General Secretary La Ja explained that taxes from the timber and mining companies funded infrastructure development.[12] According to him, the KIO did not tax Kachin civilians initially unless they

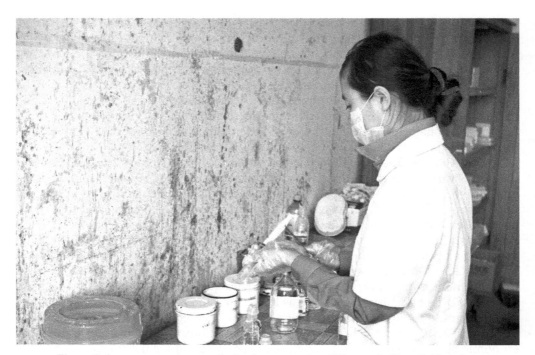

Figure 6 A nurse preparing anesthetics for surgery in a KIO-operated hospital in Laiza. Photograph by the author.

were selling large amounts of land.[13] While taxing Kachin civilians might have been alienating, reliance on and entanglement with incoming business interests damaged leadership cohesion, which in turn affected legitimate authority relations between elites and grassroots following the cease-fire.

To be sure, the KIO's post-cease-fire dependence on the natural resource trade was a continuation of its pre-cease-fire dependence on jade mining and small commodity smuggling on the Myanmar–Chinese border.[14] But the 1994 cease-fire stabilized the area to an extent that enabled Chinese, Myanmar, and Kachin companies to exploit natural resources on an unprecedented scale and pace (Buchanan, Kramer, and Woods 2013, 17–18). Since then the Myanmar government has gradually taken control of the most resource-rich parts of the region, including the world's largest jade mines in Hpakant. The head of the KIO's Economics Department, Zawng Buk Than, explained that it still receives taxes from that region through clandestine means that are neither formal nor legal. On the basis of reports on the natural resource industry I surmised that he was referring to protection rackets the KIO has imposed on companies operating within its reach as well as KIA mobile and stationary tollgates along illicit trade routes leading to the Chinese border (cf. Global Witness 2015). Zawng Buk Than said as well that the KIO relies more heavily on timber logging than on jade mining because of the intrusion of the Tatmadaw in that industry (figure 7). A newly imposed logging ban in China has made Chinese consumers amenable to higher prices, which raises profits (Buchanan, Kramer, and Woods 2013, 18). Global Witness (2009) reports that KIO territories have experienced massive deforestation; when I asked Zawng Buk Than about that, he nodded and said, "We

Figure 7 Timber smuggling at an illegal border crossing from Kachin State to China.
Photograph by the author.

know that it's not good for the environment, and environment agencies prohibit timber cutting like that, but we need to manage our income. So we need to do it. We need that business." Since the cease-fire Chinese companies have also been engaged in large-scale hydraulic gold mining in Kachin State. Taxing them has given the KIO new sources of income.[15]

Reverend Zau Toi, a well-connected leader of the Kachin Baptist Convention (KBC), the most important religious institution in Kachin State, explained to me how these new opportunities turned rebel leaders into businesspeople: "The KIO has many departments, and the department heads know the Chinese businessmen well. Until 2008–9 many KIO leaders became big businessmen, including the heads of the mining and forest department. They became rich. . . . They have many nice houses in the cities and a lot of land. They worked very close with the Myanmar leaders [and in this respect were] not faithful to the KIO."[16]

Rebel leaders could not advance their business interests without cooperating with Myanmar officials, as the Tatmadaw were still the gatekeepers to the most profitable resources in the region. While the state had formally transferred power to the rebels who supported the cease-fires, the Tatmadaw had a cachet of officialdom that allowed them to sell land concessions with ostensible investment security to foreign companies in ways that rebel armies cannot (International Crisis Group 2004, 10). Foreign investors are thus mostly forced into joint ventures with companies owned by senior Tatmadaw officers or by Myanmar crony businesspeople who themselves are often retired Tatmadaw officers. Observers noted that Kachin elites came to see collaboration with the Myanmar government as socially acceptable (Farrelly 2012, 55).

As many Kachin leaders developed intimate ties with their erstwhile enemies, competing business interests sparked rivalry among them. Individual strongmen often lined the pockets of their families first. This led to the fragmentation of the movement's leadership. In the early 2000s these tensions turned violent. In 2001 Lt. Gen. N'ban La ousted Gen. Zau Mai, the organization's top leader since the cease-fire, in a coup. According to Zau Toi, this happened because of rival business interests:

> Inside the KIO they had many individual conflicts, you know. Zau Mai, he took too much opportunities, advantage to do business, working with the Chinese, and also his own relatives, very close relatives. This is why the power struggle happened in the KIO. . . . Many people viewed him as too selfish, giving our jade mining concessions to his relatives. That's why N'ban La took over the power from him. This is one reason. And the second reason is . . . he came very close to Myanmar leaders. That is why the KIO Central Committee worried about that. This was the foundation for the conflict.[17]

Zau Toi also attributed the subsequent assassination of the rebel army's vice chief of staff and head of intelligence in 2004 following another coup attempt to business interests, saying that "all the conflicts within the KIO back then were based on business, based on personal business interests."[18]

Joint–General Secretary U La Nan told me that he understands that the economic opportunities proffered by the state were part of a "government policy to weaken us as well as the other armed groups." As he admitted, "We thought that the [1994] cease-fire will lead to a political settlement. But as time went by without [political] talks, we were given incentives, such as business, whatever you want. In that time, some of us wanted to do business."[19] He conceded that the government had been successful, in the KIO as well as in other organizations, in dividing every organization that signed a cease-fire at that time because of business interests. In fact, the Tatmadaw has long sought to divide and rule ethnic armies to weaken their opponents, and cease-fire economies became part of this agenda. This business-focused agenda crucially affected the Kachin grassroots' perception of their leaders. Duwa Mahkaw Hkun Sa, a prominent Kachin activist in the diaspora who refers to the coup against Zau Mai as the beginning of a "decade of challenge for the KIO," writes that the overthrow was supported by the KIO grassroots because Zau Mai's "autocratic, sometimes even brutal style of leadership was diminishing trust and confidence in the KIO among Kachin people" (2016, 341). A local elder in Laiza agreed. Reflecting on the cease-fire period, he said, "Some of our leaders back then behaved just like warlords."[20]

New Grievances and Growing Alienation

The KIO's increased entanglement in the region's lucrative cease-fire economies did more than spark disastrous infighting among the movement's leadership. It also weakened the KIO by damaging its legitimate authority relations between the movement's elites and their grassroots. The business dealings that enriched rebel leaders infringed on the livelihoods of local communities. Although the resentments were a continuation of those directed against Yangon before the cease-fire, now they settled on the KIO leadership itself. The rebel leaders' legitimacy among their grassroots crumbled, and in turn the group's previously stable support networks among the wider Kachin public eroded.

Increased security and welfare could have benefited the standing of KIO leaders. The people I spoke with recalled a feeling of optimism among Kachin civilians in 1994, when decades of brutal civil war ended.[21] And the end of fighting neutralized the most central source of insecurity. The development agenda of the KIO contributed to increased access to education, health, and electricity in the areas they administered. Moreover, incoming investments and better transport links made many towns in Kachin State more prosperous than ever before (Farrelly 2012, 56). Despite these tangible benefits, many ordinary Kachin today feel that the cease-fire did not improve their lives.[22] I spoke about this with a priest in Laiza, Father Paul, who attributed eroding support for KIO leadership more to the continuation of displacement and repression after 1994 than to the fact that leaders grew rich while the grassroots remained poor.[23] The large-scale unsustainable resource exploitation and further militarization after the cease-fire largely erased the sense of improvement.

The KIO could not protect communities from forced displacement and other insecurities. A man I met in 2014 at one of the many internally displaced persons (IDPs) camps in Kachin State told me that his family had fled violence four times since the 1994 cease-fire. Two of his five children had died in the course of this upheaval. He acknowledged that the most recent displacement was prompted by the return to war in 2011, "but before that we had to leave because the companies and Burmese soldiers took our land for doing business."[24] Before the cease-fire this displaced man had been part of a community that depended on smallholder and subsistence farming. His account reflects the experience of many Kachin civilians and illustrates how civilians' insecurities continued throughout the cease-fire period. Armed conflict led to forced displacement that undermined his livelihood before the cease-fire. After the cease-fire, the logging and mining sectors led to a new uprooting. The environmental impacts of large-scale natural resource extraction have since squeezed the livelihoods of local farming communities as well. The use of heavy machinery and explosives in industrialized jade mining has degraded entire mountain ranges (Global Witness 2015, 38).

Gold mining has become the second largest mineral extraction activity in Kachin State. Whereas at the time of the cease-fire in 1994 fourteen small-scale gold mines existed in western Kachin State's Hugawng Valley, by 2003 there were thirty-one, all of them industrialized operations. Relying on mercury as a chemical reagent to loosen the gold, hydraulic mining has polluted the rivers and soil on which local livelihoods depend. Deforestation from timber logging also increased. The assignment of the most profitable mining areas to the Tatmadaw and the resulting loss of revenue to the KIO increased timber logging as a means of making up lost KIO revenue (Global Witness 2009). Large monocrop plantations for cash and food crops have benefited Chinese businessmen and local authorities but further marginalized local communities, who have since come to experience soil degradation, land encroachment, and dependence on volatile market forces (Buchanan, Kramer, and Woods 2013, 47).

The uncodified status of communal landownership among ethnic minority communities in Myanmar's border areas, as in many other places where swidden agriculture is traditionally practiced, has made large-scale landgrabs easier, in effect dispossessing more than half of the rural population in most areas of Kachin State (Buchanan, Kramer, and Woods 2013, 47). The Kachin Development Networking Group, a local civil society organization, provides an example of landgrabbing in its reports on the Hukawng Valley. In 2001 the Myanmar government officially designated the valley as the world's largest tiger reserve and established a conservation zone on the initiative of and in cooperation with a US-based NGO, the Wildlife Conservation Society. The Kachin civil society report calls the reserve a sham (Kachin Development Networking Group 2012). This is because the creation of the preserve has restricted local people's access to forests, including to resources like game and timber. But the Myanmar-based Yuzana Company has experienced no such restriction. Since 2006 the state has given the company access to most parts of the valley, where it established eighty-one thousand hectares of monocrop plantations in cassava and sugarcane. The Kachin Development Networking Group organization writes, "Bulldozers have razed forest areas, animal corridors, and farmlands of ethnic people living in the valley for generations. . . . Local people have been forced from their homes into a relocation camp" (2012).

In addition to the environmental costs and investment-induced displacement, the cease-fire economies brought new social problems. The most obvious one relates to the spread of drugs and, consequently, HIV/AIDS. The area has been known as the "golden triangle" since the 1950s, when opium production started to boom.[25] The KIO officially stopped growing poppies in 1991, but heroin and amphetamine production have flourished in Shan and Kachin States as part of cease-fire capitalism (Woods 2011). Richard Synder describes drug production as a "lucrative 'exit option'" that the Tatmadaw granted to cease-fire groups, effectively legalizing the narcotics industry (2006, 959). Drugs have become cheap and plentiful in Kachin State, and poverty and insecurity have driven demand.[26] Opium bans by various cease-fire groups, including the KIO, led to a decline in the opium industry beginning in 1994, but it has resurged since 2006, doubling its output by 2012.[27] Progovernment militias have largely been driving the trade since (Meehan 2011, 2015). Measures to decrease output have included crop substitution programs that have involved Chinese investment in monoculture rubber plantations. Studies show that these estates have created new economic dependencies and environmental degradation that damage the livelihood of local farmers who depended on poppy cultivation (Buchanan, Kramer, and Woods 2013, 47).

The expansion of labor-intensive extractive industries, which have attracted droves of migrant workers from all over the country to the mining towns of Kachin State, has led to a surge in the local demand for narcotics among impoverished workers facing inhumane working conditions. Prostitution and needle sharing are rampant in these commercial hubs, and an HIV/AIDS epidemic has swept northern Burma (Kachin Development Networking Group 2007, 37–56). A local social worker who is working with drug-addicted youth in the government-controlled capital Myitkyina told me that almost half of the local university students were drug addicts. When I visited Myitkyina University in February 2014 heroin and amphetamines were readily available on campus. Many local Kachin feel that government officials have turned a blind eye to this epidemic because drugs make mounting ethnic resistance difficult. The social worker said, "The army has stopped killing us directly. Now they leave us to destroy ourselves."[28]

Even if Kachin blame the Tatmadaw for the epidemic, they see KIO leaders as having been complicit in the emergence of predatory economies over the cease-fire years (see Duwa Mahkaw Hkun Sa 2016, 341). Likewise, the fact that the Tatmadaw used the cease-fires of the 1990s to build up its military capacities in northern Myanmar, focusing on areas of economic interests, did not endear the locals to the KIO leaders who had signed the cease-fire. In Bhamo District of southern Kachin State the Tatmadaw maintained four battalions before the 1994 cease-fire. Ten years later it had ten battalions, each of which confiscated approximately three hundred acres of land (Human Rights Watch 2005, 55). Local communities often experienced abuses by Tatmadaw soldiers, including extortion, forced labor, and expropriation (Global Witness 2009, 64–66). Sitting at his desk in the KIO's Pentagon, the abandoned Chinese casino in Laiza, La Nan said to me, "[Under] the cease-fire it was very difficult for the KIO to maneuver between the government and the civilians. They were trying to get trust from the civilian side but also not to break down the cease-fire with the government. . . . From the civilians' view, the KIO sometimes even looked like a [Burman] government agency."[29]

Another senior KIA officer in the movement's liaison office in Chiang Mai in Thailand had equally bad memories of those days, admitting during a conversation that one of the biggest problems arising from this situation was that "we could not provide security for the public. We simply had no power to protect them."[30] According to Father Paul in Laiza, the lack of protection was indeed one of the major reasons "people became very disillusioned about the KIO and thought it lost its revolutionary goals." Protecting the community is arguably the highest essential moral principle of a rebel movement built on ethnonational ideology. The KIA's inability to protect Kachin civilians from abuses by government troops, from the landgrabs of Chinese companies, and from the rampant environmental and social problems arising out of the cease-fire economy, eroded not only the trust of local communities in the movement but also that of KIA foot soldiers in their leadership.[31] Unable to protect the Kachin people and being associated with leadership the grassroots mistrusted, KIA soldiers no longer derived positive social identities from affiliation to the rebel collective.

Although civilian departments in the KIO expanded during the cease-fire years and individual leaders enriched themselves, the KIA, as the organization's armed wing, lost out. Young officers and foot soldiers did not receive the same payoffs from the cease-fire economies as their superiors, and the KIO paid them only one hundred Chinese renminbi per month, equivalent to US$16. In order to feed their families, they began operating petty businesses like small-scale cross-border jade smuggling. Some had to depend on remittances from family networks.[32] As a Kachin elder summarized, "The KIO, the organization itself, was poor, but the leaders, personally, they became rich."[33] Morale among the middle and lower ranks plunged as they witnessed the leaders' self-enrichment, amicable ties with Myanmar's establishment, complicity in exploiting their own territories, and internal feuds. Equally disheartening was the soldiers' inability to protect Kachin civilians. Father Paul noted that such pessimism led to mass desertions in the early 2000s as many soldiers went home to their families.[34] The armed wing Lintner had praised for its discipline was near collapse by the early 2000s. As a local journalist recalled, "[The soldiers] really didn't like the cease-fire [and] wanted to continue fighting for their rights." A Kachin soldier himself remembered the cease-fire years as "really dark. . . . We just didn't know what to fight for anymore."[35]

REBUILDING POPULAR REBELLION

The Kachin cease-fire had ruptured reciprocal relations between the rebel leaders and their grassroots. The implicit social contract between the KIO and local communities had broken down, and the rebellion's previously stable support networks among the Kachin public crumbled. A disillusioned group of young officers gathered around a charismatic leader and realigned with the powerful Kachin churches, the only political institution that retained any legitimacy among the Kachin public during the cease-fire years. This alliance enabled the aspiring rebel leaders to rebuild legitimate authority relations with local communities, to remobilize the movement by recruiting a new generation of revolutionaries on a large scale, and ultimately to take over the KIO leadership. One man who was part of this remobilization effort in Maijayang described the situation in the waning days of the cease-fire as a generational conflict: "There was a gap between old officers and young officers, their ideas and many other things. . . . The old men acted just like Burmese soldiers. They wanted to control the organization and make profit. But the young officers wanted to change that behavior."[36]

Ranked in the middle of a top-down military organization in a strictly age-based traditional society, young KIA officers were largely excluded from the power and wealth more senior commanders enjoyed. They also faced the potential collapse of their army, a disintegrating central leadership, and the erosion of overall support among local communities. Against this background, they had little to lose. To rebuild legitimate authority relations with the movement's grassroots, they treated Kachin civilians in a consciously respectful and dignifying way. The rank and file began to derive positive social identities through affiliation with the rebel movement again.

Widespread discontent afforded the young officers fertile ground from which to launch an attack on the incumbent leadership. Yet, as one of their confidants told me, it was difficult to reestablish support in Myitkyina while the people there still feared the KIA. He attributed the wariness of the population to the fact that most of the KIA leaders had become unscrupulous businesspeople by then.[37]

The large Kachin Baptist Convention (KBC) and the smaller local Catholic Church provided the support the young KIA officers needed. Ever since the arrival of Christian missionaries in the late nineteenth century Christian churches have had notable influence on Kachin society, including in the production of Kachin ethnonationalism. Most early Kachin ethnonationalist leaders were educated in church institutions, such as the Kachin Theological College in Myitkyina. And while the Kachin conflict had issues unrelated to religion, the interests of the KIO and the Kachin churches have historically overlapped to a substantial degree. In fact, Christianity has long distinguished the Kachin from the Buddhist Bamar majority. It served as a vessel for nationalism itself with its inherent promise of Western-style modernity (Sadan 2007). Reverend Zau Toi, the Kachin Baptist leader from Myitkyina, told me that the Kachin Baptist Convention has thus always had a good relationship with the KIO: "A good relationship because we all belong to Christianity. And most of the KIO are Kachin, very few are non-Kachin, almost all are Christian. We are all relatives. So KIO, KBC, we became the same. Same motivation, same goal."[38]

Since the inception of the Kachin revolution, Christianity has indeed offered a remedy for the most profound problem KIO leaders faced, namely, uniting the six major ethnic subgroups within Kachin State: Jinghpaw, Lawngwaw, Zaiwa, Nung Rawang, Lisu, and Lachik (Sadan 2013, 331–60). The majority Jinghpaw community generally dominates. One Lachik youth leader at the Jinghpaw-dominated KBC explained to me that the Jinghpaw language was the first to receive an orthography, as devised by the American-Swedish missionary Ola Hanson in the late nineteenth century. Ever since, the youth continued, the Jinghpaw have thought of themselves as being more educated than anyone else among the Kachin, and thus it was only natural that they were taking the lead in the Kachin rebellion. The fact that the Lachik youth leader himself accepted this civilizational discourse suggests that these hierarchies are well established across Kachin society.[39] Nevertheless, Jinghpaw domination has created resentments. Members of the Lisu community, for example, often feel discriminated against. Many Lisu do not even regard themselves as Kachin, and support for the KIO is low among Lisu people. A Lisu community leader in Myitkyina, for instance, told me in bitter terms about an invitation he received in January 2017 inviting him to Kachin State Day celebrations. The invitation featured titles in English, Burmese, and Jinghpaw. While two of the titles read "Kachin State Day" in English and Burmese, the third one, in Jinghpaw, read *Jinghpaw Mungdaw Nhtoi,* or "Jinghpaw State Day." The leader explained that he abstained from the festivities because he did not feel welcome.[40] The intra-ethnic divides are a politically sensitive issue in contemporary Kachin society. In a conversation I had with a Jinghpaw friend who works with a KIO-affiliated relief organization in Laiza, for instance, he used the term "Lisu-cycle" to describe his cheap but sturdy motorbike. He thought the word fit because that model of bike was popular among Kachin foot soldiers and in Lisu communities for its reliability on long hauls (many Lisu live on both sides of the Myanmar–Chinese border and thus travel frequently to Yunnan). When I naively referred to the bike as a Lisu-cycle some days later he hushed me up. He said the term was "politically incorrect." The Lisu, he went on, have historically been the group that has experienced the most discrimination in Kachin society, and I should not make such tactless jokes.[41] Intra-ethnic tensions between subgroups of the Kachin community are real and have seemingly increased since my conversation in 2014. But they did not play a major role in the internal leadership struggle of the KIO in the early 2000s. Young rebel officers stood up to their superiors because of their corruption and profiteering, which were threatening the movement.[42]

Christianity is still one of the principal unifying factors in Kachin society. Church leaders actually played a central role in pushing for a cease-fire in 1994 as well as in mediating during the negotiations.[43] The role of the churches changed, however, over the course of the cease-fire. Father Paul recounted a complex history. While saying that the KIO and the church are "very, very friendly . . . [and have] great trust in one another," he conceded that the warmth between the church and the KIO leadership dissipated during the cease-fire years.[44] He explained that during the cease-fire senior KIO leaders were "increasingly secretive," cutting "the younger leaders [and] the public" out of their decisions, and that they stopped listening to religious leaders.[45]

Sumlut Gun Maw, the leader of the young officers, focused on partnering with local churches and youth groups to regain the trust of the Kachin public. Holding the rank of brigadier in the early 2000s, he commanded the 3rd Brigade of the KIA at the time and allied with some individuals in the more senior ranks of the KIA, including General Gam Shawng. Gun Maw was also in good standing with the Kachin grassroots. In fact, he had cultivated close relations with Kachin student networks since the early 1990s. Gun Maw was thus particularly well known and popular among young Kachin across the country (see Hkanhpa Tu Sadan 2016, 312–13). Father Paul emphasized his approachability and popularity: "[In 2002] he was a very active young officer. He had a lot of friends in the towns. He is a very friendly person also, he had a lot of friends among the university students, even though they were very much younger. . . . Everybody was talking: Du Kaba [officer] Gun Maw, Du Kaba Gun Maw!"

To Father Paul, the young leaders contrasted sharply with the nontransparent and authoritarian incumbent leadership. He quoted the young officers as saying, "Let the people know all the ideas, people should know what we are discussing and where we are going. Only then they will come and cooperate with us."[46] A Kachin political activist in the diaspora explained the importance of Gun Maw's approach: "If you want to understand the Kachin rebellion, you need to understand Kachin society first. We are very loyal but we want to be asked. The leaders cannot leave us out of their decisions. But once a decision is made we will follow."[47] In her account of traditional Kachin society she referred to Edmund Leach's (1954) work, which stresses the constant fluctuation of traditional Kachin political organization between hierarchical forms (*gumsa*) and egalitarian ones (*gumlao*) in which consultative councils play a central role. The accuracy of Leach's foundational depiction of Kachin society is a matter of ongoing debate. But my interlocutors believe in the historical existence of egalitarian social orders and consultative decision making, and this belief appears to have helped Gun Maw build legitimacy.

In this project of restoration, Gun Maw and his followers relied heavily on the wide-ranging networks of the Kachin churches, which, unlike the KIO, have not suffered a loss of legitimacy during the cease-fire years. Father Paul proudly explained why: "I read Ho Chi Minh and advised [Gun Maw] about the importance of organizing the local, the village level. Just like the Vietnamese [meaning Viet Cong] did. But here we need to organize through the religious churches. So our churches became a great force in that. Because when the people from the different towns and the different villages when they came here and saw me with my clothes in white among the other people [the KIO officers] who came for the meeting [consultation], they were very inspired. They saw that there is change."[48]

I attended such a meeting in "the Pentagon" in Laiza. I saw young men and women in colorful traditional costumes welcoming the families of KIA soldiers as they gathered in one of the large casino rooms now turned into a meeting hall. In the courtyard heavily armed commando units waited for the arrival of a senior KIO leader who was to address the soldiers' families. Eventually a general arrived in a $300,000 bullet-proof, luxury-edition Hummer SUV. To my surprise he was not one of the young officers but Gen. N'ban La, the senior KIO leader who overthrew Zau Mai in 2011. N'ban La was a strongman who had made a fortune in jade mining and had also, according to a member of the new leadership, lost his revolutionary ideals. He delivered a long speech about the need to endure current hardships for the freedom of future generations, then patiently responded to the questions of worried parents asking about recent developments on the front line, where their sons and daughters were battling the militarily much superior Tatmadaw. When the meeting ended more than three hours later, the general disappeared as quickly as he had appeared.

I asked a local aid worker who had accompanied me to the meeting to explain why people trusted N'ban La. He shrugged and said, "Sure he is a gangster, but he is a good gangster!"[49] A local journalist and KIO insider overheard this comment and agreed that N'ban La was a good gangster "because he is guided by some good people these days. . . . He has a lot of money. . . . But now, Du Kaba Gun Maw and Du Kaba Gam Shawng, they advise him and organize him in the right way." The journalist said that the leader had overthrown Zau Mai in 2001 to gain an advantage in the jade trade but "now he changed. His political stand is good. Just now."[50] Similarly, a Kachin activist living in London told me that some of the new KIO leaders were also profiting from the jade industry. He said I should not be so naïve as to think otherwise: "They are no angels. They also profit from the jade. But these days, they show that they care about the local population and the KIO."[51]

These opinions illustrate that elite interaction with the grassroots can build authority within nonstate armed groups even when elites continue to profit while the masses remain impoverished. In essence, they show that grassroots' material interests and binary judgments about the morality of elite behavior do not necessarily shape perceptions about the legitimacy of rebel rulers among the grassroots of the Kachin movement. While the enrichment of the elites during the cease-fire years seems to have fed the resentment of the movement's impoverished rank and file and local communities, their willingness to accept a member of the old elite once he shows them respect implies that ignoring the grassroots was the elites' most crucial mistake. The rebel grassroots might have maintained a positive social identity through affiliation to the rebellion if the elites had shown greater respect for their dignity. Yet the grassroots don't necessarily need to feel that rebel leaders are treating them with respect because of their own moral convictions. The old leader could become a good gangster by demonstrating a certain respect.

MOBILIZING THE YOUTH

After gradually regaining popular support by tapping into the social networks and legitimate standing of the Kachin churches and implementing consultative mechanisms, Gun Maw and his young officers have used their authority to rebuild the faltering movement and recruit a new generation of rebels from among the disillusioned Kachin youth. Their recruitment strategies directly addressed the social pressures and problems, and ultimately the claim to recognition, of many young Kachin. In doing so, they infused the Kachin revolution anew with moral values and high social standing. That made it a cause worth fighting and dying for again.

The most instrumental recruitment tool for achieving this revival was the establishment of a KIO youth wing, the so-called Education and Economic Development for Youth (EEDY). Gun Maw and Gam Shawng jointly established this organization in 2003, but it did not start operating on a large scale until several years later. EEDY has targeted youth across Kachin State, with special emphasis on government-controlled areas, where recruiting often happened among school, college, and university students. More than three thousand youths have traveled to KIO-controlled areas to attend forty-five-day workshops in which they are taught Kachin history and the ethnonational political agenda of the KIO while being trained in basic guerrilla warfare.[52] U La Nan has run EEDY since Gun Maw began focusing on the movement's military campaign after the cease-fire broke down. He explained what the purpose of its educational offerings was: "The Burmese government teaches only the Burman language, history, culture, and religion and so on. . . . [W]e Kachin youth have little or no knowledge of Kachin culture, customs, history, [or] literature even when graduating from universities. If we are following this kind of Burmese system, we will gradually end up with the extinction of our identity. So our Kachin youth should understand Kachin affairs such as history, literature, language, and culture. . . . [W]e focus on our youth."[53]

Youth mobilization was about more than filling the decimated lower ranks of the rebellion's armed wing. Indeed, the emphasis on youth rebuilt the wider social movement behind the Kachin rebel organization. It was instrumental in reviving ethnonational ideology and rebel political culture in Kachin State. I observed this myself when I visited Myitkyina in 2014. At a pop-up stand decorated with KIO flags Kachin students from Myitkyina University were selling T-shirts, mugs, key ring holders, and smartphone covers with the insignia of the Kachin rebellion printed on them. Local youth, zipping by on their scooters, frequently stopped to stock up on the accessories. I was surprised to see this in a state-controlled provincial capital. Military intelligence and special branch police units are omnipresent in the city that for decades had been the headquarters of the dreaded Northern Command of the Tatmadaw. Arbitrary arrests and interrogations have long created a climate of fear among Kachin civilians, and I certainly did not expect to see young people publicly exhibiting their support for the rebellion. I told one of the students that I was studying the Kachin conflict and asked her why she was selling rebel insignia so openly. She was quite surprised that I questioned her backing of the KIO. To her, it seemed self-explanatory. Evidently the KIO has succeeded in garnering the support of her social set.

U La Nan stressed that Gun Maw's close relations with the movement's grassroots were crucial to establishing EEDY in the first place. He said, "Gun Maw performed this role better [than I do], organizing youth and the general public from towns and villages to become more united. He could perform so well because of his innate ability to relate to the people. . . . Although I am not as popular as him because I cannot perform like him, I am completing the job as good as I can."[54]

In fact, Gun Maw had help in organizing EEDY. One of the founders, Brang Awng, is a journalist.[55] I met him in a KIO hospital in Maijayang where he was being treated for a wound he had received while reporting from the front line. He told me that some young officers had approached him because of his media expertise and asked for his help in coordinating the youth wing's public outreach. This led to the establishment and operation of the Laiza-based television station Laiza TV, which screens regular news of the ongoing armed conflict between the Kachin rebels and the Myanmar government. Brang Awng is an example of how EEDY improved the movement as a whole; he said that when he joined the rebellion in 2002 the young members of the movement were still using typewriters. He trained the media department in how to use the radio equipment it had purchased and how to write news for an audience.[56]

To reach out to Kachin youth in government-held areas of Kachin State the KIO resorted to social media platforms. For example, they created karaoke versions of classic Kachin revolutionary songs, using visuals and audio that resembled Asian popular music videos from across eastern Asia. The videos are available on Laiza TV and on YouTube and can be bought as DVDs in local shops. The contrast between the 1970s lyrics and the contemporary video was odd. "Shanglawt Sumtsaw Ga Leh" (Love for the revolution), for example, relies on archaic gender roles, emphasizing that beautiful young Kachin women want to marry daring KIA soldiers and thereby do their part for the revolution and that the male commanding officer will share his troops' rations with the women.[57] The verses promise that revolution will bring economic security, physical safety, and harmony, pledges that today's Kachin are unlikely to believe. Yet the visuals appeal to the desires of Kachin urban youth. Besides featuring ethno-nationalist and revolutionary symbols, including dashing uniforms, minority national costumes, and a traditional Manau ceremonial ground, they frequently resemble the videos of popular Asian boy bands. The handsome young KIA officers lean on expensive cars and switch from military camouflage to blue jeans and sunglasses. Girls in makeup and fashionable clothes watch from the balcony of a seemingly luxurious building (see Brenner 2018).

These images stand in vivid contrast to the stark realities urban Kachin youth face. Cities are characterized by rampant drug abuse and widespread disillusionment over the dire state of the local economy. Myitkyina University students whom I interviewed seemed generally unenthusiastic about their chosen majors. A physics student said, "It does not matter what I study. I could study philosophy or law. There won't be a job for me."[58] Indeed, Myitkyina in February 2014, three and half years into the renewal of conflict, showed signs of stress. Many of the trains arriving at the train station came from Mandalay. The cars were full of Tatmadaw soldiers on their way to fight Kachin rebels on the nearby front lines just north of Myitkyina, where both rebel and government forces are dug into trenches and clash over hilltop positions. Transferred to cargo trucks, the soldiers rode past intimidated civilians, who rushed by without raising their heads. After dark, the streets emptied quickly as curfews took effect.

Young Kachin born after the 1994 cease-fire had a paucity of options. Their susceptibility to EEDY's promises of bringing an end to injustice, improving security, and affording greater economic opportunities through revolution seems predictable. Graduates of EEDY training courses who return home often operate as recruiters and multipliers in their home communities. Others continue working in the bureaucratic KIO apparatus or join the KIA as part of a three-year voluntary enlistment service.

Many of the young soldiers defending Laiza in hilltop positions outside the town joined the rebellion by way of EEDY. A twenty-one-year-old KIA soldier who lived in the muddy trenches for more than two years told me that before joining the rebellion he had been a student in a college in Myitkyina, where he had used heroin and amphetamines. He declared that EEDY and, later, the KIA had saved his life.[59] Father Paul, who teaches classes in religion and ethics at EEDY, explained that many Kachin youth were addicted when they arrived at EEDY or had acquaintances in their immediate social circles who were addicts. He attributed EEDY's success in attracting students to its ability to give young people who feel lost a purposeful alternative. EEDY, he said, "is about reformation, moral reformation. The youth became very weak in their morality, so we needed to correct this. We teach them the value of God."[60] Indeed, the KIO youth wing does more than disseminate rebel propaganda in the effort to convert Kachin youth into gun-toting rebel soldiers. It promotes positive social identification with the rebel movement and the coproduction of rebel political culture. In addition to the karaoke videos EEDY produces, since about 2007 independent Kachin singers and musicians outside the rebel organization have begun to produce mobilization videos they circulate on social media platforms. The music videos often picture the suffering of Kachin civilians in the renewed conflict, and many of the singers wear rebel insignias and profess unambiguously to side with the KIO. They sing original songs featuring lyrics that are more radical than those of the revolutionary oldies. For example, the song "Share Shagan Nampan Lahkawng" (Two heroic flowers) by Ah Tang grieves over two female volunteer teachers who were raped and murdered by Tatmadaw soldiers in northern Shan State in January 2015. The incident sparked protests across Kachin State, not least because government investigators acquitted the army of responsibility (Lawi Weng 2015b). The video shows footage of the crowded funeral march and rally the KBC organized in Myitkyina. Wearing a cap with KIO insignia, the singer appeals to the Kachin public to fight against their repressors and avenge the two women:

> It hurts a lot. Two heroic flowers who sacrificed their lives. Tears drop from everyone [. . .] the two flowers had no opportunity to blossom. We will claim blood debt. All the people who love their country and serve their duties. Forward!!! . . . in harmonious manner . . . Fight, fight, fight!!! We will fight the enemy while holding up the winning flag . . . the unjust abusers will lose/fall . . . we will get rid of the enemies . . . there will be no footprints of them . . . fight all the devils . . . We will win this unjust war. God is with us.[61]

Laiza TV broadcasts these videos of the marshaling of independent youth because they dovetail with the KIO agenda. The rebels' mobilization has taken on a life of its own, giving additional impetus to the social process of rebellion (see Brenner 2018).

The Kachin people's efforts to end the narcotics epidemic, locally referred to as the Kachin War on Drugs, illustrates the impact of youth discourse. The movement has mostly made headlines in the form of the so-called Pat Jasan (block and clean) movement, a vigilante movement that emerged in 2014 and is known for its violent methods. It burns poppy fields and arrests drug users, who are sent to extrajudicial rehabilitation camps to reform their behavior. Pat Jasan is embedded in a wider discourse that calls out the central state for its unwillingness and the KIO for its inability to stop the scourge. The movement has used music videos to spread its message, calling narcotics *katsi hpyen,* or, the "cold enemy" of the Kachin people, and the narcotics industry a *katsi majan,* or, a "cold war" against them. Though not openly condoning Pat Jasan tactics, KIO propaganda uses these terms and others the vigilante movement employs.[62] For instance, a KIO video shows a band of young Kachin soldiers playing hard rock tunes in front of an IDP camp, intoning their intention to join the struggle against drugs: "It is our duty to fight against the cold enemy who has destroyed many of our young beautiful lives and happy families. . . . Let us prevent this awful disease, let us fight the cold enemy!"[63]

TAKEOVER

By the mid-2000s Gun Maw and Gam Shawng had managed to repair the movement's ruptured authority relations with local communities and were creating a strong internal force through the successful recruitment of young Kachin soldiers. However, this accomplishment created new interdependencies and reciprocal power relations in the movement. Buoyed by their successful recruitment of Kachin youth, Gun Maw and his followers focused on rebuilding the movement's armed wing. They established an officer training school in the mountains surrounding Laiza in 2006. The facility has trained a new generation of motivated KIA officers. Kachin analysts attribute the KIA's battlefield success since the reescalation of conflict in 2011 mostly to this training facility (Duwa Mahkaw Hkun Sa 2016, 347). Most of the school's new cadets are loyal to Gun Maw and have assumed key positions within the expanding rebel army. While the old guard retained some positions of apparent power, young officers dominated the rank and file and were faithful in their allegiance to Gun Maw. Brang Awng attributed this power of persuasion to education through EEDY and the new officer training school.

As it has for most of the cease-fire period, in the mid-2000s the group still looked to outsiders: a significantly weakened, business-minded, and conciliatory cease-fire group. Yet the new internal realities soon became visible when heightened tension with the Myanmar government led to the actual dethroning of the old guard in 2008. In an attempt to exert tighter control over nonstate armed groups within its borderlands, Naypyidaw demanded that the cease-fire organizations transform themselves into BGFs, saying it would legalize them and register them as political ethnic minority parties, promising the opportunity to compete in elections. This change subordinated armed groups as militias under Tatmadaw command. Perceiving ethnic armies as weakened, fourteen years after the cease-fire with KIO it appeared Myanmar's generals believed they could finally bring the country's borderlands under more direct control (Jones 2014a). This eventuality brought the internal struggle for leadership to a head. According to KIO insiders, many within the old elite were initially inclined to accept the offer.[64] Some of them had taken part in other government initiatives, including the National Convention process in 2003, which was tasked with drafting the country's 2008 constitution. As the International Crisis Group noted, the KIO did not actually influence the language of the constitution, but it maintained "a fairly cooperative stance" throughout the process (2012, 6). The same old guard that had helped draft the constitution felt that accepting the transformation to a government militia and establishing a political party were better than risking a return to armed conflict.[65]

The new faction of young officers vehemently opposed the old guard. U La Nan said they thought it would be a "deathblow to the KIO."[66] The officers mobilized the KIA brigades against the old guard's attempts to deescalate the situation by promoting demobilization. The youth faction had become a formidable, coherent force whereas years of infighting had weakened the established leadership. But to prevail in the tug-of-war over the government's demand they had to overcome the resistance of the elder cohort. Even if, as Reverend Zau Toi told me, the senior leaders had "become very soft" (by which he meant submissive to the government) some still wielded power and commanded small but strong units loyal to them.[67] Brang Awng told me the young officers developed a secret plan to topple their superiors without a direct coup.[68] The old cease-fire KIO leaders were fragmented, and the young officers incorporated those they could, forced others to retire, and sidelined still others while letting them keep their formal standing.

Many senior leaders proved to be interested in joining forces with the young officers, especially after they saw that the KIO's strength and popularity were surging. The KIO general secretary, Brig. Gen. La Ja, was among them. He told me he had long felt alienated by the conciliatory approach of the KIO leadership during the cease-fire because he sensed the government would not make political changes. He concluded that the Kachin would never have rights if they did not resort to military force.[69]

Vice Chairman Manam Tu Ja, part of the movement's old guard, left the KIO and formed a political party known as the Kachin State Democracy Party (KSDP). He told me that in the discussion of his status the ultimate decision for him to withdraw was unanimous. A young officer that was part of the faction that took over corroborated his account but also made clear that he was glad about Tu Ja's retirement from the revolution.[70] The KSDP struggled to mobilize voters in the 2015 general elections. Winning only four seats in Kachin State, it came in a distant third after the NLD and the military-affiliated Union Solidarity and Development Party. Tu Ja lost to the NLD's candidate in Myitkyina constituency (Thuta 2015). N'ban La, the KIO's long-term strongman and "bad gangster" turned "good gangster" whom I witnessed consoling the soldiers' families at one of the movement's new consultative meetings in Laiza, was among the officers deemed too powerful to oust. N'ban La had emerged triumphant from the leadership's disastrous infighting over competing business interests in the early 2000s. Brang Awng told me that the "gangster" had decided everything in the KIO during his rule in the cease-fire years.[71] While he did not enjoy much backing among the young rebel generation, there were strong units who remained loyal to him personally.[72] The new leadership tried to keep him out of the center of decision making but allowed him to retain his title and rank. After the young officers took over, N'ban La initially spent most of his time in the group's liaison office in Chiang Mai in Thailand, working with the UNFC ethnic armed alliance organization until he resettled to Kachinland in 2016. As the KIO leadership makes most of its decisions in KIO territory, N'Ban La's sojourn in Chiang Mai was described to me as a form of temporary exile. According to Brang Awng, N'ban La had learned to toe the line in at least pretending to support the new path of the revolution.[73] The intelligent decisions the new leadership made in terms of prompting some old leaders to retire and incorporating others point to their skill in managing dissent. Their complex power calculations also highlight the multiplicity of interests within rebel groups and the fluid relations among differently situated rebels over time.

After the young officers took control, the KIO refused Naypyidaw's requests. It began to fiercely oppose the 2008 constitution and made known their dissatisfaction over the detrimental effects of joint Myanmar–Chinese infrastructure projects in the region. In an open letter to China's then president Hu Jintao the KIO demanded that the construction of a megadam at Myitsone be halted. The site lies at the confluence of two rivers, the source of Myanmar's main waterway, the Irrawaddy, and a sacred place in Kachin culture. The letter warned that the project could spark full-blown civil war, as KIO would not allow government troops to secure the construction site (Kachin News Group 2011).[74] In June 2011 Tatmadaw troops attacked KIA positions at a Chinese hydropower plant already in operation in Tarpein in an attempt to clear the site of rebel units. This is the incident mentioned earlier that triggered the new round of fighting that displaced more than 120,000 civilians in the ensuing three years (Burma News International 2014, 23) (figure 8).

Despite the humanitarian toll, the KIO has garnered immense popularity across Kachin State as well as in other ethnic minority areas of Myanmar since the outbreak of conflict.[75] Many Kachin once again view the organization as their legitimate representative. In November 2013 thousands of Kachin civilians evidenced their renewed

Figure 8 IDP camp in KIO-controlled territory. One of the many makeshift camps that sprang up to accommodate the tens of thousands of citizens displaced since fighting escalated again in 2011. Photograph by the author.

faith by waving KIO flags and cheering a KIO envoy arriving for negotiations in government-held Myitkyina (Saw Yan Naing 2013a). Newfound popular support, the revival of ethnonationalist ideology, and the rekindled morale and loyalty within the organization have transformed a business-driven cease-fire group on the brink of collapse back into a capable, popular rebel fighting force. These developments also impacted the movement's negotiations over a new cease-fire with the government. The young leadership has produced a resurgence of a strong ethnonational identity and uncompromising rebel political culture across wide parts of the Kachin public and Kachin youth in particular. According to Revered Zau Toi, Kachin society has again become the revolutionary backbone of the KIO movement and is making it difficult for KIO leaders to negotiate another cease-fire. In consultation meetings the KIO held with representatives of Kachin civil society the KIO grassroots urged the leadership to seek political concessions.[76] A local newspaper reported that a community leader had urged Gun Maw not to sign any agreement unless the state established a firm date for "political dialogue" and committed to withdrawing its troops from Kachinland (*Kachinland News* 2013). Zau Toi explained that the memory of the past cease-fire made the KIO's grassroots wary. He warned that "it is very dangerous for the Kachin leaders to agree to another cease-fire now. We have experienced this before you know: seventeen years of cease-fire. This brought a lot of business opportunities, and many leaders got involved with business. So they became rich but lost their target."[77]

One of the KIO's chief negotiators confirmed that increasing pressure from the Kachin street indeed complicates the movement's ability to negotiate a new cease-fire, let alone a federal settlement with the government. According to him, the KIO grassroots have become more radical than its leadership. He explained that KIO policy seeks to negotiate a federal constitution with the government, while a growing segment of Kachin society demands independence by force of arms.[78] The situation of today's Kachin rebel movement illustrates the dynamism and reciprocity that underpin power relations within the social process of rebellion. It highlights figurational pressures within which rebel leaders make decisions. By reembedding the rebellion in wider social networks, including the powerful local churches, and by creating a vibrant youth movement the young KIA officers surrounding Gun Maw and Gam Shawng were able to rebuild a legitimate authority relationship to the rebel grassroots. Yet at the same time they created new dependencies by empowering the KIO grassroots vis-à-vis the higher echelons of the movement. In negotiations with the government they have to respond to these pressures.

This chapter has shown that the seventeen-year cease-fire in Kachin State produced a façade of stability that actually contained the seeds of its own destruction. Despite years of conciliatory policies and near organizational collapse, the KIO emerged strengthened and willing to fight. The main reason was the ripple effects of the co-optation of some KIO leaders across the rest of the movement, most centrally the erosion of leadership legitimacy, which gave rise to a new faction determined to rebuild the movement.

Economic incentives drove cooperation between the KIO and the government after the cease-fire of 1994. Yet the grassroots did not enjoy the fruits of development—on the contrary, they suffered displacement and witnessed the destruction of their native lands—and the lack of political gains took a toll on the legitimacy of leadership. They came to see Kachin elites who initially followed a developmental agenda but soon collaborated in their personal interests as corrupt. Their co-optation led to factionalism within the Kachin leadership, weakening it. Ordinary Kachins' suffering eroded the movement's legitimacy among local communities. The combination of these factors sparked a social identity crisis among the lower and middle ranks of the KIO.

Plunging morale and mass desertions in the KIA created fertile ground for a group of young KIA officers to mobilize. They rebuilt legitimate authority relations by reembedding rebellion within wider social networks with the help of the powerful, authoritative Kachin churches. In combination with the creation of a strong youth movement and new organizational institutions, the aspiring faction managed to recruit new members to the movement on a large scale and place them in key positions within the movement, creating their own power base within the KIO. By utilizing this internal coalition for change and simultaneously sidelining or accommodating the incumbent leaders, the internal opposition took control.

Reembedment within wider social alliances and the organization of disillusioned Kachin youth have rebuilt not only the movement's capacities to confront the state militarily but also its inclination to do so. The mobilization of the KIO's grassroots indeed revived rebel political culture to the extent that it created a momentum of its own. But that rebuilding has made it more difficult for KIO leaders to negotiate another cease-fire.

CHAPTER FIVE

THE SOCIAL FOUNDATIONS OF WAR AND PEACE

In December 2018 I returned to northern Karen State's Mutraw, the stronghold of the Karen rebellion. The KNU had just suspended its participation in the peace process. Since earlier that year, the region has witnessed a reescalation of severe fighting. The resurgence of war had ignited around a strategic road project with which Myanmar's military sought to connect its bases in the north and south of Mutraw's inaccessible hills. To secure the road construction, which was cutting deep into KNU territory, the Tatmadaw deployed fifteen hundred soldiers, who found themselves battling the KNLA's 5th Brigade and affiliated local defense units. Yet again thousands of Karen villagers were forced to flee their homes and seek shelter in the thick forests of Kawthoolei.

I sat with one of the KNU's internal opposition leaders, who has mobilized against the movement's rapprochement with Naypyidaw since the cease-fire in early 2012. He explained that the relapse into war was the inevitable outcome of the Tatmadaw's continued violations of the cease-fire code of conduct. Fighting the army's aggressive intrusion into the last bastion of the Karen revolution was a matter of survival. The escalation of conflict also contributed to a more general shift of political realities within the KNU. Years of cease-fire have enabled militarized state territorialization and played into the hands of outside business interests. The political demands of the Karen revolution and the grievances of its grassroots, however, remained unaddressed. The KNU opposition leader explained that the movement's decision to suspend peace talks with the government was ultimately the result of increasing frustration among its rank and file, particularly among its armed wing. These sentiments have enabled the internal opposition to remobilize against the incumbent conciliatory leadership of General Mutu.

At the time of writing, it is not entirely clear what the revitalization of KNU resistance means for the movement and its cease-fire. Nor do I know what the future holds for the Kachin rebellion. Internal contestation has also continued to shape the organization since the breakdown of the cease-fire in 2011. For example, its old strongman N'ban La, who was exiled to the groups' alliance bureau in Chiang Mai, staged a comeback in January 2016. Moreover, long-standing ideological differences between Gun Maw and Gam Shawng have divided the former companions. A Kachin analyst says the threesome has set off a new "tripartite power struggle" within the KIO (Kumbun 2017). It is far from clear how these ongoing struggles within the Karen and Kachin rebel movements will play out in the future or impact Myanmar's fragile peace process. Their social figurations are not static. On the contrary, the interaction of interdependent actors continuously creates and recreates a multitude of social pressures that drive the trajectories of rebel movements in often-unforeseen ways. What is clear, however, is that forces internal and external to both revolutions work in tandem in producing the tides of war and peace in Myanmar's changing borderlands.

Although it does not necessarily draw a map of the future, the history of the two rebel movements I have presented here will advance scholars' understanding of the state of politics and society in Myanmar and resonate in conflict and security studies. In addition, my findings have implications for conflict resolution and peace-building practitioners in Myanmar and elsewhere.

BETWEEN CO-OPTATION AND RESISTANCE

Two main factors are at the root of the puzzling conflict dynamics in Myanmar's Karen and Kachin borderlands. The first is the internal contestations between rival rebel factions, which have driven the strategies of both the Karen and the Kachin rebel movements with regard to negotiation and conflict vis-à-vis the state. The second is the challenges that cease-fire politics creates in each rebellion. They have already led to the breakdown of the Kachin cease-fire and may in time lead to the dissolution of the more recent Karen cease-fire.

The 2012 KNU cease-fire was the result of leadership contestation after power relations inside the movement shifted considerably from central to northern brigade territories within the Karen movement. Central brigade leaders who sought to compensate for their declining power and authority led the rapprochement with the government, while leaders affiliated with northern units opposed conciliation. Increasing military and geopolitical pressures along the Thai–Myanmar border that have built up since the early 1990s and fragmented the organization along its individual brigades resulted in changing power relations and a factional split. These external pressures impacted central and southern rebel units more severely than those in the remote northern mountains of Karen State, and this disparity was true with respect to leadership authority among their grassroots. This circumstance has effectively shifted the KNU's internal power balance from its traditional backbone in central Karen State to the north and has given rise to two competing factions in the KNU leadership and their diverging strategies toward the state. Leaders linked to central Karen brigades sought to compromise with the state in order to compensate for their loss of power and authority and therefore signed the 2012 cease-fire with Naypyidaw.

In the case of the KIO, the breakdown of the 2011 cease-fire followed internal contestations and leadership change. After the Kachin leaders pursued an accommodating strategy in dealing with the government during most of its seventeen-year cease-fire in the early 2000s, young rebel leaders began to oppose their superiors in order to remobilize a faltering movement characterized by eroding power and authority as well as the waning of the revolutionary agenda. This generational split resulted from the modalities of the cease-fire. Tied to the changing political economy along the Chinese–Myanmar border, the cease-fire benefited the higher echelons of the Kachin leadership but left the underlying grievances of the rebel grassroots unaddressed. This state of affairs eroded both the authority of Kachin cease-fire leaders among their own rank and file and the movement's standing among local communities as a whole. It also gave rise to a faction of young leaders who set out to reverse these developments by mobilizing against their superiors' cease-fire policies. They reembedded the rebellion in local networks and recruited a new generation of rebels in conjunction with whom they managed to take over the leadership of the KIO. Since then, the KIO has renounced its conciliatory stance toward the state and remobilized militarily, thereby contributing to the reescalation of conflict.

Internal contestations between rival rebel factions are essential to explaining why the KNU signed a cease-fire in 2012 and why the Kachin cease-fire broke down the year before. At the core of these struggles lay shifting internal authority and power relations that were largely driven by politico-economic changes in both borderlands.

An analysis of the dynamics inside the two rebel movements revealed that the Karen cease-fire faces challenges similar to those that led to the breakdown of the Kachin cease-fire. In both cases the halt in hostilities involved the partial co-optation of rebel leaderships, which aggravated existing internal conflict and caused new organizational fragmentation and contestation over authority. While the case of the KNU sheds light on the movement's fragmentation and contestation over authority following partial leadership co-optation, that of the KIO shows how such processes can unfold over time and lead to renewed resistance from within the movement. While the two movements proceeded through different stages at different times, they essentially followed a similar trajectory along four tracks: leadership co-optation; group fragmentation; contention over authority; and renewed resistance from within.

PARTIAL LEADERSHIP CO-OPTATION

Partial leadership co-optation seemed to be a central mechanism in the cease-fires of both movements.[1] Co-opting rebel elites by way of economic incentives played a crucial role in the cease-fire politics of Myanmar's northern border areas in the 1990s, including Kachin State. The coalescing economic interests of state and rebel elites as well as outside business networks transformed decades-long violent conflict in these borderlands into a mutual enterprise. Post–Cold War rapprochement between China and Myanmar, which occurred rapidly, made this possible. Commercial interests seeking profit from resource exploitation, border trade, and infrastructure construction in these borderlands had driven the two countries' reconciliation. While the KIO signed the 1994 cease-fire for a variety of reasons, economic benefits granted to its leaders have been widely cited as a key driver of the cessation and the group's subsequent conciliatory stance toward the state (Smith 1999, 441; Sherman 2003; Woods 2011).

Political economy dynamics have featured less prominently in analyses of the Karen cease-fire. Outside observers and pro-cease-fire KNU leaders maintain that the Karen halt to fighting in 2012 was the direct result of wider political transition in Myanmar (see International Crisis Group 2011, chap. 5; Burke 2012; Mydans 2012). But dynamics of co-optation by economic means seemed to play a role as well. Mirroring developments at the Chinese border, large parts of the Karen borderlands have witnessed resource exploitation, border trade, and infrastructure developments that financially benefit KNU leaders as well as domestic and foreign businesspeople. These politico-economic changes began in the 1990s and increased after the turn of the millennium. Pro-cease-fire KNU leaders acknowledged these powerful forces and presented themselves as partners in regional economic development. They also established companies to tap into the expanding cease-fire economy. Business actors have also promoted and financed the armistice negotiations between the KNU and Naypyidaw. From this perspective, the political economy of the Karen cease-fire resembles that of previous settlements in northern Myanmar.[2] Many Karen rebel grassroots told me they worried that some of their leaders are negotiating with the government to maximize personal gains rather than bearing collective interests in mind.

GROUP FRAGMENTATION

Partial leadership co-optation aggravated existing dynamics of group fragmentation and sparked new ones in both movements. It is difficult now to ascertain the extent of such division within the KIO at the time it signed the cease-fire in 1994. The southern brigades' defection had certainly weakened the KIO and weighed heavily on leaders' decision to sign an armistice. Reports suggest that the Kachin organization at the time was nevertheless more coherent and centralized than the Karen rebellion in 2012 (South 2011). That the 1994 cease-fire triggered organizational segmenting inside the KIO is clearer. On the one hand, there was horizontal fragmentation among top leadership over rival business interests, which caused severe internal strife in the early 2000s. On the other hand, leadership co-optation eroded the vertical authority relations between KIO leaders and the grassroots of their movements. The KIO no longer offered security from state violence, and investment in large-scale resource extraction caused displacement. The grassroots increasingly perceived KIO leaders as being disrespectful, and positive social rebel identity from affiliation with the KIO eroded among the grassroots as well as rank-and-file soldiers.

The KNU was already highly fragmented when it signed the pact in 2012. The movement's leadership sought accommodation with the U Thein Sein government largely because of its eroding military strength and authority. But the cease-fire has exacerbated organizational fissures along existing fault lines between leaders as well as between rebel elites and grassroots. The accord further increased horizontal fragmentation between the more accommodating leaders linked to the central and southern brigades and the less conciliatory ones in the northern brigades. But at the same time it widened the vertical gap between pro-cease-fire leaders and the movement's grassroots. These authority relations between rebel elites and nonelites in the central and southern brigades had already suffered in the face of military and geopolitical pressures along the Thai border in the 1990s, disembedding the rebellion from local communities in those areas. The alienation ruptured the KNU's support networks, its traditional reciprocal exchange relations with local communities in these areas. The organization's declining authority among its grassroots incentivized leaders linked to central and southern units, including Chairman General Mutu Say Poe and General Secretary Kwe Htoo Win, to reach rapprochement with Naypyidaw. The movement's remote northern units face fewer challenges and have remained more embedded in local communities, maintaining their vertical social ties to a much greater extent. Their relative power and authority explain why leaders affiliated with these units, including the former vice chairperson Naw Zipporah Sein and the armed wing's vice chief of staff Lt. Gen. Baw Kyaw Heh, have been less eager to accommodate Naypyidaw. Thus while it appears that group fragmentation has facilitated the co-optation of individual KNU leaders who lacked vertical social ties to their grassroots, their rapprochement with the state has, in turn, provoked further horizontal and vertical fragmentation of the Karen rebellion. It widened the rift between incumbent leaders and the KNU grassroots while driving an even larger wedge between the two existing internal rival factions.

CONTENTION OVER AUTHORITY

In both rebel movements partial leadership co-optation and group fragmentation stimulated internal contention between incumbent and aspirant leaders. In both of these internal power struggles one leadership faction sought alliances with state forces by promoting conciliatory cease-fire policies; the other mobilized its movement's grassroots from below against such cooperation. In the Kachin rebellion intergenerational grievances and interorganizational schisms between the political and military wings delineated the main fault lines along which an internal opposition materialized in the early 2000s. During this period top KIO leaders were preoccupied with lining their pockets with the spoils of an unleashed cease-fire economy. This new oppositional faction initially emerged from within the organization's armed wing at the initiative of young KIA officers. These officers were largely excluded from the power and wealth their superiors enjoyed in the movement, a fact which merged the top-down hierarchies of a military organization with those of a strictly age-based society. Their subordinates, KIA foot soldiers, deserted by the hundreds at a time of rapidly eroding leadership authority due to widespread alienation among the movement's grassroots. Faced with the disintegration of their army, the young KIA officers surrounding the equally youthful brigadier Sumlut Gun Maw and the more senior general Gam Shawng set out to change this unpromising situation: they rebuilt authority among the grassroots in order to mobilize against the group's incumbent leadership and to reassemble a coherent movement that was willing and able to resist the state again.

In the Karen rebellion KNU leaders who were demoted to second rank after the 2012 cease-fire but remained backed by relatively strong northern brigade units opposed the group's top leaders and their appeasing line by seeking to appeal to the wider Karen grassroots. At the time of my field research many traditional members and supporters of the KNU were indeed inclined to tout the internal opposition to the new leadership's appeasing stance. Considering that local Karen communities have borne the brunt of the armed conflict in previous decades, their support for what has often been called the KNU's hardliners might initially seem counterintuitive. They did so because the growing rapprochement between the pro-cease-fire leadership and Naypyidaw had, for several reasons, given rise to large-scale alienation among the movement's rank and file. First, the KNU grassroots saw their pro-cease-fire leadership being co-opted by economic means, including through personal gifts and benefits. Second, they regarded the KNU's post-cease-fire collaboration in economic development as being opposed to their own interests due to investment-related social problems, including landgrabs and environmental degradation. Third, they viewed the new leadership's abrupt reconcilement with former Tatmadaw generals with deep suspicion, not least because militarization had increased in cease-fire areas. Fourth, the KNU grassroots took the secrecy surrounding the negotiations between pro-cease-fire leaders and Naypyidaw as a signal that leadership was ignoring their interests and concerns. They perceived the internal opposition to be more legitimate for various reasons, including its association with the northern units. These remained embedded in local communities. Its vocal disagreement with the new leadership and conciliatory policies with Naypyidaw, including resistance to destructive mega-development projects and increasing militarization, also appealed to local communities.

RESISTANCE FROM WITHIN

Both the Kachin and Karen cease-fires involved the partial co-optation of rebel leaderships, and this sparked organizational fragmentation and internal contention over authority between rival rebel factions. My field research in 2013–14 took place midst heightened tensions within the KNU after it signed a cease-fire agreement in early 2012. When I was researching the KIO in 2014 the Kachin accord had already broken down, and less conciliatory rebel leaders like Gen. Sumlut Gun Maw had risen to power. During the time I spent with the KNU I observed firsthand how the cease-fire fomented internal struggles over authority. By comparison, the time I spent with the KIO allowed me to trace how the cease-fire in practice had led to renewed resistance from within, against both pro-cease-fire leaders and the Myanmar state.

In the KIO disaffected young officers managed to rebuild the rebellion's unity from within. This enabled them to assume power then reject the movement's conciliatory cease-fire policies and remobilize resistance against the state. Essential to their success was the rebuilding of authority relations between the new leadership and the movement's grassroots. By tapping into the authority and reach of the local churches the young officers established consultative mechanisms with local communities. These served to reembed the rebel movement in the wider Kachin society and to counter widespread feelings of alienation among the rebellion's members and supporters. The movement was therefore able to recruit a new generation of rebels from among disillusioned Kachin youth. The young KIA officers built stable support networks for their faction, a crucial resource the factionalized old guard of the KIO lacked at the time. When a leadership power struggle erupted in 2008, aspiring leaders were able to mobilize a strong coalition, bringing together young rebel soldiers, local communities, and the powerful Kachin churches. At the same time, these emerging leaders managed to integrate, sideline, or retire potential opponents among the old guard. The young officers took over the helm without much resistance and steered the revitalized rebellion back into confrontation with the state.

Within the heavily segmented and deeply fractured KNU internal fights between rival rebel factions had also surfaced at the time of my research. There were stark disagreements between pro-cease-fire leaders and leaders who opposed making overtures to Naypyidaw. The Karen rebel grassroots appear to have been inclined to back the KNU opposition linked to its northern stronghold. Whether the internal opposition to Gen. Baw Kyaw Heh and Vice Chairperson Naw Zipporah Sein will be able to retake power and revitalize resistance against the state will depend on their ability to mobilize the Karen grassroots. It will also be contingent on whether the conciliatory incumbent leadership can accommodate the aspirants' claim to power within the current cease-fire order and on the degree to which they can counter widespread alienation among their grassroots and regain authority among them. At the time of writing, the KNU's future trajectory is highly uncertain. The movement's withdrawal from the peace process and severe fighting in Mutraw in 2018 signify how fragile the Karen cease-fire is. My insights from the Kachin case also suggest that Naypyidaw, international organizations, and scholars should take the likelihood of renewed KNU resistance seriously.

THE PERSPECTIVE FROM WITHIN ARMED STRUGGLE

Ever since Myanmar embarked on its transition from military rule, the country has attracted renewed scholarly interest. While questions surrounding democratization and political change in the country's central lowlands have become the primary focus (for example, Cheesman, Skidmore, and Wilson 2012; Cheesman, Farrelly, and Wilson 2014), many scholars with a long-term interest in Myanmar point out that solving ethnic conflict in the border areas is of central importance to the country's wider transition (for example, Jones 2014a; Farrelly 2012; Sadan 2016b). Yet scholars and analysts have struggled to explain the shifting tides of conflict the country has witnessed since the eve of transition. My book thus contributes to our understanding of Myanmar's conflict and some of its most important actors at a crucial time. Explaining the breakdown of the Kachin cease-fire, which led to a major escalation of conflict between various ethnic armed groups and Myanmar's armed forces in the country's north at a time when other groups, such as the Karen, have entered negotiations, seems particularly significant for the wider scholarship on Myanmar. My findings show how intramural relations within both of the country's ethnic armed groups drive wider dynamics of war and peace.

Analyzing the internal politics and social dimensions of rebellion offers a corrective to explanations that infer the strategies of Myanmar's ethnic armed groups primarily from their strategic external environments, most commonly the country's political transition and its changing borderland economies. Policy and media analysts have mostly highlighted political liberalization in Naypyidaw when explaining why KNU leaders signed a cease-fire in 2012 and subsequently pushed for a peace process (for example, International Crisis Group 2011; Burke 2012; Mydans 2012). Viewed through this lens, Karen rebel leaders have seized the opportunity presented by an overall shift in the political incentive structure, which enabled them to negotiate a peaceful settlement to their six decades of guerrilla war. But the concurrent outbreak of conflict with previous cease-fire groups on the Chinese border, including the KIO, belies this narrative of a trending toward peace and democracy (see Sadan 2016a for a critical discussion).

Scholars of Myanmar's conflict have long pointed to the centrality of borderland economies in understanding nonstate armed groups (Woods 2011; Sherman 2003; Jones 2014a). A political economy perspective has become prominent since rapprochement between China, Thailand, and Myanmar at the end of the Cold War brought increased economic investments in Myanmar's borderlands. This train of thought poses the notion that the increased integration of borderland economies has created pressures on the ethnic rebel armies, whose peripheral location had generally benefited them militarily and financially during the Cold War. Incoming foreign investments have also allowed the state to co-opt rebel leaders with economic incentives. The economic interests of rebel leaders have thus become a crucial factor in explaining the relative stability on the Myanmar–Chinese border between the 1990s and 2011. My account largely agrees with this analysis and also shows that the same logic might be applied to the new cease-fires in eastern Myanmar, including that of the KNU.

That said, the social ruptures that "cease-fire capitalism" creates in the long run—dynamics that dialectical political economy analyses also illuminate—are important in clarifying the situation of many ethnic rebel movements in Myanmar (see Woods 2011; Jones 2016). In highlighting these rifts, I have shown how they can lead to renewed armed conflict, as happened in the case of the KIO. By looking to social dynamics internal to armed movements I have sought to contribute to an understanding of conflict by asking questions of identity, dignity, and voice. The point is not to discard structural factors of political economy altogether. In fact, my relational approach not only appreciates the ways in which external forces shape the social context within which political violence takes place but also underscores the impact of powerful external economic forces on the contestations within the KNU and KIO. My account thus elucidates why cease-fire capitalism leads to renewed conflict despite yielding economic benefits to key elites on all sides.

The ethnographic bent of my research is crucial to understanding these nonlinear dynamics unfolding on the micro level. Immersion was essential to identifying how internal contention within the Kachin and Karen movements has shaped their external conduct vis-à-vis the state in ways that cannot be identified from the outside. My close-range investigation stresses the agency and power of rebel grassroots, including the middle and lower ranks of both organizations and a variety of rebel affiliates and supporters in wider society. This revealed the complex social fabric underpinning political violence in the Karen and Kachin borderlands and pushed the analysis beyond a focus on strategizing elites and their modes of decision making. Most important, it underlined the interdependencies of rebel elites and their rebel grassroots and how these often uneasy relations have driven the strategies of the two movements.

THE SOCIAL DYNAMICS OF POLITICAL VIOLENCE

This book adopts the relational heuristics of Elias and Bourdieu. Their ontological perspective revealed intertwined, multicausal social forces operating at various levels within the wider networks of rebellion and driving collective trajectories. Instead of seeing differently situated elite and grassroots actors as self-propelled individuals, I understand them as being ontologically embedded in rebel social figurations, which themselves are inextricably rooted in the broader sociotemporal spaces of rebellion. Despite these structural attributes, I show that rebel figurations are by no means static. On the contrary, uneven, constantly shifting power relations continuously rework them along chains of interdependencies between differently situated elite and nonelite actors who are part of or affiliated with the rebel social network. These figurational dynamics create forces of their own in driving the collective conduct of rebel movements in ways that individual actors never intended or foresaw.

A focus on interdependencies stresses the reciprocal nature of power located within social relations as opposed to regarding it as the sole property of rebel leaders. While rebel grassroots might not direct or intend to direct the rebel collective in the same ways as incumbent and aspirant rebel leaders, they possess agency and indeed power. This is because their willing support and obedience are crucial to sustaining a movement's asymmetric struggle against the state as well as the leaders' clashes with their internal rivals. An emphasis on the reciprocal and dynamic nature of power relations pointed to the most fundamental challenge rebel elites face in their parallel struggle against both incumbent states and rival rebel elites: building and maintaining active support for, or at least passive compliance with, their rebel social order among their rebel grassroots. Questions of legitimate authority have therefore become the focus of analyses of the power dynamics propelling the social processes of the rebel movements in question. I focus my account of the Kachin and Karen rebellions on explaining those conditions under which rebel grassroots take an interest in supporting, joining, or obeying rebel rulers and their social orders and those under which they do not. I have found two interlaced, relational processes at the core of leadership authority in both rebel groups: social embeddedness and social identification.

EMBEDDEDNESS: REBELLION AS PRACTICE

The Karen and the Kachin have built sophisticated quasi states in the territory they controlled. This serves to embed the movements in local communities by way of reciprocal exchange relations, which can generate legitimacy for the rebel collective among local communities as well as rebel elites' leadership authority among their rank and file. Thus the rebel movements have political and administrative departments that are in charge of wide-ranging governance activities, such as the provision of public goods like health care and education and the creation and management of revenues through taxation. The degree of embeddedness in and the reciprocal exchange relations with local communities has varied across time and space within the same movement. For example, a rebel movement that provided security and welfare to a local community at one time might lose that ability. Such ruptures of reciprocal exchange relations can undermine both the rebels' legitimacy among local communities and the authority of leaders within the movement.

The notion of embeddedness explains why the breakdown of governance arrangements between the organization and local communities undermines authority relations between rebel elites and their lower ranks. Embedding rebellion in the wider social field by way of basic public goods provision, including security and health care, shapes local social identities to the extent that the distinctions between rebels and civilians are increasingly blurred. In other words, rebellion itself becomes part of the wider social context, and its internalization shapes identities, interests, and practices. This phenomenon seems to be of particular import in protracted armed conflicts and conditions of limited statehood, in which rebel movements are intertwined with other nonstate governance arrangements. In such areas the rebellion "proper," in governing local communities, often relies on community-based relief, development, and activist organizations as well as on traditional social institutions like local churches and village elders. In addition, these institutions play roles in the movement beyond service provision, including capacity building, legitimization, and even mobilization. Nonstate authorities can thus become nodes of the wider rebel social network. Hence commonly assumed distinctions, as between civilians and combatants or active support and passive obedience, may be inherently blurred. In fact, the social spaces of rebellion and nonrebellion can sometimes be conflated to the extent that it is impossible to conceptually delineate strict boundaries between in-group and out-group.

Long-term embeddedness of rebel groups in local communities thus turns rebellion itself into an intrinsic part of the past and present social context through whose internalization a rebel habitus evolves in local communities. Material exchange by way of service provision can play a central role in embedding movements in the local context and in this way establishing legitimate authority relations. But the link between reciprocity and authority is not primarily or even necessarily based on material payoffs. Local communities do not deliberately sell their allegiance to the highest bidder among local authorities. This is so because many members and supporters of rebellion neither enter nor leave contractual arrangements in a conscious manner based on distributional outcomes. Protracted armed conflict and limited statehood make rebellion an intrinsic part of the social fabric, and choice becomes even less conscious. Grassroots affiliation to, support of, and taking part in rebellion can, then, be better understood as a prereflexive, routinized practice flowing from the rebel habitus rather than as the result of conscious deliberations over material payoffs. In areas where rebel movements have been entrenched in local communities for generations, for example, in Mutraw in northern Karen State, people do not necessarily *choose* to support or engage in rebellion because of the better quality of rebel-operated hospitals and schools. In fact, studying or teaching at a school run by rebels, working as a nurse in a hospital operated by rebels, or joining the ranks of the rebel army might simply appear as the right or normal thing to do.

The rebel habitus matches the rebel grassroots' subjective expectations with the objective opportunities they have derived from their position within the rebel social figuration (see Bourdieu and Wacquant 1992, 130; Elias 1994, 446). Many shortcomings and injustices underlying rebel social orders, such as the unequal allocation of wealth between elites and nonelites of rebel groups, are therefore commonly naturalized and often remain unquestioned, which, in turn, stabilizes rebel authority. This explains why the existence of stark inequalities between wealthy leaders and impoverished grassroots alone do not necessarily undermine legitimate authority relations. The rebel habitus allows the grassroots to describe the wealthy rebel general who remained in power after the cease-fire that had enriched him as a "good gangster." When the matching mechanism between expectations and chances produced by the rebel habitus breaks down, however, leadership authority is undermined. In the Kachin and Karen movements that eventuality happened when the cease-fire did not end displacements, and the rebel movements could no longer offer security to the grassroots, a deficit that damaged the self-perceived positive rebel social identities of the rank-and-file soldiers. Thus the second relational process at the core of leadership authority in both rebellions, social identification, came into play.

IDENTIFICATION: THE STRUGGLE FOR RECOGNITION

Leadership authority in rebel movements is inherently linked to social identities and the struggle for recognition. In ethnocratic states that discriminate against ethnic minorities, it is difficult or even impossible for ethnic minority communities to derive a positive social identity through affiliation with the dominant political order. In Axel Honneth's view, the struggle for due and proper recognition becomes the "moral grammar" of social conflict and serves as the motivational basis of collective resistance (1996). Affiliation with the alternative, rebel political order can then generate positive social identities for grassroots rebels if the rebel collective is associated with moral principles. These principles can, for instance, be about the protection of a community, the fight against unjust state structures, and the creation of a political order that is perceived as more just than the incumbent state. Feeling recognized as a valued member of a rebel collective can therefore lead rebel grassroots to experience feelings of self-esteem and self-worth. This, in turn, generates legitimacy for the rebel social order and authority for its leaders. But threats to positive social identification with the rebel collective undermine the authority of rebel leaders. In line with social identity theory (see Branscombe et al. 1999, 46–55), social rebel identities are threatened when (a) sources both within and without the group question the moral principles and social standing of the rebel collective, and/or (b) the grassroots perceive elite interactions as being disrespectful, thus conveying misrecognition rather than recognition of valued group membership in their grassroots.

A threat to external social identity that questions the moral standing and social status of the rebel collective can, for instance, occur when rebel soldiers fail to protect their local communities. Such a failure not only undermines the rebellion's standing among members of the local communities but also estranges the movement's rank and file: their feelings of powerlessness counteract their sense of self-esteem derived from being part of a collective that is associated with the ability to effectuate political agency against powerful, unjust structures. As Wood suggests, rebel soldiers who are unable to protect their communities are threatened in their rebel identities precisely because they can no longer take "pleasure in agency," a source of self-esteem based on the successful assertion of intention (2003, 235). The rebel grassroots I observed, like those Wood (2003, 235) analyzed in El Salvador, are seeking to assert an intention to further the cause of justice. Losing the sense of rebel agency poses a severe challenge to the perceived moral principles and social standing of the rebel collective among its grassroots. This threatens their self-perceived positive social identities derived through affiliation with the movement, which in turn erodes the authority of rebel leaders.

Threats to social identity can also emerge from within the rebel group itself. For instance, rebel leaders who appear to seek personal gain instead of collective goods undermine their grassroots' understanding of the rebellion as being associated with moral principles and social standing. In addition, if the rebel grassroots see elite interaction and communication as being disrespectful, this will hamper self-perceived positive social identification with the rebel collectives. Highlighting the importance of dignity in understanding human motivation points to the powerful role such interactions play in communicating recognition as a respected member of a rebel movement. Analogous to the ways in which the struggle for due and proper recognition can form the motivational bedrock of collective resistance against the state is how it can form the moral context for rebel grassroots to turn against their rebel leaders. If rebel leaders manage to satisfy their grassroots' claim to recognition, their rebel social orders are stable. If they do not, their authority erodes and becomes vulnerable to challenge from below.

IDENTITY AND POLITICAL VIOLENCE

This book has significant implications for the study of political violence beyond the immediate confines of ethnic conflict in Myanmar. An analysis of how internal contestation over authority drives the conflict and negotiation strategies of rebel groups highlights the importance of microlevel dynamics in explaining wider instances of war and peace. Tracing the effects of changing politico-economic structures on the social relations within armed groups, moreover, sheds light on the ways in which micro- and macrolevels of conflict interact. My study of the ways in which rebel leaders struggle over legitimacy among their rank and file addresses a little-understood phenomenon in the scholarship on rebellion: the workings of power and authority inside rebel movements. Whereas the literature on armed group fragmentation focuses primarily on the horizontal relations between rival rebel leaders and their factions, the literature on rebel governance primarily treats the vertical relations between rebels and local communities. My findings help to conceptualize how rival rebel leaders gain and lose legitimacy within their movements.

In addition, this book demonstrates the merits of sociological approaches to the study of conflict and security. In particular, it shows how a relational framework can be helpful in analyzing multifarious social processes of violence, including the reciprocal flows of power within constantly fluctuating figurations that are embedded in a wider social space. The insights of Honneth's recognition theory proved highly useful in interpreting the perspectives of rebel grassroots. Scholars of international relations have demonstrated the relevance of recognition in explaining dynamics of political conflict on an interstate level (for example, Haacke 2005; Gustafsson 2015; Lindemann and Ringmar 2015). In the analysis of nonstate violence the use of recognition theory has hitherto been surprisingly limited (see Strömbom 2014). Nevertheless, understanding the struggle for recognition as a core motivation of social conflict dovetails with early scholarship in the field of conflict and security studies. One of the founding fathers of the discipline, Edward Azar, has, for instance, identified the "denial of separate identity of parties involved in the political process" as the core driver of protracted social conflicts (1986, 30). In connecting to the roots of the discipline, my account calls for paying greater attention to process over outcome and identity over interests in order to explain dynamics of political violence in what has become an increasingly rationalist field of inquiry.

The ethnographic bent of my account implies that unconventional methods can illuminate such identity politics. My close-range research has produced primary source data on the internal life of rebel movements, the lack of which is one of the biggest challenges in the study of internal armed group politics. More important, my ethnographic immersion and sensitivity opened a window into the everyday lives of rebel grassroots, including the middle and lower ranks and a variety of rebel affiliates and supporters. This fostered an appreciation of the complex social fabric that underlies political violence. Most significant, it revealed the agency of rebel grassroots and their interdependencies with rebel elites, which constitute the social process of rebellion that develops a momentum of its own in driving political violence. The same ethnographically informed approach points to the existence of many more unidentified political objects that remain concealed in Myanmar's restive borderlands as well as in other conflicts. To be sure, close-range research on armed conflict in general and on nonstate armed groups in particular entails practical and ethical challenges. Yet there seem to be few alternatives for generating deep, meaningful knowledge about the actual actors involved in political violence. While this book contributes to the emerging interest in ethnographic inquiry in conflict and security studies, it also suggests that the potential of ethnography for adjusting the discipline's traditional bird's-eye view remains far from exhausted.

IMPLICATIONS FOR POLICY

My findings have two main implications for engaging rebel movements in Myanmar and elsewhere. First, counterinsurgency approaches that aim at fragmenting rebel groups and eroding rebel authority might weaken rebellion but are likely to be counterproductive to finding peaceful solutions to civil war. They might even reproduce violence. Second, in a similar vein, economic development is not a silver bullet for ending civil wars. While economistic approaches to counterinsurgency, conflict resolution, and peace building can achieve temporary stabilization of armed conflict, they are inadequate for addressing the root causes of political violence. In fact, they might exacerbate existing grievances if unaccompanied by political concessions.

FRAGMENTATION AND VIOLENCE

Counterinsurgency approaches aimed at fragmenting rebel groups, my findings show, are unsuitable for bringing about a durable settlement to civil wars. On the contrary, organizational coherence and leadership authority within rebel groups are pivotal to transforming violent organizations into nonviolent ones. States and international stakeholders involved in peace processes therefore need to be careful not to erode their negotiating partners' authority within the latter's own movements. Hence inclusivity in peace negotiations cannot be limited to inviting representatives of all warring parties to the negotiating table. To prevent spoiling dynamics by excluded actors, mediators and interlocutors must take care to also engage factions internal to armed groups. Taking that step ensures that their leaders can garner support for a peaceful settlement within their movement.

This approach stands in contrast to conventional counterinsurgency practices, many of which aim at breaking the organizational structures of rebel movements by assassinating their key leaders and disembedding rebellion from local support networks by denying them access to local communities (see Staniland 2014, 39–41). These tactics might weaken rebel movements militarily, but they are ill-suited to end conflict and in fact are likely to produce new violence. This is so because group fragmentation incites outbidding and spoiler dynamics, which prolong rather than shorten civil wars.[3] The civil war in Syria is a case in point. Part of its intractability stems from the extremely fractured actor landscape, in which rebel groups have proliferated as a result of organizational splintering. Competing for local support, these multiple groups increase their use of violence in order to sway local communities by signaling their strength and resolve (Perkoski 2015). At the same time, the multiplicity of warring factions complicates peace negotiations by increasing the likelihood of spoiling dynamics in which hardline factions use violence to derail talks between moderates (Berti 2013b).

My analysis of the Karen and Kachin rebellions in Myanmar has shown that the internal fragmentation of rebel groups further exacerbates these dynamics. It also demonstrates that settlements that seem stable from the outside might be highly contested from within a fragmented movement. This is so because leaders of such groups represent only part of their rebel collective. Even though they might enter peace negotiations with the state, their contentious relationship with rival coleaders and their limited authority among their rank and file bring into question their ability to implement decisions reached at the negotiating table. In addition, taking an accommodating stance toward the state can further erode moderate rebel leaders' authority among their rank and file and exacerbate factional tensions with less accommodating elements inside the same movement. While rebel schisms thus complicate peace negotiations, they might also derail agreed-upon settlements at a later point in time.

In the case of Myanmar, peace negotiators should therefore expand negotiations to include all ethnic armed groups, including those previously excluded from the NCA, such as, for instance, the Ta'ang National Liberation Army and the groups that did not sign the accord in 2015, such as the KIO. Negotiators also need to secure the participation of factions internal to the groups that are officially negotiating already, such as the internal opposition of the KNU surrounding the KNLA's Fifth Brigade and the KNDO. These findings are relevant to peace negotiations beyond the Myanmar context. In the Israeli–Palestinian conflict, for instance, the leadership competition between Fatah and Hamas has complicated negotiations (Pearlman 2009). Factional tensions within both organizations have further complicated negotiations and contributed to the escalation of conflict on several occasions. These tensions include those between the political and armed wings of Hamas as well as its Gaza- and diaspora-based arms (Berti 2013a, 125; 2014). In the run-up to the 2016 peace accord between the Fuerzas Armadas Revolucionarias de Colombia and the Colombian government political commentators worried that fragmentation would lead to internal spoiling dynamics of disaffected elements within the movement (Findley, Ponce de Leon, and Denly 2016). The historic signing of Colombia's peace accord may have taken place, but organizational fragmentation nonetheless poses one of the greatest challenges to the country's fragile peace.

THE PITFALLS OF ECONOMISTIC APPROACHES TO PEACE

The second implication of my study is linked to the first. Organizational coherence and leadership authority are vital to ensuring the stability of peace agreements. Attempts to buy rebel leaders out of violence via economic incentives can be counterproductive to peace in the long run because they can trigger organizational division and erode the authority of moderate rebel leaders who are engaging in negotiations.

Yet contemporary practices of counterinsurgency, conflict resolution, and peace building have often been grounded in overly economistic assumptions. This is true not least because scholars and policy makers have increasingly viewed economic profiteering rather than ideology or political grievances as the main fomenter of contemporary civil wars. That outlook has effectively depoliticized political violence (Collier and Hoeffler 1998; Duffield 2002; Kaldor 1999). Most prominently, Paul Collier and Anke Hoeffler (1998) argued that present-day rebellion is motivated by economic greed rather than by political grievances. Their statistical study has been criticized on theoretical, methodological, and normative grounds (Cramer 2002; Keen 2012). Quantitative research has also refuted their core argument, showing that grievances, if measured differently, are indeed a major driver of civil wars (Stewart and Fitzgerald 2001; Cederman, Weidmann, and Gleditsch 2011). Nevertheless, economistic understandings of conflict have become deeply ingrained in conflict studies, while identity explanations have taken a backseat. As Siniša Malešević (2008, 107) points out, contemporary conflict analyses thus generally consider identity to be at most a secondary cause of social action.

The development of the spoiler concept is telling. Originally proposed by Stephen Stedman (1997), spoilers attempt to sabotage peace negotiations in their self-interest. Given the popularity of economistic explanations of violence, spoilers have also come to be understood as having vested interests in maintaining their assets in war economies (Zahar 2008). Scholars have since asked how peace can come about if conflict is so profitable. One seemingly obvious answer is to buy off greedy spoilers with economic incentives (Le Billon and Nicholls 2007; Wennmann 2009). In addition to propounding the idea that rebels can be corrupted into accepting peace through economic incentives, the economistic strand of conflict studies has shaped the practice of peace building. As observed in the cases of Afghanistan and Sri Lanka, the international donor community has often come to view economic development as a shortcut to peace (Goodhand 2013, 234).

The idea that rebel leaders can be co-opted via business opportunities and marginalized communities swayed with the fruits of economic development has also taken root in counterinsurgency doctrine around the world. Myanmar's generals have based their cease-fire politics on mutual business collaboration with rebel leaders and securitized development of borderland peripheries. Analogously, Turkish state officials have long viewed economic underdevelopment and societal backwardness as the core causes of conflict in Turkey's Kurdish periphery (Aydin and Emrence 2015, 89–106). This framing invited a two-pronged counterinsurgency approach against the rebel Kurdish Partiya Karkerên Kurdistanê. In much the same way Naypyidaw has engaged with restive ethnic minorities in its borderlands, Ankara has committed to the co-optation of Kurdish elites by offering material benefits and a developmentalist agenda aimed at bringing peace by way of "civilizing" the Kurds through increased prosperity in their underdeveloped regions (Aydin and Emrence 2015, 89–106 at 90). Similarly, Sri Lanka's government attempted to co-opt leaders of the Liberation Tigers of Tamil Eelam and win the support of local Tamil communities during the country's failed peace process in the early and mid 2000s, wrongly believing that the spoils of economic development would not only corrupt the Tigers' leadership but also undermine their desire to establish their own state among the wider Tamil population (Goodhand 2013, 234).

Distilling the lessons he learned from the war in Iraq, Gen. David Petraeus, a US counterinsurgency mastermind, also stressed the importance of economic strategies in winning counterinsurgency wars by equating money to ammunition. He wrote that at times "[money can be] more important than real ammunition" (Petraeus 2006). The recent histories of the Karen and Kachin movements, however, point to the pitfalls of this point of view. Some political economy scholars have indeed referred to the economic dimensions of Myanmar's cease-fires as examples of how the harnessing of economic interests can foster accommodation between warring factions (Sherman 2003; Snyder 2006; Le Billon and Nicholls 2007). My findings, however, demonstrate that such interests have become part and parcel of the conflict's intractability. The co-optation of rebel leaders by offering business incentives tends to undermine their leadership authority by alienating their grassroots. Estrangement owing to such co-optation is likely to drive dynamics of organizational fragmentation and internal contention leading to further violence. Economic development, moreover, cannot override political grievances centered on political marginalization and competing nationalisms. On the contrary, if the political demands and grievances of rebel movements and their support base are not appreciated, the economistic engagement of armed groups is likely to cause new violence, as was evident in the case of the KIO.

To end the cycle of conflict, Myanmar's government needs to strengthen moderate elements within ethnic armed movements by creating trust among ethnic minority communities in a genuine peace process. It must break with the country's overly economistic engagement with rebellion and focus on the political solution of conflict, including negotiations of federal constitutional amendments. That approach must address the claims to the due and proper recognition of minority rights and identities that have long been the core stimulus of ethnic minority nationalism and armed rebellion against an authoritarian and ethnocratic state. This is not to deny that economic issues are of major importance. The conflict is as much about the political sources of economic marginalization as it is about ethnicity. But instead of business agendas surrounding resource extraction for the profit of a small elite, the state should employ inclusive economic development and the institutionalization of revenue sharing that contributes to overcoming the tangible grievances of local communities.

When I started this project in 2012 it was unclear where Myanmar's transition process was heading and how it would affect the country's decades-old civil war. As I write this, there are still no easy answers to these questions. Since Aung San Suu Kyi and her NLD came to power in March 2016, she has pushed to reform the country's peace process. Her efforts have so far culminated in two large peace conferences, styled as the twenty-first-century Panglong. In contrast to the relatively small original Panglong conference of 1947, the first meeting, held in August and September 2016 in Naypyidaw, featured some eighteen hundred delegates from government, the Tatmadaw, and seventeen ethnic armed organizations. Unsurprisingly, it did not end with a binding agreement. At best, it marked the beginning of a long, winding road toward national conciliation. Progress along this road, however, is uncertain. Fierce battles are regularly taking place in Kachin State, the Tatmadaw pushing against KIA positions with heavy artillery shelling and aerial bombardment. Moreover, re-escalating clashes between the KNLA and Myanmar armed forces in northern Karen State threaten the embryonic stability at the Thai border.

To be sure, a major reason for the continuation of armed conflict is the limited control Myanmar's government exerts over the country's armed forces. As Tatmadaw generals have long profited from perpetuating conflict, it was naïve to think they would simply give up their sources of power and wealth. It has also become clear that the political reform process has not altered the violent, ethnocratic character of Myanmar's state institutions and elites in any significant ways. If at all, state violence against ethnic minorities has intensified since the country embarked on political reforms in 2011. This is reflected in the ongoing discrimination against and marginalization of ethnic minorities across the country, the continuation of brutal counterinsurgency campaigns that indiscriminately target civilians in Kachin, Karen and Shan States, and the large-scale ethnic cleansing campaign in Rakhine State.

Suu Kyi and her NLD administration not only have remained silent about the atrocities committed by the Tatmadaw but have actively defended them. It is thus not surprising that Myanmar's ethnic minorities have lost trust in the country's political transition and rebel movements do not exhibit much willingness to demobilize. In fact, many ethnic armed groups seem determined to continue the armed struggle and receive significant support from local communities. Ending this cycle of violence not only demands a genuine willingness by all sides to make peace. It may also, I suggest, require rethinking what rebellion is. Rebellions are social phenomena. Revolutionary leaders do not unilaterally determine the strategies of their movements. Rather, a social interaction process between differently situated rebel elites and their grassroots drives the collective trajectory of rebellion. That process includes rebel soldiers on the front line, teachers in rebel-held schools, civil society activists, and local youth singing revolutionary songs in karaoke bars. These grassroots find their motivation above all in the struggle to have their identities recognized. Finding peaceful solutions not only to Myanmar's civil war but also to civil wars everywhere will require policy makers to push for settlements that address the identity needs of rebel grassroots. Scholars can contribute to this endeavor by developing a better understanding of rebellion and its social foundations. An important first step in that direction, as this book advocates, is to listen to rebels themselves.

INTERVIEWS

KAREN NATIONAL UNION (KNU)

Colonel, KNLA central command, Mae Sot, Thailand, 12 October 2013

Padoh Saw Dot Lay Mu, Head of Agriculture Department, Mae Sot, Thailand, 12 October 2013

KNLA officer, Mutraw (Brigade 5), 21 October 2013

KNU education workers (group interview), Mutraw (Brigade 5), Karen State, Myanmar, 21 October 2013

KNU administrator, Mutraw (Brigade 5), 23 October 2013

Anonymous KNU leader 1, Mae Pa, Thailand, 25 October 2013

Padoh Saw David Tharckabaw, Head of Alliance Affairs Department, Mae Sot, Thailand, 8 November 2013

Padoh Saw Lah Say, Head of Education and Culture Department, Mae Sot, Thailand, 15 November 2013

Chairman of Thaton District (Brigade 1), Mae Sot, Thailand, 24 November 2013

Chairman of Duplaya District (Brigade 6), Law Keeh Lah, Karen State, Myanmar, 4 December 2013

Saw Mahn Nyei Maung, Executive Committee, Law Keeh Lah, Karen State, Myanmar, 4 December 2013

Saw Roger Khin, Executive Committee, Law Keeh Lah, Karen State, Myanmar, 4 December 2013

Padoh Saw Hkwe Htoo Win, General Secretary, Law Keeh Lah, Karen State, Myanmar, 4 December 2013

Chairman of Toungoo District (Brigade 2), Law Keeh Lah, Karen State, Myanmar, 5 December 2013

Padoh Saw Mahn Ba Tun, Head of Forestry Department, Law Keeh Lah, Karen State, Myanmar, 5 December 2013

Padoh Saw Ker Ler, Head of Mining Department, Law Keeh Lah, Karen State, Myanmar, 5 December 2013

Anonymous KNU leader 2, Law Keeh Lah, Karen State, Myanmar, 5 December 2013

Lt. Gen. Baw Kyaw Heh, KNLA Vice Chief of Staff, Law Keeh Lah, Karen State, Myanmar, 6 December 2013

Col. Ner Dah Bo Mya, KNDO, Mae Sot, Thailand, 30 January 2017

Anonymous KNU leader 1, Mutraw, Karen State, Myanmar, 19 December 2018.

OTHER KAREN

Col. Saw Dah, KNU/KNLA Peace Council (KPC), Mae Sot, Thailand, 11 November 2013

Teacher, Mae La refugee camp, Thailand, 10 December 2013

Headmaster, Mae La refugee camp, Thailand, 10 December 2013
Activist, Yangon, Myanmar, 22 January 2014
NGO worker, Yangon, Myanmar, 22 January 2014
Priest, Dawei, Karen State, Myanmar, 28 January 2014
NGO worker, Dawei, Karen State, Myanmar, 28 January 2014

KACHIN INDEPENDENCE ORGANIZATION (KIO)

Dr. La Ja, General Secretary, Chiang Mai, Thailand, 14 November 2013
Member of Technical Advisory Team, Myitkyina, Kachin State, Myanmar, 10 February 2014
Member of Technical Advisory Team, Myitkyina, Kachin State, Myanmar, 12 February 2014
Deputy Manager, BUGA Company, Myitkyina, Kachin State, Myanmar, 14 February 2014
Salang Kaba Doi Pisa, Head of Humanitarian Affairs, Laiza, Kachin State, 14 March 2014
Sara Kaba Sum Lut Gam, Senior Negotiator, Laiza, Kachin State, 17 March 2014
KIA Officer, officer training school outside Laiza, Kachin State, Myanmar, 17 March 2014
Zawng Buk Than, Head of Economics Department, Laiza, Kachin State, 25 March 2014
KIA Officer, drug eradication center outside Laiza, Kachin State, Myanmar, 27 March 2014
U La Nan, Joint–General Secretary, Laiza, Kachin State, 29 March 2014
Cofounder of the Education and Economic Development for Youth (EEDY), Maijayang, Kachin State, Myanmar, 4 April 2014
Activist, Chiang Mai, Thailand, 30 October 2014
Activist, Chiang Mai, Thailand, 31 October 2014
KIO officer, KIO Technical Advisory Team, Myitkyina, 11 January 2017

OTHER KACHIN

Kachin elder, Myitkyina, Kachin State, Myanmar, 7 February 2014
Dr. Manam Tu Ja, Chairman of the Kachin State Development Party (KSDP), Myitkyina, Kachin State, Myanmar, 10 February 2014
Staff, Kachin Baptist Convention, Myitkyina, Kachin State, Myanmar, 10 February 2014
Religious leader, Myitkyina, Kachin State, Myanmar, 13 February 2014
Kachin businessmen and members of Peace Talk Creation Group (group interview), Myitkyina, Kachin State, Myanmar, 13 February 2014
Humanitarian worker, Laiza, Kachin State, Myanmar, 12 March 2014
Activist, Laiza, Kachin State, Myanmar, 28 March 2014
Religious leader, Laiza, Myanmar, 29 March 2014
Journalist, Maijayang, Kachin State, Myanmar, 3 April 2014
Two Kachin student leaders, Myitkyina, 5 January 2017
Kachin historian, Myitkyina, 6 January 2017
Kachin elder and singer, Myitkyina, 7 January 2017
Kachin elder, Myitkyina, 16 January 2017
Kachin Baptist Convention youth leader, Myitkyina, 17 January 2017

OTHER

Paul Keenan, independent researcher, Chiang Mai, Thailand, 31 October 2013

Chairmen of the Tak Chamber of Commerce (group interview), Mae Sot, Thailand, 3 December 2013

Consultant, Myanmar Peace Support Initiative (MPSI), Yangon, Myanmar, 22 January 2014

Lisu politician, Myitkyina, 12 January 2017

Shanni politician, Myitkyina, 13 January 2017

NOTES

INTRODUCTION

1. Myanmar's military rulers changed the name of the country from Burma to Myanmar in 1989. They also renamed several places, including Rangoon, now Yangon, and Karen State, now Kayin State. While many people in Myanmar have since come to use the new and old terms interchangeably, opposition movements have refused to employ the new terminology for many years, fearing it would confer legitimacy on the military junta. Since 2011, however, the new terms, including Myanmar and Yangon, have become common among people on all sides of the political landscape. I thus follow the emerging scholarly consensus and use *Burma* in discussing events that took place before 1989 and *Myanmar* for those that came after that year. The sole exception to this practice is my use of *Karen State*—because that is the preference of many Karen people who are at the heart of this book.

1. REBELLION AS A SOCIAL PROCESS

1. Charles Tilly employed a similar notion of collective repertoires in the context of contentious politics. These entities are historically developed patterns of public claim making by collective social actors, such as protests, strikes, or the taking up of arms: "Repertoires vary from place to place, time to time, and pair to pair. But on the whole, when people make collective claims, they innovate within limits set by the repertoire already established for their place, time, and pair" (2008a, 14–15).
2. This idea stands in contrast to normative theories of legitimacy, i.e., what legitimate authority ought to look like, which is common in political thought.
3. Renato Rosaldo introduced the term "deep hanging out" as a common denominator of ethnographic methodology before James Clifford and Clifford Geertz made it more widely known as a term of art.
4. Interview with Karen activist, Chiang Mai, Thailand, 30 October 2015.

3. KAREN REBELLION

1. *Saw* (male) and *Naw* (female) are Sgaw Karen honorifics equivalent to *U* or *Daw* in Burmese.
2. *Padoh* is Sgaw Karen for "leader" and is usually used as an honorific for KNU leaders without military rank. Joint statement of U Aung Min and Padoh Kwe Htoo Win: http://www.knuhq.org/pdoh-kwe-htoo-win-and-minister-u-aung-min-reading-aloud-together/.
3. Conversation with KNU officer, Thai–Myanmar border, 19 October 2013.
4. Interview with KNU leader from Duplaya, Law Khee Lar, 4 December 2013.
5. While sectarian divides have not played a major role in the current fragmentation of the movement, they certainly did so in the early and mid 1990s. A Karen civil society leader and KNU insider told me that in the past there was a cynical saying within the movement: "Everything is controlled by the Seven-Day Adventists, everything is managed by the Baptists, the Anglicans have to fight, and those who have to die are Buddhists." Interview with Karen civil society leader, Yangon, 23 January 2014.
6. Conversation with KNU officer, Thai--Myanmar border, 19 October 2013.
7. Interview with Karen activist, Chiang Mai, Thailand, 30 October 2015.
8. International NGOs documented the severe human rights abuses accompanying the construction of the pipeline and filed lawsuits against Total and the US-based Unocal in Europe and the United States for "complicity in crimes against humanity" (Kolås 2007, 630).

9. Interview with KNU leader from Duplaya, Law Khee Lar, 4 December 2013.
10. Conversation with KNU officer, Mutraw, 20 October 2013.
11. Interview with retired KNLA central command officer, Mae Pa, 12 October 2013.
12. Group interview with Thai businessmen, Mae Sot, Thailand, 3 December 2013.
13. Interview with retired KNLA central command officer, Mae Pa, 12 October 2013. According to a Human Rights Watch (2005) report, the Tatmadaw have used other cease-fires as a similar opportunity.
14. Group interview with KNU education workers, Mutraw, October 2013.
15. Conversation with Karen teacher in Mae Sot, Thailand, 12 November 2013.
16. This is the estimation of the 2014 Myanmar Population and Housing Census.
17. Interview with KNU administrator, Mutraw, 23 October 2013.
18. Interview with KNU member, Mae Pa, 14 October 2013. Various other KNU members expressed similar resentment of the 15th Congress election in conversations and interviews between September 2013 and December 2013.
19. Conversation with KNU chairman Gen. Mutu Say Poe, Law Khee Lar, 5 December 2013.
20. Interview with Padoh Mahn Nyein Maung, Law Khee Lar, 5 December 2013.
21. Interview with Padoh Mahn Nyein Maung, Law Khee Lar, 5 December 2013.
22. Interview with KNU general secretary Padoh Kwe Htoo Win, Law Khee Lar, 4 December 2013.
23. Interview with David Tharckabaw, Mae Sot, 8 November 2013.
24. Interview with anonymous KNU leader 2, Law Khee Lar, 5 December 2013.
25. Interview with anonymous KNU leader 2, Law Khee Lar, 5 December 2013. See also Kean and Zaw Win Than 2012.
26. Interview with anonymous KNU leader 2, Law Khee Lar, 5 December 2013.
27. The Central Committee member Padoh David Taw died in the meantime due to a long-standing health condition.
28. Group interview with KNU education workers, Mutraw, 24 October 2013.
29. Interview with Karen activist, Chiang Mai, 30 October 2015.
30. Interview with KNU administrator, Mutraw, 23 October 2013.
31. Interview with retired KNLA colonel, central command officer, Mae Pa, 12 October 2013.
32. Group interview with KNU education workers, Mutraw, 24 October 2013.
33. Group interview with KNU education workers, Mutraw, 24 October 2013.
34. I have changed his name.
35. Interview with Karen activist, Chiang Mai, Thailand, 30 October 2015.
36. Interview with Karen activist, Chiang Mai, 30 October 2015.
37. Conversation with KNDO sergeant, Mutraw, 23 October 2013.
38. Conversation with KDHW member, Mae Sot, 2 November 2013.
39. Conversation with KDHW member, Mae Sot, 2 November 2013.
40. See, for instance, Eh Na 2013, Karen News 2013, Saw Yan Naing 2014.
41. Interview with KNU leader, Mae Pa, 25 October 2013.
42. Interview with KNLA vice chief of staff Lt. Gen. Baw Kyaw Heh, Law Keeh Lar, 6 December 2013.
43. Interview with MPSI consultant, Yangon, 22 January 2014.
44. Interview with KNU leader, Mae Pa, 25 October 2013.
45. Karen National Union Supreme Headquarters, Central Standing Committee after 15th KNU Congress Third Emergency Meeting Statement, 29 October 2014. Obtained by the author.
46. Interview with KNU leader 1, Mutraw, 19 December 2018.
47. Interview with KNU leader 1, Mutraw, 19 December 2018.
48. The interview can be found at https://www.facebook.com/knuheadquartersofficial/posts/2272439329705170?__tn__=K-R, last accessed 4 February 2019.

4. Kachin Rebellion

1. Concrete numbers are difficult to obtain, not least because many Kachin flee behind rebel-held lines, where international humanitarian agencies have limited access. Government figures from 2014 estimate that the renewed conflict in Kachin State alone has displaced

123,000 civilians. About 43,000 of them were living in government-controlled camps and 80,000 in KIO-controlled camps. Burma News International 2014, 23; 2015, 25–29.

2. In theory the KIA is subordinate to the KIO, but in practice the distinction between the military and political arms of the organization is hazy. Since the resumption of fighting in 2011 the two branches have overlapped to the extent that local people use the two names interchangeably, although in the cease-fire years the distinction was more significant.

3. Conversation with KIA officer, Laiza, 15 March 2014.

4. Various KIO insiders with decidedly different roles in the movement, among them a Kachin religious leader, confirmed this review. I interviewed them in Laiza, Kachin State, Myanmar, in March 2014.

5. Interview with Brig. Gen. La Ja, the KIO general secretary, Chiang Mai, Thailand, November 2013.

6. Interview with KIO Joint–General Secretary U La Nan, Laiza, 29 March 2014.

7. Interview with Kachin elder, Myitkyina, 7 February 2014.

8. Interview with Kachin religious leader, Myitkyina, 13 February 2014.

9. Interview with KIO General Secretary Brig. Gen. La Ja, Chiang Mai, Thailand, 14 November 2013.

10. Interview with BUGA company representative, Myitkyina, 14 February 2014. Interview with KIO General Secretary Brig. Gen. La Ja, Chiang Mai, Thailand, 14 November 2013.

11. While the cease-fire made BUGA possible, the KIO-run company still provides electricity to government-controlled towns despite the resumption of war in 2011. The head of the KIO Economics Department, Zawng Buk Than, openly told me that the company, which exists because of the cease-fire and continues to exist legally in spite of the breakdown, provides a lot of income to the KIO. Interview with Zawng Buk Than, Laiza, 25 March 2014.

12. Interview with KIO General Secretary Brig. Gen. La Ja, Chiang Mai, Thailand, 14 November 2013.

13. Interview with the head of the KIO Economics Department, Zawng Buk Than, Laiza, 25 March 2014.

14. While other cease-fire groups, including the Shan, Kokang, and Wa as well as Kachin militias, have relied on de facto legalized narcotics production to fund themselves, the KIO was never a big player in the narcotics industry and has refrained from drug-related business since 1991. Interview with the head of the KIO Economics Department, Zawng Buk Than, Laiza, 25 March 2014).

15. Interview with the head of the KIO Economics Department, Zawng Buk Than, Laiza, 25 March 2014.

16. Interview with Kachin religious leader to whom I have given the name Reverend Zau Toi, Myitkyina, 13 February 2014.

17. Interview with Kachin religious leader, Myitkyina, 13 February 2014.

18. Interview with Kachin religious leader, Myitkyina, 13 February 2014.

19. Interview with KIO Joint–General Secretary U La Nan, Laiza, 29 March 2014.

20. Interview with Kachin religious leader, Laiza, 29 March 2014. Interview with Kachin religious leader, Myitkyina, 13 February 2014.

21. Interviews and conversations with several civilians in Laiza and Myitkyina between February and April 2014.

22. Whether or not people were objectively better off as the result of the cease-fire is not as important as the way they feel about it. In addition, Ted Gurr's concept of relative deprivation suggests that the situation for the grassroots might have improved during the cease-fire period but not to the same extent as their expectation did (Gurr 1971).

23. Interview with Kachin religious leader, Laiza, 29 March 2014. Father Paul is not his real name.

24. Conversation with IDP at KIO-administered IDP camp outside Laiza, 15 March 2014.

25. The region has produced opium for many centuries. Industrial production initially grew as the French and British turned to the opium trade to finance their conquests of South and Southeast Asia (Chin 2016). Regional governments clamped down on narcotics production in the first half of the twentieth century, but the trade boomed again since the Chinese Kuomintang attempted to finance their reinvasion of Maoist China after the Chinese Civil War, with support from the CIA. McCoy 1972, 166–67; Chin 2016.

26. Interview with the head of the KIO Economics Department, Zawng Buk Than, Laiza, 25 March 2014.
27. Buchanan, Kramer, and Woods 2013, 2; United Nations Office on Drugs and Crime 2014.
28. Conversation with Kachin social worker, Myitkyina, 10 February 2014.
29. Interview with KIO Joint–General Secretary U La Nan, Laiza, 29 March 2014.
30. Interview with KIO General Secretary Brig. Gen. La Ja, Chiang Mai, Thailand, 14 November 2013.
31. Interview with Kachin religious leader, Laiza, 29 March 2014.
32. Conversation with KIA soldier, Laiza, 20 March 2014.
33. Interview with Kachin religious leader, Myitkyina, 13 February 2014.
34. Interview with Kachin religious leader, Laiza, 29 March 2014.
35. Conversation with KIA soldier, Laiza, 20 March 2014.
36. Interview with the cofounder of EEDY, Maijayang, 14 April 2014.
37. Interview with the cofounder of EEDY, Maijayang, 14 April 2014.
38. Interview with Kachin religious leader, Myitkyina, 13 February 2014.
39. Kachin Baptist Convention youth leader, Myitkyina, 17 January 2017. This is a politically sensitive issue in contemporary Kachin society.
40. Interview with Kachin/Lisu politician, Myitkyina, 12 January 2017.
41. Conversation with relief worker, Laiza, 20 March 2014.
42. Smith (1999, 330) reports that this motive is also not unheard of in the long history of the movement.
43. Interview with Kachin religious leader, Myitkyina, 13 February 2014.
44. Interview with Kachin religious leader, Laiza, 29 March 2014.
45. Interview with Kachin religious leader, Laiza, 29 March 2014.
46. Interview with Kachin religious leader, Laiza, 29 March 2014.
47. Conversation with member of the Kachin diaspora, London, 28 October 2015.
48. Interview with Kachin religious leader, Laiza, 29 March 2014.
49. Conversation with local aid worker, Laiza, 2 April 2014.
50. Interview with local journalist, Maijayang, 14 April 2014.
51. Conversation with a member of the Kachin diaspora, London, 12 November 2014.
52. By *youth* I mean people in their late teenage years to their late twenties.
53. Interview with KIO Joint–General Secretary U La Nan, Laiza, 29 March 2014.
54. Interview with KIO Joint–General Secretary U La Nan, Laiza, 29 March 2014.
55. I have changed his name.
56. Interview with the cofounder of EEDY, Maijayang, 14 April 2014.
57. Video found at https://www.youtube.com/watch?v=cRpUq8ozgcw, last accessed 2 October 2015.
58. Conversation with university student, Myitkyina, 10 February 2014.
59. Conversation with KIA soldier, front-line position near Laiza, 8 April 2014.
60. Interview with Kachin religious leader, Laiza, 29 March 2014.
61. Video of "Share Shagan Nampan Lahkawng" (Two heroic flowers) by Ah Tang at https://www.facebook.com/856928137743956/videos/858292547607515/?theater, last accessed 2 October 2015.
62. See, for instance, "Katsi Majan," a song produced by the youth group of a Kachin church congregation, at https://www.youtube.com/watch?v=VA0XjH2_mCU.
63. The video is at https://www.youtube.com/watch?v=rRMUCCwR14Q, translated by member of the Kachin diaspora in London, 17 May 2016.
64. Interview with Kachin religious leader, Myitkyina, Myanmar, 13 February 2014. Interview with the cofounder of EEDY, Maijayang, 14 April 2014.
65. Interview with the chairman of the KSDP and the former KIO vice chairman Manam Tu Ja, Myitkyina, 10 February 2014.
66. Interview with KIO Joint–General Secretary U La Nan, Laiza, 29 March 2014.
67. Interview with Kachin religious leader, Myitkyina, 13 February 2014.
68. Interview with the cofounder of EEDY, Maijayang, 14 April 2014.
69. Interview with KIO General Secretary Brig. Gen. La Ja, Chiang Mai, Thailand, 14 November 2013.
70. Interview with the chairman of the KSDP and the former KIO vice chairman Manam Tu Ja, Myitkyina, 10 February 2014. Interview with KIO Joint–General Secretary U La Nan, Laiza, 29 March 2014.

71. Interview with the cofounder of EEDY, Maijayang, 14 April 2014.
72. Conversation with a member of the Kachin diaspora, London, 12 November 2014.
73. Interview with the cofounder of EEDY, Maijayang, 14 April 2014.
74. While the letter marked the first time the KIO voiced its resistance to the Myitsone dam publicly, many young KIA officers started to oppose the project as early as 2007.
75. This appeared to be the case in both government and rebel-held parts of Kachin and Karen States as well as in Thailand during field research I conducted between September 2013 and April 2014.
76. Interview with Kachin religious leader, Laiza, 29 March 2014.
77. Interview with Kachin religious leader, Myitkyina, 13 February 2014.
78. KIO officer, KIO Technical Advisory Team, Myitkyina, 11 January 2017.

5. THE SOCIAL FOUNDATIONS OF WAR AND PEACE

1. While co-optation is always a matter of degree, I use the term *partial leadership co-optation* to stress that some leaders were more receptive to co-optation than others.
2. Bertil Lintner and Tom Kramer, longtime observers of Myanmar's ethnic conflict, have also drawn these parallels (Lintner 2013).
3. For a theoretical discussion of outbidding and spoiling, see Kydd and Walter 2006.

References

Adam Smith International. 2015. "Institutional Regulatory Assessment of the Extractive Industries in Myanmar." Accessed 14 October 2015. http://www-wds.worldbank. org/external/default/WDSContentServer/WDSP/IB/2015/05/14/090224b082e83 01f/1_0/Rendered/PDF/Main0report.pdf.

Allina-Pisano, Jessica. 2009. "How to Tell an Axe Murderer: An Essay on Ethnography, Truth, and Lies." In Schatz 2009, 53–75.

Almond, Gabriel A., and G. B. Powell. 1978. *Comparative Politics: System, Process, and Policy*. London: Little, Brown.

Anderson, Robert, and Mandy Sadan. 2016. "Historical Perspectives on War and Peace in Kachin Space: The First Kachin Ceasefire, 1944–1961." In Sadan 2016b, 34–53.

Apter, David. 1997. "Political Violence in Analytical Perspective." In *The Legitimization of Violence*, edited by David Apter and M. Nicholson, 1–32. New York: New York University Press.

Arjona, Ana, Nelson Kasfir, and Zachariah Mampilly. 2015. *Rebel Governance in Civil War*. Cambridge: Cambridge University Press.

Asad, Talal. 1972. "Market Model, Class Structure and Consent: A Reconsideration of Swat Political Organisation." *Man* 7 (1): 74–94.

Asian Development Bank. 2010. "Strategy and Action Plan for the Greater Mekong Subregion East–West Economic Corridor." Accessed 19 January 2016. https:// openaccess.adb.org/bitstream/handle/11540/1035/gms-action-plan-east-west. pdf?sequence=1.

Aung Naing Oo. 2014. "Myanmar's Labyrinthine Peace Process." *Irrawaddy*, June 5. Accessed 10 July 2014. http://www.irrawaddy.org/contributor/myanmars-labyrinthine-peace-process.html.

Aydin, Aysegul, and Cem Emrence. 2015. *Zones of Rebellion: Kurdish Insurgents and the Turkish State*. Ithaca: Cornell University Press.

Azar, Edward E. 1986. "Protracted International Conflicts: Ten Propositions." In *International Conflict Resolution: Theory and Practice*, edited by Edward E. Azar and Tom W. Burton, 28–39. Brighton, UK: Wheatsheaf.

Bakke, Kristin M., Kathleen G. Cunningham, and Lee J. M. Seymour. 2012. "A Plague of Initials: Fragmentation, Cohesion, and Infighting in Civil Wars." *Perspectives on Politics* 10 (2): 265–83.

Bakonyi, Jutta, and Berit Bliesemann de Guevara, eds. 2014a. *A Micro-Sociology of Violence: Deciphering Patterns and Dynamics of Collective Violence*. London: Routledge.

——. 2014b. "The Mosaic of Violence: An Introduction." In *A Micro-Sociology of Violence: Deciphering Patterns and Dynamics of Collective Violence*, edited by Jutta Bakonyi and Berit Bliesemann de Guevara, 1–17. London: Routledge.

Barth, Fredrik. 1959. *Political Leadership among Swat Pathans.* London: Athlone.

Bayard de Volo, Lorraine, and Edward Schatz. 2004. "From the Inside Out: Ethnographic Methods in Political Research." *Political Science and Politics* 37 (2): 267–71.

Beck, Teresa K. 2009. "Staging Society: Sources of Loyalty in the Angolan UNITA." *Contemporary Security Policy* 30 (2): 343–55.

Beech, Hannah. 2012. "A Cease-Fire in Burma: Is One of the World's Oldest Insurgencies About to End?" *Time*, 1 December. Accessed 7 May 2012. http://world.time.com/2012/01/12/a-ceasefire-in-burma-is-one-of-the-worlds-oldest-insurgencies-about-to-end/.

Berti, Benedetta. 2013a. *Armed Political Organizations: From Conflict to Integration.* Baltimore: Johns Hopkins University Press.

——. 2013b. "Syria' Rebels: Between Talks and a Hard Place." *National Interest*, 8 November. Accessed 8 October 2015. https://nationalinterest.org/commentary/syrias-rebels-between-talks-hard-place-9378.

——. 2014. "Hamas and Israel at the Brink." Accessed 7 November 2014. http://carnegieendowment.org/sada/2014/07/08/hamas-and-israel-at-brink/hfe3.

Boehler, Patrick. 2012. "The Kachin Borderlands." *Le Monde diplomatique (English Edition)*, June 2012. Accessed 22 January 2016. http://mondediplo.com/2012/06/12 kachin.

Bourdieu, Pierre. 1990. *The Logic of Practice.* Stanford: Stanford University Press.

——. 1998. *On Television and Journalism.* London: Pluto.

Bourdieu, Pierre, and Loïc J. D. Wacquant. 1992. *An Invitation to Reflexive Sociology.* Chicago: University of Chicago Press.

Branscombe, Nyla R., Naomi Ellemers, Russell Spears, and Bertjan Doosje. 1999. "The Context and Content of Social Identity Threat." In Ellemers, Spears, and Doosje 1999, 35–58.

Brenner, David. 2017. "Rohingya 'Terrorists' and the Hierarchies of Legitimate Resistance in Myanmar." *Political Violence @ a Glance*, 5 September. Accessed 9 July 2018. https://politicalviolenceataglance.org/2017/09/05/rohingya-terrorists-and-the-hierarchies-of-legitimate-resistance-in-myanmar/.

——. 2018. "Performing Rebellion: Karaoke as a Lens into Political Violence." *International Political Society* 12 (4): 401–17.

Buchanan, John, Tom Kramer, and Kevin Woods. 2013. "Developing Disparity: Regional Investment in Burma's Borderlands." Accessed 28 April 2018. http://www.tni.org/sites/www.tni.org/files/download/tni-2013-burmasborderlands-def-klein-def.pdf.

Burke, Jason. 2012. "Burma Signs Ceasefire with Karen Rebels in Step towards Ending Isolation." *The Guardian*, December 2. Accessed 3 August 2016. http://www.theguardian.com/world/2012/jan/12/burma-ceasefire-karen-rebels-isolation.

Burma News International. 2013a. "Deciphering Myanmar's Peace Process." Accessed 5 October 2015. http://mmpeacemonitor.org/images/pdf/deciphering_english_2013.pdf.

——. 2013b. "Economics of Peace and Conflict." Accessed 21 July 2014. http://www.mmpeacemonitor.org/images/pdf/economics_peace_and_conflict_eng.pdf.

——. 2014. "Deciphering Myanmar's Peace Process." Accessed 5 October 2015. http://mmpeacemonitor.org/images/pdf/deciphering_myanmar_peace_process_2014.pdf.

——. 2015. "Deciphering Myanmar's Peace Process." Accessed 5 September 2016. http://mmpeacemonitor.org/images/2015/august/deci-myan-peace-process-2015-eng.pdf.

Callahan, Mary P. 2003. *Making Enemies: War and State Building in Burma.* Ithaca: Cornell University Press.

——. 2007. *Political Authority in Burma's Ethnic Minority States: Devolution, Occupation and Coexistence.* Washington: East–West Center; Singapore: Institute of Southeast Asian Studies.

Chachavalpongpun, Pavin. 2011. "Look East Meets Look West: Indian–Southeast Asian Relations in Flux." *International Spectator* 46 (2): 91–108.

Chandra, Kanchan. 2006. "What Is Ethnic Identity and Does It Matter?" *Annual Review of Political Science* 9: 397–424.

Cederman, Lars-Erik, Nils B. Weidmann, and Kristian Skrede Gleditsch. 2011. "Horizontal Inequalities and Ethnonationalist Civil War: A Global Comparison." *American Political Science Review* 105 (3): 478–95.

Cheesman, Nick, Nicholas Farrelly, and Trevor Wilson, eds. 2014. *Debating Democratization in Myanmar.* Singapore: Institute of Southeast Asian Studies.

Cheesman, Nick, Monique Skidmore, and Trevor Wilson, eds. 2012. *Myanmar's Transition: Openings, Obstacles and Opportunities.* Singapore: Institute of Southeast Asian Studies.

Chenoweth, Erica, and Adria Lawrence, eds. 2010. *Rethinking Violence: States and Non-State Actors in Conflict.* Belfer Center Studies in International Security, edited by Adria Lawrence. Cambridge: MIT Press.

Chin, Ko-Lin. 2016. *The Golden Triangle: Inside Southeast Asia's Drug Trade.* Ithaca: Cornell University Press.

Chouvy, Pierre-Arnaud. 2009. *Opium: Uncovering the Politics of the Poppy.* Cambridge: Harvard University Press.

Christie, Clive J. 2001. *Ideology and Revolution in Southeast Asia 1900–80.* Richmond, Surrey: Curzon.

Clifford, James. 1996. "Anthropology and/as Travel." *Etnofoor* (2): 5–15.

——. 1997. "Spatial Practices: Fieldwork, Travel, and the Disciplining of Anthropology." In *Anthropological Locations: Boundaries and Grounds of a Field Science,* edited by Akhil Gupta and James Ferguson, 185–222. Berkeley: University of California Press.

Clifford, James, and George E. Marcus. 1986. *Writing Culture: The Poetics and Politics of Ethnography: A School of American Research Advanced Seminar.* Berkeley: University of California Press.

Collier, Paul. 1999. "Doing Well Out of War." Paper presented at the Conference on Economic Agendas in Civil Wars, London, 26–27 April 1999. http://siteresources. worldbank.org/INTKNOWLEDGEFORCHANGE/Resources/491519-119981844 7826/28137.pdf.

Collier, Paul, and Anke Hoeffler. 1998. "On Economic Causes of Civil War." *Oxford Economic Papers* 50 (4): 563–73.

——. 2004. "Greed and Grievance in Civil War." *Oxford Economic Papers* 56 (4): 563–95.

Connor, Walker. 1994. *Ethnonationalism: The Quest for Understanding.* Princeton: Princeton University Press.

Core, Paul. 2009. "Burma/Myanmar: Challenges of a Ceasefire Accord in Karen State." *Journal of Current Southeast Asian Affairs* 28 (3): 95–105.

Cramer, Christopher. 2002. "Homo Economicus Goes to War: Methodological Individualism, Rational Choice and the Political Economy of War." *World Development* 30 (11): 1845–64.

——. 2006. *Civil War Is Not a Stupid Thing: Accounting for Violence in Developing Countries.* London: Hurst.

Cunningham, David E., Kristian S. Gleditsch, and Idean Salehyan. 2009. "It Takes Two: A Dyadic Analysis of Civil War Duration and Outcome." *Journal of Conflict Resolution* 43 (5): 570–97.

Cunningham, Kathleen G., Kristin M. Bakke, and Lee J. M. Seymour. 2012. "Shirts Today, Skins Tomorrow: Dual Contests and the Effects of Fragmentation in Self-Determination Disputes." *Journal of Conflict Resolution* 56 (1): 67–93.

Dapice, David. 2012. "China and Yunnan Economic Relations with Myanmar and the Kachin State: Powering the Peace Process." Ash Center, Harvard University. Accessed 30 April 2016. http://www.ash.harvard.edu/extension/ash/docs/chinayunnan.pdf.

Dean, Karin. 2005. "Spaces and Territorialities on the Sino–Burmese Boundary: China, Burma and the Kachin." *Political Geography* 24 (7): 808–30.

——. 2012. "Struggle over Space in Myanmar: Expanding State Territoriality after the Kachin Ceasefire." In *Autonomy and Armed Separatism in South and Southeast Asia,* edited by Michelle A. Miller, 113–35. Singapore: Institute of Southeast Asian Studies.

Deignan, Herbert G. 1943. *Burma: Gateway to China.* War Background Studies 17. Washington DC: Smithsonian Institution Press.

Driscoll, Jesse. 2012. "Commitment Problems or Bidding Wars? Rebel Fragmentation as Peace Building." *Journal of Conflict Resolution* 56 (1): 118–49.

Duffield, Mark R. 2001. *Global Governance and the New Wars: The Merging of Development and Security.* London: Zed Books.

——. 2002. "War as a Network Enterprise: The New Security Terrain and Its Implications." *Cultural Values* 6 (1–2): 153–65.

Duncan, Christopher R., ed. 2004. *Civilizing the Margins: Southeast Asian Government Policies for the Development of Minorities.* Ithaca: Cornell University Press.

——. 2004. "Legislating Modernity among the Marginalized." In *Civilizing the Margins: Southeast Asian Government Policies for the Development of Minorities,* edited by Christopher R. Duncan, 1–23. Ithaca: Cornell University Press.

Duwa Mahkaw Hkun Sa. 2016. "The Founding of the KNO and the Development of a Diaspora Activist Network." In *War and Peace in the Borderlands of Myanmar: The Kachin Ceasefire 1994–2011,* edited by Mandy Sadan, 330–60. Copenhagen: Nordic Institute of Asian Studies Press.

Egreteau, Renaud. 2006. "Instability at the Gate: India's Troubled Northeast and Its External Connections." CSH India Occasional Papers. Accessed 30 April 2016. http://egreteau.com/images/Documents%20PDF/CSH%20OP%20-%20 n%B016.pdf.

Eh Na. 2013. "KNU Gen. Baw Kyaw Heh Exposes How Ceasefire Agenda Has Shifted to Business." *Karen News*, 9 May. http://karennews.org/2013/09/knu-gen-baw-kyaw-heh-exposes-how-ceasefire-agenda-has-shifted-to-business.html/.

Ei Ei Toe Lwin. 2014a. "Will Karen National Union Stay in UNFC?" *Myanmar Times*, 9 August. Accessed 19 January 2016. http://www.mmtimes.com/index.php/in-depth/11574-will-karen-national-union-stay-in-unfc.html.

———. 2014b. "KNU to Meet amid Split Fears." *Myanmar Times*, 17 October. Accessed 19 January 2016. http://www.mmtimes.com/index.php/national-news/11982-knu-calls-urgent-meeting-for-reunification.html.

Elias, Norbert. 1978. *What Is Sociology?* New York: Columbia University Press.

———. 1983. *The Court Society.* Oxford: Blackwell.

———. 1994. *The Civilizing Process.* New ed. Edited by Edmund Jephcott. Oxford: Blackwell.

Ellemers, Naomi, Russell Spears, and Bertjan Doosje, eds. 1999. *Social Identity: Context, Commitment, Content.* Malden, MA: Blackwell Publishers.

Emirbayer, Mustafa. 1997. "Manifesto for a Relational Sociology." *American Journal of Sociology* 103 (2): 281–317.

Farrelly, Nicholas. 2012. "Ceasing Ceasefire? Kachin Politics Beyond the Stalemate." In *Myanmar's Transition: Openings, Obstacles and Opportunities*, edited by Nick Cheesman, Monique Skidmore, and Trevor Wilson, 52–71. Singapore: Institute of Southeast Asian Studies.

Findley, Mike, Alejandro Ponce de Leon, and Mike Denly. 2016. "Spoiler Alert: Combatant Fragmentation and the Colombian Peace Process." *Political Violence @ a Glance*, September 5. Accessed 8 September 2016. https://politicalviolenceataglance. org/2016/05/09/spoiler-alert-combatant-fragmentation-and-the-colombian-peace-process/.

Florento, Hector, and Maria I. Corpuz. "Myanmar: The Land Bridge." In *Connecting Asia: Infrastructure for Integrating South and Southeast Asia*, edited by Michael G. Plummer, Peter J. Morgan, and Ganeshan Wignaraja, 215–244. Asian Development Bank Institute. Northampton, MA: Edward Elgar.

Formoso, Bernard. 2010. "Zomians or Zombies? What Future Exists for the Peoples of the Southeast Asian Massif?" *Journal of Global History* 5 (2): 313–32.

41 Karen Civil Society Organisations. 2015. "Karen Civil Society Has Lost Trust in the Nationwide Ceasefire Agreement (NCA) Negotiations as a Gateway to Political Dialogue." News release. 10 April. Accessed 5 July 2016. http://www.burmapart nership.org/2015/10/karen-civil-society-has-lost-trust-in-the-nationwide-ceasefire-agreement-nca-negotiations-as-a-gateway-to-political-dialogue/.

Geertz, Clifford. 1974. "From the Native's Point of View": On the Nature of Anthropological Understanding." *Bulletin of the American Academy of Arts and Sciences* 28 (1): 26–45.

Gerring, John. 2007. *Case Study Research: Principles and Practices:* Cambridge: Cambridge University Press.

Global Witness. 2003. "A Conflict of Interest: The Uncertain Future of Burma's Forests." Accessed 22 January 2016. https://www.globalwitness.org/en-gb/archive/conflict-interest-english/.

———. 2005. "A Choice for China: Ending the Destruction of Burma's Northern Frontier Forests." Accessed 22 January 2016. https://www.globalwitness.org/documents/11694/a_choice_for_china_low_res.pdf.

———. 2009. "A Disharmonious Trade: China and the Continued Destruction of Burma's Northern Frontier Forests." A Review by Global Witness 2006–2009. Accessed 30 September 2014. http://www.globalwitness.org/library/disharmonious-trade-china-and-continued-destruction-burmas-northern-frontier-forests.

———. 2014. "What Future for Rubber Production in Myanmar?" Accessed 19 January 2016. https://www.globalwitness.org/documents/10527/what_future_english_version_april_2014_0.pdf.

———. 2015. "Jade: Myanmar's 'Big State Secret.'" Accessed 22 January 2016. https://www.globalwitness.org/documents/18153/Jade_full_report_online_hi_res_xDRGxt7.pdf.

Goodhand, Jonathan. 2000. "Research in Conflict Zones: Ethics and Accountability." *Forced Migration Review* 8 (4): 12–16.

———. 2005. "Frontiers and Wars: The Opium Economy in Afghanistan." *Journal of Agrarian Change* 5 (2): 191–216.

———. 2008. "War, Peace and the Places in Between: Why Borderlands Are Central." In *Whose Peace? Critical Perspectives on the Political Economy of Peacebuilding*, edited by Michael Pugh, Neil Cooper, and Mandy Turner, 225–44. London: Palgrave Macmillan.

———. 2013. "Stabilising a Victor's Peace." In *Stabilization Operations, Security and Development: States of Fragility*, edited by Robert Muggah, 215–43: Routledge.

Gravers, Mikael. 1999. *Nationalism as Political Paranoia in Burma: An Essay on the Historical Practice of Power.* 2nd ed. Richmond, Surrey: Curzon.

———. 2016. "The Karen and the Ceasefire Negotiations: Mistrust, Internal Segmentation, and Clinging to Arms." In *War and Peace in the Borderlands of Myanmar: The Kachin Ceasefire 1994–2011*, edited by Mandy Sadan, 388–407. Copenhagen: Nordic Institute of Asian Studies Press.

Guevara, Ernesto. 2002. *Guerrilla Warfare.* London: Rowman and Littlefield.

Guha, Ranajit. 1988. "The Prose of Counter-Insurgency." In *Selected Subaltern Studies*, edited by Ranajit Guha and Gayatri C. Spivak, 45–88. Oxford: Oxford University Press.

Gurr, Ted R. 1971. *Why Men Rebel.* Princeton: Princeton University Press.

Gustafsson, Karl. 2015. "Recognising Recognition through Thick and Thin: Insights from Sino-Japanese Relations." *Cooperation and Conflict* 51 (3): 255–71.

Haacke, Jürgen. 2005. "The Frankfurt School and International Relations: On the Centrality of Recognition." *Review of International Studies* 31 (1): 181–94.

———. 2006. "Myanmar's Foreign Policy towards China and India." *Adelphi Paper* 46 (381): 25–39.

———. 2010. "China's Role in the Pursuit of Security by Myanmar's State Peace and Development Council: Boon and Bane?" *Pacific Review* 23 (1): 113–37.

Hagmann, Tobias, and Didier Péclard. 2010. "Negotiating Statehood: Dynamics of Power and Domination in Africa." *Development and Change* 41 (4): 539–62.

Hkanhpa Tu Sadan. 2016. "Kachin Student Life at Yangon University in the Mid-1990s." In *War and Peace in the Borderlands of Myanmar: The Kachin Ceasefire, 1994–2011*, edited by Mandy Sadan, 308–29. Copenhagen: Nordic Institute of Asian Studies Press.

Honneth, Axel. 1996. *The Struggle for Recognition: The Moral Grammar of Social Conflicts.* Cambridge: MIT Press.

Horowitz, Donald L. 1985. *Ethnic Groups in Conflict.* Berkeley: University of California Press.

Human Rights Watch. 2002. "My Gun Was as Tall as Me: Child Soldiers in Burma." Accessed 19 January 2016. https://www.hrw.org/reports/2002/burma/Burma0902.pdf.

———. 2005. "'They Came and Destroyed Our Village Again': The Plight of Internally Displaced Persons in Karen State." Accessed 19 January 2016. http://www.hrw.org/reports/2005/burma0605/burma0605.pdf.

International Crisis Group. 2003. "Myanmar Backgrounder: Ethnic Minority Politics." Accessed 10 January 2014. http://www.crisisgroup.org/~/media/Files/asia/south-east-asia/burma-myanmar/052%20Myanmar%20Backgrounder%20Ethnic%20Minority%20Politics.pdf.

———. 2004. "Myanmar: Aid to the Border Areas." Accessed 4 February 2019. https://www.crisisgroup.org/asia/south-east-asia/myanmar/myanmar-aid-border-areas.

———. 2011. "Myanmar: A New Peace Initiative." Accessed 21 July 2014. http://www.crisisgroup.org/~/media/Files/asia/south-east-asia/burma-myanmar/214%20Myanmar%20-%20A%20New%20Peace%20Initiative.pdf.

———. 2012. "A Tentative Peace in Myanmar's Kachin Conflict." Accessed 30 September 2014. http://www.crisisgroup.org/~/media/Files/asia/south-east-asia/burma-myanmar/b140-a-tentative-peace-in-myanmars-kachin-conflict.pdf.

———. 2014. "Myanmar's Military: Back to the Barracks." Accessed 14 October 2015. http://www.crisisgroup.org/~/media/Files/asia/south-east-asia/burma-myanmar/b143-myanmar-s-military-back-to-the-barracks.pdf.

Jones, Lee. 2014a. "Explaining Myanmar's Regime Transition: The Periphery Is Central." *Democratization* 21 (5): 780–802.

———. 2014b. "The Political Economy of Myanmar's Transition." *Journal of Contemporary Asia* 44 (1): 144–70.

———. 2016. "Understanding Myanmar's Ceasefires: Geopolitics, Political Economy and State-Building." In Sadan 2016b, 95–113.

Jost, John T., and Brenda Major. 2001. "Emerging Perspectives on the Psychology of Legitimacy." In Jost and Major 2001, 3–32.

———, eds. 2001. *The Psychology of Legitimacy: Emerging Perspectives on Ideology, Justice, and Intergroup Relations.* Cambridge: Cambridge University Press.

Jourde, Cédric. 2009. "The Ethnographic Sensibility: Overlooked Authoritarian Dynamics and Islamic Ambivalences in West Africa." In Schatz 2009, 201–16.

Justino, Patricia, Tilman Brück, and Philip Verwimp. 2013. *A Micro-Level Perspective on the Dynamics of Conflict, Violence, and Development*. Oxford: Oxford University Press.

Kachin Development Networking Group. 2007. "Valley of Darkness: Gold Mining and Militarization in Burma's Hugawng Valley." Accessed 10 February 2014. http://www.burmacampaign.org.uk/reports/ValleyofDarkness.pdf.

——. 2012. "Sham Tiger Reserve in Burma: A Lesson on American Aid in Myanmar." Accessed 10 January 2014. http://www.kdng.org/publication/286-sham-tiger-reserve-in-burma-a-lesson-on-american-aid-in-myanmar-.html.

Kachin News Group. 2011. "KIO Appeals to China to Stop Myitsone Dam Construction." *Kachin News Group*, November 24. Accessed 10 February 2014. http://www.kachinnews.com/news/1916-kio-appeals-to-china-to-stop-myitsone-dam-construction.html.

Kachinland News. 2013. "No Ceasefire Agreement without Reaching the Stage for Political Discussions, Said Kachin Public." *Kachinland News*, 29 May. Accessed 22 January 2016. http://kachinlandnews.com/?p=23286.

Kaiser, Tania. 2013. "Researching Social Life in Protracted Exile: Experiences with Sudanese Refugees in Uganda 1996–2008." In *Research Methods in Conflict Settings: A View from Below*, edited by Mazurana, Jacobsen, and Gale 2013, 106–28. Cambridge: Cambridge University Press.

Kaldor, Mary. 1999. *New and Old Wars: Organized Violence in a Global Era*. Cambridge, UK: Polity Press.

Kalyvas, Stathis N. 2001. "New" and "Old" Civil Wars: A Valid Distinction?" *World Politics* 54 (1): 99–118.

——. 2003. "The Ontology of 'Political Violence': Action and Identity in Civil Wars." *Perspective on Politics* 1 (3): 475–94.

——. 2006. *The Logic of Violence in Civil War*. Cambridge: Cambridge University Press.

——. 2010. "Foreword: Internal Conflict and Political Violence: New Developments in Research." In Chenoweth and Lawrence 2010, xi–xiii.

Karen Human Rights Group. 2014. "Truce or Transition? Trends in Human Rights Abuse and Local Response in Southeast Myanmar since the 2012 Ceasefire." Accessed 14 October 2015. http://khrg.org/sites/default/files/khrg_-_truce_or_transition_-_english.pdf.

——. 2015. "'With Only Our Voices, What Can We Do?': Land Confiscation and Local Response in Southeast Myanmar." Accessed 30 August 2015. http://www.khrg.org/2015/06/with-only-our-voices-what-can-we-do-land-confiscation-and-local-response.

Karen News. 2013. "KNU Leader—Govt's Labels Nationwide Ceasefire 'Untimely' . . . : Interview with Padoh Naw Ziporah Sein." 10 July. Accessed 19 January 2016. http://karennews.org/2013/10/knu-leader-govts-labels-nationwide-ceasefire-untimely.html/.

——. 2014a. "KNU Decision to Withdraw from UNFC Undemocratic Claims Karen Women's Organisation." 10 March. Accessed 19 January 2016. http://karennews.org/2014/10/knu-decision-to-withdraw-from-unfc-undemocratic-claims-karen-womens-organisation.html/.

——. 2014b. "Karen Army General Explains Rational behind Reformation of Ethnic Alliance and Recent Conflict with Govt Troops." 21 October. Accessed 21

October 2014. http://karennews.org/2014/10/karen-army-general-explains-rational-behind-reformation-of-ethnic-alliance-and-recent-conflict-with-govt-troops.html/.

Karen Peace Support Network. 2018. "The Nightmare Returns: Karen Hopes for Peace and Stability Dashed by Burma Army's Actions." Accessed 28 January 2019. http://www.kesan.asia/index.php/resources/download/13-reports/122-the-nightmare-return-karen-hopes-for-peace-and-stability-dashed-by-burma-army-s-actions

Kean, Thomas, and Zaw Win Than. 2012. "Govt, KNU Sign Ceasefire." *Myanmar Times*, 16 January. Accessed 19 January 2016. http://www.mmtimes.com/index.php/national-news/1258-govt-knu-sign-ceasefire.html?start=1.

Keen, David. 2005. *Conflict and Collusion in Sierra Leone*. Oxford: James Currey.

——. 2006. *Endless War? Hidden Functions of the War on Terror*. London: Pluto Press.

——. 2012. "Greed and Grievance in Civil War." *International Affairs* 88 (4): 757–77.

Keyes, Charles F. 2004. "Afterword: The Politics of 'Karen-ness' in Thailand." In *Living at the Edge of Thai Society: The Karen in the Highlands of Northern Thailand*, edited by Claudio Delang, 210–18. London: Routledge Curzon.

King, Gary, Keohane O. Robert, and Sidney Verba. 1994. *Designing Social Inquiry: Scientific Inference in Qualitative Research*. Princeton: Princeton University Press.

Kolås, Åshild. 2007. "Burma in the Balance: The Geopolitics of Gas." *Strategic Analysis* 31 (4): 625–43.

Korf, Benedikt. 2011. "Resources, Violence and the Telluric Geographies of Small Wars." *Progress in Human Geography* 35 (6): 733–756.

Korf, Benedikt, and Timothy Raeymaekers. 2013. *Violence on the Margins: States, Conflict, and Borderlands*. London: Palgrave Macmillan.

Kramer, Tom. 2009. "Neither War nor Peace: The Future of the Cease-Fire Agreements in Burma." Accessed 22 January 2013. http://www.tni.org/sites/www.tni.org/files/download/ceasefire.pdf.

Krause, Keith, and Jennifer Milliken. 2009. "Introduction: The Challenge of Non-State Armed Groups." *Contemporary Security Policy* 30 (2): 202–20.

Kudo, Toshihiro. 2013. "Border Development in Myanmar: The Case of the Myawaddy–Mae Sot Border." In *Border Economies in the Greater Mekong Sub-region*, edited by Masami Ishida, 186–206. London: Palgrave Macmillan.

Kumbun, Joe. 2017. "The Tripartite Power Struggle in the KIO." *Irrawaddy*, 30 June. Accessed 6 September 2017. https://www.irrawaddy.com/opinion/guest-column/tripartite-power-struggle-kio.html.

Kydd, Andrew H., and Barbara F. Walter. 2006. "The Strategies of Terrorism." *International Security* 31 (1): 49–80.

Lambrecht, Curtis W. 1999. "Destruction and Violation: Burma's Border Development policies." *Watershed* 5(2).

——. 2004. "Oxymoronic Development: The Military as Benefactor in the Border Regions of Burma." In *Civilizing the Margins: Southeast Asian Government Policies for the Development of Minorities*, edited by Christopher R. Duncan, 150–81. Ithaca: Cornell University Press.

Lawi Weng. 2015a. "Karen Leader: 'If They Keep Attacking Us, There Will Be No Peace': Interview with David Tharckabaw." *Irrawaddy*, 11 May. Accessed 5 July

2016. http://www.irrawaddy.com/burma/karen-leader-if-they-keep-attacking-us-there-will-be-no-peace.html.

——. 2015b. "Kachin Group Questions Govt Murder Probe, Forms Investigation Team." *Irrawaddy,* 2 November. Accessed 22 January 2016. http://www.irrawaddy.com/burma/kachin-group-questions-govt-murder-probe-forms-investigation-team.html.

——. 2015c. "A Taxing Trip in Karen State." *Irrawaddy,* 6 December. Accessed 19 January 2016. http://www.irrawaddy.com/burma/a-taxing-trip-in-karen-state.html.

Le Billon, Philippe, and Eric Nicholls. 2007. "Ending 'Resource Wars: Revenue Sharing, Economic Sanction or Military Intervention?" *International Peacekeeping* 14 (5): 613–32.

Leach, Edmund. 1954. *Political Systems of Highland Burma: A Study of Kachin Social Structure.* Cambridge: Harvard University Press.

——. 1960. "The Frontiers of 'Burma.'" *Comparative Studies in Society and History* 3 (1): 49–68.

Lieberman, Victor. 2010. "A Zone of Refuge in Southeast Asia? Reconceptualizing Interior Spaces." *Journal of Global History* 5 (2): 333–46.

Lindemann, Thomas, and Erik Ringmar, eds. 2015. *The International Politics of Recognition.* New York: Routledge.

Lintner, Bertil. 2013. "Rain for Myanmar's Peace Parade." *Asia Times Online,* 25 June. Accessed 10 April 2014. http://www.atimes.com/atimes/Southeast_Asia/SEA-01-250613.html.

——. 2015a. *Great Game East: India, China, and the Struggle for Asia's Most Volatile Frontier.* New Haven: Yale University Press.

——. 2015b. "The Core Issues Not Addressed." *Irrawaddy,* 5 May. Accessed 30 August 2015. http://www.irrawaddy.org/magazine/the-core-issues-not-addressed.html.

Lintner, Bertil, and Hseng N. Lintner. 1990. *Land of Jade: A Journey through Insurgent Burma.* Edinburgh: Kiscadale.

MacGinty, Roger, and Oliver Richmond. 2013. *The Liberal Peace and Post-War Reconstruction: Myth or Reality?* London: Routledge.

Malešević, Siniša. 2008. "The Sociology of New Wars? Assessing the Causes and Objectives of Contemporary Violent Conflicts." *International Political Sociology* 2 (2): 97–112.

Mamdani, Mahmood. 1996. *Citizen and Subject: Contemporary Africa and the Legacy of Late Colonialism.* Princeton: Princeton University Press.

Mampilly, Zachariah C. 2011. *Rebel Rulers: Insurgent Governance and Civilian Life during War.* Ithaca: Cornell University Press.

Marcus, George E. 1995. "Ethnography in/of the World System: The Emergence of Multi-Sited Ethnography." *Annual Review of Anthropology,* 95–117.

Marx, Karl, Friedrich Engels, and Robert C. Tucker, eds. 1978. *The Marx–Engels Reader.* 2nd ed. New York: W. W. Norton.

Maton, Karl. 2014. "Habitus." In *Pierre Bourdieu: Key Concepts*, edited by Michael J. Grenfell, 48–64. London: Routledge.

Maung Aung Myoe. 2009. *Building the Tatmadaw: Myanmar Armed Forces since 1948*. Singapore: Institute of Southeast Asian Studies.

Mazurana, Dyan, Lacey Gale, and Karen Jacobsen. 2013. "A View from Below: Conducting Research in Conflict Zones." In Mazurana, Jacobsen, and Gale 2013, 3–26.

Mazurana, Dyan, Karen Jacobsen, and Lacey Gale, eds. 2013. *Research Methods in Conflict Settings: A View from Below*. Cambridge: Cambridge University Press.

McCoy, Alfred W. 1972. *The Politics of Heroin in Southeast Asia*. New York: Harper and Row.

McElwee, Pamela. 2004. "Becoming Socialist or Becoming Kinh? Government Policies for Ethnic Minorities in the Socialist Republic of Viet Nam." In *Civilizing the Margins: Southeast Asian Government Policies for the Development of Minorities*, edited by Christopher R. Duncan, 182–213. Ithaca: Cornell University Press.

Meehan, Patrick. 2011. "Why the Drugs Trade Is Central to Burma's Changing Political Order." *Journal of Southeast Asian Studies* 42 (3): 376–404.

——. 2015. "Fortifying or Fragmenting the State? The Political Economy of the Opium/Heroin Trade in Shan State, Myanmar, 1988–2013." *Critical Asian Studies* 47 (2): 253–82.

Menkhaus, Ken. 2007. "Governance without Government in Somalia: Spoilers, State Building, and the Politics of Coping." *International Security* 31 (3): 74–106.

Michaud, Jean. 2010. "Editorial—Zomia and Beyond." *Journal of Global History* 5 (2): 187–214.

Millen, Raymond A., and Steven Metz. 2004. *Insurgency and Counterinsurgency in the 21st Century: Reconceptualizing Threat and Response*. Carlisle, PA: Strategic Studies Institute.

Moore, Barrington. 1978. *Injustice: The Social Bases of Obedience and Revolt*. London: Macmillan.

Muckian, Martin J. 2006. "Structural Vulnerabilities of Networked Insurgencies: Adapting to the New Adversary." *Parameters* 36 (4): 14.

Mutu Say Poe. 2015. "KNU Chairman Speech at the Nationwide Ceasefire Agreement Signing Ceremony." News release, 15 October. Accessed 5 July 2016. http://www.knuhq.org/knu-chairman-speech-at-the-nationwide-ceasefire-agreement-signing-ceremony/.

Myanmar Peace Monitor. n.d. "DKBA-5: Democratic Karen Benevolent Army." Accessed 1 October 2016. http://www.mmpeacemonitor.org/background/ethnic-grievances/159-dkba-5.

Mydans, Seth. 2012. "Burmese Government and Ethnic Rebel Group Sign Cease-Fire." *New York Times*, 2 December. Accessed 5 July 2016. http://www.nytimes.com/2012/01/13/world/asia/myanmar-signs-truce-with-ethnic-rebel-group.html?_r=0.

Myers, Steven L., and Seth Mydans. 2012. "U.S. Restores Full Ties to Myanmar after Rapid Reforms." *New York Times*, 13 January Accessed 7 May 2016. http://www.

nytimes.com/2012/01/14/world/asia/united-states-resumes-diplomatic-relations-with-myanmar.html.

Nair, Deepak. 2015. "Saving the States' Face: An Ethnography of the ASEAN Secretariat and Diplomatic Field in Jakarta." PhD diss., London School of Economics and Political Science.

Neumann, Cecilie B., and Iver B. Neumann. 2015. "Uses of the Self: Two Ways of Thinking about Scholarly Situatedness and Method." *Millennium: Journal of International Studies* 43 (3): 798–819.

Neumann, Iver B. 2012. *At Home with the Diplomats: Inside a European Foreign Ministry.* Ithaca: Cornell University Press.

Nyein Nyein. 2016. "Burma Army Offensive Continues in Kachin State: KIA Spokesman." *Irrawaddy*, 23 September. Accessed 26 September 2016. http://www.irrawaddy.com/burma/burma-army-offensive-continues-in-kachin-state-kia-spokesman.html.

Obama, Barack. 2012. "Statement by the President on the Release of Burmese Political Prisoners." News release, 13 January. Accessed 7 May 2016. https://www.white house.gov/the-press-office/2012/01/13/statement-president-release-burmese-political-prisoners.

Pachirat, Timothy. 2009. "The Political in Political Ethnography: Dispatches from the Kill Floor." In Schatz 2009, 143–62.

Panglong Agreement. 1947. Accessed 7 July 2018. http://www.mmpeacemonitor.org/~mmpeac5/images/pdf/PangLong-Agreement.pdf.

Paulle, Bowen, Bart van Heerikhuizen, and Mustafa Emirbayer. 2012. "Elias and Bourdieu." *Journal of Classical Sociology* 12 (1): 69–93. https://doi.org/10.1177/1468795X11433708.

Peace Donor Support Group. 2013. "Myanmar Joint Peacebuilding Needs Assessment." Accessed 26 September 2016. http://www.themimu.info/sites/themimu.info/files/documents/Ref_Doc_Desktop_Review_of_Needs_and_Gaps_in_Conflict-Affected_Parts_PDSG_Jul2013.pdf.

Pearlman, Wendy. 2009. "Spoiling Inside and Out: Internal Political Contestation and the Middle East Peace Process." *International Security* 33 (3): 79–109.

——. 2010. "A Composite-Actor Approach to Conflict Behavior." In Chenoweth and Lawrence 2010, 212–35.

Perkoski, Evan. 2015. "Militant Proliferation and the Consequences of Fragmentation." *Political Violence @ a Glance*, 30 July. Accessed 8 September 2016. https://politicalviolenceataglance.org/2015/07/30/militant-proliferation-and-the-consequences-of-fragmentation/.

Petraeus, David. 2006. "Learning Counterinsurgency: Observations from Soldiering in Iraq." http://www.army.mil/professionalWriting/volumes/volume4/april_2006/4_06_2.html.

Rabinow, Paul. 2007. *Reflections on Fieldwork in Morocco.* Berkeley: University of California Press.

Radio Free Asia. 2012. "Three Karen Officials Removed." *Radio Free Asia*, 10 April. Accessed 19 January 2016. http://www.rfa.org/english/news/myanmar/karen-10042012152054.html.

Rampton, Dave. 2016. "Social Orders, State Formation and Conflict: Buddhist Nationalism in Sri Lanka and Myanmar." Working Paper.

Ranger, Terence O. 1983. "The Invention of Tradition in Colonial Africa." In *The Invention of Tradition*, edited by Terence O. Ranger and Eric J. Hobsbawm. Cambridge: Cambridge University Press.

Reno, William. 2009. "Explaining Patterns of Violence in Collapsed States." *Contemporary Security Policy* 30 (2): 356–74.

Richmond, Oliver. 2012. *A Post-Liberal Peace.* London: Routledge.

Richmond, Oliver P., Stefanie Kappler, and Annika Björkdahl. 2015. "The 'Field' in the Age of Intervention: Power, Legitimacy, and Authority Versus the 'Local.'" *Millennium: Journal of International Studies*, 0305829815594871.

S' PhanShaung. 2013. "KNU 7th Brigade—Open for Business." *Karen News*, 7 September. Accessed 19 January 2016. http://karennews.org/2013/07/knu-7th-brigade-open-for-business.html/.

Sadan, Mandy. 2007. "Constructing and Contesting the Category 'Kachin' in the Colonial and Post-Colonial Burmese State." In *Exploring Ethnic Diversity in Burma*, edited by Mikael Gravers, 34–73. Copenhagen: Nordic Institute of Asian Studies Press.

——. 2013. *Being and Becoming Kachin: Histories beyond the State in the Borderworlds of Burma.* Oxford: British Academy and Oxford University Press.

——. 2016a. "Introduction." In Sadan 2016b, 1–28.

——, ed. 2016b. *War and Peace in the Borderlands of Myanmar: The Kachin Ceasefire 1994–2011.* Copenhagen: Nordic Institute of Asian Studies Press.

Sai Wansai. 2015. "Panghsang Summit Meeting, Joint Monitoring Committee and Military Offensives." *Panglong*, 4 November. Accessed 5 July 2016. http://english.panglong.org/?p=13087.

Sakhong, Lian Hmung. 2003. *In Search of Chin Identity: A Study in Religion, Politics and Ethnic Identity in Burma.* Copenhagen: Nordic Institute of Asian Studies.

Saw Yan Naing. 2012. "KNU Bridges Internal Rift." 29 October. Accessed 19 January 2016. http://www.irrawaddy.com/burma/knu-bridges-internal-rift.html.

——. 2013a. "Thousands Greet Convoy of Ethnic Leaders in Myitkyina." *Irrawaddy*, 11 March. Accessed 10 February 2014. http://www.irrawaddy.org/kia/thousands-greet-convoy-ethnic-leaders-myitkyina.html.

——. 2013b. "Who's Behind the Bombings in Burma?" *Irrawaddy*, 18 October. Accessed 30 August 2014. http://www.irrawaddy.org/news-analysis/whos-behind-bombings-burma.html.

——. 2014a. "Is Naypyidaw Learning from Sri Lanka to End Civil War?" *Irrawaddy*, 29 January. Accessed 19 January 2016. http://www.irrawaddy.com/interview/naypyidaw-learning-sri-lanka-end-civil-war.html.

——. 2014b. "The Growing Friendship between Naypyidaw and the KNU." *Irrawaddy*, 6 June. Accessed 18 June 2014. http://www.irrawaddy.org/burma/multimedia-burma/growing-friendship-naypyidaw-knu.html.

——. 2014c. "Karen Rebel Groups Plan Military Cooperation." *Irrawaddy*, 14 October. Accessed 10 January 2015. http://www.irrawaddy.com/burma/karen-rebel-groups-plan-military-cooperation.html.

———. 2016. "More Than 3,000 Villagers Flee Escalating Conflict in Karen State." *Irrawaddy,* 12 September. Accessed 26 September 2016. http://www.irrawaddy.com/burma/more-than-3000-villagers-flee-escalating-conflict-in-karen-state.html.

Schatz, Edward. 2009. "Introduction: Ethnographic Immersion and the Study of Politics." In Schatz 2009, 1–22.

———, ed. 2009. *Political Ethnography: What Immersion Contributes to the Study of Power.* Chicago: University of Chicago Press.

Schlichte, Klaus. 2009a. *In the Shadow of Violence: The Politics of Armed Groups.* Frankfurt: Campus Verlag.

———. 2009b. "With the State against the State? The Formation of armed Groups." *Contemporary Security Policy* 30 (2): 246–64.

———. 2012. "The Limits of Armed Contestation: Power and Domination in Armed Groups." *Geoforum* 43 (4): 716–24.

Schlichte, Klaus, and Ulrich Schneckener. 2015. "Armed Groups and the Politics of Legitimacy." *Civil Wars* 17 (4): 409–24.

Scott, James C. 1979. "Revolution in the Revolution." *Theory and Society* 7 (1–2): 97–134.

———. 1985. *Weapons of the Weak: Everyday Forms of Peasant Resistance.* New Haven: Yale University Press.

———. 2009. *The Art of Not Being Governed: An Anarchist History of Upland Southeast Asia.* Yale Agrarian Studies. New Haven: Yale University Press.

Scott, James G. 1900. *Gazetteer of Upper Burma and the Shan States.* 1 vol. Rangoon: Superintendent, Government Printing, Burma. Assisted by J. P. Hardiman.

Shah, Alpa. 2013. "The Intimacy of Insurgency: Beyond Coercion, Greed or Grievance in Maoist India." *Economy and Society* 42 (3): 480–506. https://doi.org/10.1080/03085147.2013.783662.

Shaw, Rosalind. 2007. "Memory Frictions: Localizing the Truth and Reconciliation Commission in Sierra Leone." *International Journal of Transitional Justice* 1 (2): 183–207.

Sherman, Jake. 2003. "Burma: Lessons from the Ceasefires." In *The Political Economy of Armed Conflict: Beyond Greed and Grievance,* edited by Karen Ballentine and Jake Sherman, 225–55. Boulder: Lynne Rienner.

Smith, Martin. 1999. *Burma: Insurgency and the Politics of Ethnicity.* 2nd ed. Dhaka: Dhaka University Press.

———. 2007. *State of Strife: The Dynamics of Ethnic Conflict in Burma.* Policy Papers 36. Singapore: Institute of Southeast Asian Studies.

———. 2016. "Reflections on the Kachin Ceasefire: A Cycle of Hope and Disappointment." In Sadan 2016b, 57–94.

Smith, Nicholas H. 2012. "Introduction: A Recognition-Theoretic Research Programme for the Social Sciences." In *Recognition Theory as Social Research: Investigating the Dynamics of Social Conflict,* edited by Shane O'Neill and Nicholas H. Smith, 1–20. London: Palgrave Macmillan.

Snyder, Richard. 2006. "Does Lootable Wealth Breed Disorder? A Political Economy of Extraction Framework." *Comparative Political Studies* 39 (8): 943–68.

South, Ashley. 2008. *Ethnic Politics in Burma: States of Conflict*. Routledge Contemporary Southeast Asia Series. London: Routledge.

———. 2011. "Burma's Longest War: Anatomy of the Karen Conflict." Accessed 22 January 2013. http://www.tni.org/sites/www.tni.org/files/download/ Burma's%20Longest%20War.pdf.

———. 2013. *Mon Nationalism and Civil War in Burma: The Golden Sheldrake*. London: Routledge.

Staniland, Paul. 2014. *Networks of Rebellion: Explaining Insurgent Cohesion and Collapse*. Ithaca: Cornell University Press.

Stedman, Stephen J. 1997. "Spoiler Problems in Peace Processes." *International Security* 22 (2): 5–53.

Steinberg, David I., and Hongwei Fan. 2012. *Modern China–Myanmar Relations: Dilemmas of Mutual Dependence*. Copenhagen: Nordic Institute of Asian Studies Press.

Stewart, Frances, and Valpy Fitzgerald. 2001. *War and Underdevelopment*. Oxford: Oxford University Press.

Strömbom, Lisa. 2014. "Thick Recognition: Advancing Theory on Identity Change in Intractable Conflicts." *European Journal of International Relations* 20 (1): 168–91.

Tajfel, Henri E. 1978. *Differentiation between Social Groups: Studies in the Social Psychology of Intergroup Relations*. London: Academic Press.

Taw, David. 2005. "Strategic Considerations for the Karen National Union." In *Choosing to Engage: Armed Groups and Peace Processes,* edited by Robert Ricigliano, 40–43. Accord 16. http://www.c-r.org/downloads/Accord16_9Choosingtoengage_ 2005_ENG.pdf. Accessed 1 October 2015.

Taylor, Robert H. 1982. "Perceptions of Ethnicity in the Politics of Burma." *Southeast Asian Journal of Social Science* 10 (1): 7–22.

———. 1987. *The State in Burma*. Honolulu: University of Hawaii Press.

———. 2006. "Colonial Forces in British Burma: A National Army Postponed." In *Colonial Armies in Southeast Asia,* edited by Karl Hack and Tobias Rettig, 185–200. London: Routledge.

Thant Myint-U. 2011. *Where China Meets India: Burma and the New Crossroads of Asia*. London: Macmillan.

The Border Consortium. 2012a. *Central Karen/Kayin Areas: Map*. Accessed 9 July 2016. http://www.theborderconsortium.org/media/58089/12-11-central-karen-state. pdf.

———. 2012b. *Northern Karen/Kayin Areas: Map*. Accessed 9 July 2016. http://www. theborderconsortium.org/media/58095/12-11-northern-karen-areas.pdf.

Thuta Linn. 2015. "Kachin Party Applies to Join Ethnic Political Alliance." *Burma News International,* 18 December. Accessed 12 December 2017. https://www. bnionline.net/en/2015-election/kachin-state/item/1349-kachin-party-applies- to-join-ethnic-political-alliance.html.

Tilly, Charles. 2003. *The Politics of Collective Violence*. Cambridge: Cambridge University Press.

———. 2008a. *Contentious Performances*. Cambridge: Cambridge University Press.

———. 2008b. *Explaining Social Processes*. Boulder: Paradigm.

Transnational Institute. 2015. "Political Reform and Ethnic Peace in Burma/Myanmar: The Need for Clarity and Achievement." Accessed 14 October 2015. https://www.tni.org/files/download/bpb14-web-042015.pdf.

Turner, John C. 1999. "Current Issues in Research on Social Identity and Self-Categorization Theories." In Ellemers, Spears, and Doosje 1999, 6–34.

Tyler, Tom R. 2001. "A Psychological Perspective on the Legitimacy of Institutions and Authorities." In Jost and Major 2001, 416–36.

U.S. Army. 2014. "Insurgencies and Countering Insurgencies: FM 3-24/MCWP 3-33.5, C1." Accessed 5 October 2015. https://fas.org/irp/doddir/army/fm3-24.pdf.

United Nations Office on Drugs and Crime. 2014. "Southeast Asia Opium Survey 2014: Lao PDR, Myanmar." Accessed 14 October 2014. https://www.unodc.org/documents/crop-monitoring/sea/SE-ASIA-opium-poppy-2014-web.pdf.

Uphoff, Norman. 1989. "Distinguishing Power, Authority and Legitimacy: Taking Max Weber at His Word by Using Resources-Exchange Analysis." *Polity* 22 (2): 295–322.

Van Maanen, John. 1991. "Playing Back the Tape: Early Days in the Field." In *Experiencing Fieldwork: An Inside View of Qualitative Research*, edited by William Shaffir and Robert A. Stebbins, 124. London: Sage.

Van Schendel, Willem. 2002. "Geographies of Knowing, Geographies of Ignorance: Jumping Scale in Southeast Asia." *Environment and Planning D: Society and Space* 20 (6): 647–68.

Vrasti, Wanda. 2008. "The Strange Case of Ethnography and International Relations." *Millennium: Journal of International Studies* 37 (2): 279–301.

Walton, Matthew J. 2008. "Ethnicity, Conflict, and History in Burma: The Myths of Panglong." *Asian Survey* 48 (6): 889–910.

——. 2013. "The 'Wages of Burman-ness:' Ethnicity and Burman Privilege in Contemporary Myanmar." *Journal of Contemporary Asia* 43 (1): 1–27.

——. 2016. "Reflections of Ceasefires Past, Present, and Future." In Sadan 2016b, 461–74.

Weber, Max. 1947. *The Theory of Economic and Social Organization.* London: W. Hodge. Part 1 of *Wirtschaft und Gesellschaft,* translated from the German by A. R. Henderson and Talcott Parsons.

——. 1980. *Wirtschaft und Gesellschaft: Grundriss der verstehenden Soziologie.* Tübingen: Mohr.

Wedeen, Lisa. 2009. "Ethnography as Interpretive Enterprise." In Schatz 2009, 75–94.

Weinstein, Jeremy M. 2006. *Inside Rebellion: The Politics of Insurgent Violence.* Cambridge: Cambridge University Press.

Wennmann, Achim. 2009. "Getting Armed Groups to the Table: Peace Processes, the Political Economy of Conflict and the Mediated State." *Third World Quarterly* 30 (6): 1123–38.

Wickham-Crowley, Timothy. 1987. "The Rise (And Sometimes Fall) of Guerrilla Governments in Latin America." *Sociological Forum* 2 (3): 473–99.

Wood, Elisabeth J. 2003. *Insurgent Collective Action and Civil War in El Salvador.* Cambridge: Cambridge University Press.

——. 2006. "The Ethical Challenges of Field Research in Conflict Zones." *Qualitative Sociology* 29 (3): 373–86.

——. 2008. "The Social Processes of Civil War: The Wartime Transformation of Social Networks." *Annual Review of Political Science* 11: 539–61.

——. 2009. "Ethnographic Research in the Shadow of Civil War." In Schatz 2009, 119–42.

Woods, Kevin. 2011. "Ceasefire Capitalism: Military–Private Partnerships, Resource Concessions and Military–State Building in the Burma–China Borderlands." *Journal of Peasant Studies* 38 (4): 747–70.

——. 2016. "The Commercialisation of Counterinsurgency: Battlefield Enemies, Business Bedfellows in Kachin State, Burma." In Sadan 2016b, 114–48.

Yanow, Dvora. 2009. "Dear Author, Dear Reader: The Third Hermeneutic in Writing and Reviewing Ethnography." In Schatz 2009.

Zahar, Marie-Joelle. 2008. "Reframing the Spoiler Debate in Peace Processes." In *Contemporary Peacemaking: Conflict, Peace Processes and Post-War Reconstruction*, 2nd ed., edited by Darby John and Roger Mac Ginty, 159–77. Basingstoke: Palgrave Macmillan.

Zartman, I. W. 1989. *Ripe for Resolution: Conflict and Intervention in Africa*. Updated ed. Council on Foreign Relations Books. New York: Oxford University Press.

Zaw Oo, and Win Min. 2007. *Assessing Burma's Ceasefire Accords*. Washington: East–West Center; Singapore: Institute of Southeast Asian Studies.

Zedong, Mao. 1961. *On Guerrilla Warfare*. Chicago: University of Illinois Press.

Zelditch, Morris. 2001. "Theories of Legitimacy." In Jost and Major 2001, 33–53.

Zoya Phan. 2013. "Listen to Us: Stop Ignoring Our Concerns." *Karen News*, 10 December. Accessed 28 April 2014. http://karennews.org/2013/10/listen-to-us-stop-ignoring-our-concerns.html/.

INDEX

Lightning Source UK Ltd.
Milton Keynes UK
UKHW030204121019
351443UK00005B/198/P